SACRIFICING THE SELF

AMERICAN ACADEMY OF RELIGION
THE RELIGIONS SERIES

SERIES EDITOR
Paul B. Courtright, Emory University

A Publication Series of
The American Academy of Religion and
Oxford University Press

Religions of Atlanta
Religious Diversity in the Centennial Olympic City
Edited by Gary Laderman

Exegesis of Polemical Discourse
Ibn Hazm on Jewish and Christian Scriptures
Theodore Pulcini

Religion and the War in Bosnia
Edited by Paul Mojzes

The Apostolic Conciliarism of Jean Gerson
John J. Ryan

One Lifetime, Many Lives
The Experience of Modern Hindu Hagiography
Robin Rinehart

Sacrificing the Self
Perspectives on Martyrdom and Religion
Edited by Margaret Cormack

AMERICAN ACADEMY OF RELIGION

SACRIFICING THE SELF

*Perspectives on
Martyrdom and Religion*

EDITED BY

MARGARET CORMACK

OXFORD
UNIVERSITY PRESS

2002

OXFORD
UNIVERSITY PRESS

Oxford   New York
Auckland   Bangkok   Buenos Aires   Cape Town   Chennai
Dar es Salaam   Delhi   Hong Kong   Istanbul   Karachi   Kolkata
Kuala Lumpur   Madrid   Melbourne   Mexico City   Mumbai   Nairobi
São Paulo   Shanghai   Singapore   Taipei   Tokyo   Toronto

and an associated company in Berlin

Library of Congress Cataloging-in-Publication Data
Sacrificing the self : perspectives on martyrdom and
world religion / edited by Margaret Cormack.
p. cm. — (AAR the religions)
Includes bibliographical references and index.
ISBN 0-19-514999-8; ISBN 0-19-515000-7 (pbk.)
1. Martyrdom—History of doctrines.   I. Cormack, Margaret (Margaret Jean)
II. AAR the religions (Unnumbered)
BL626.5 .S23 2002
291.2'3—dc21   2001036132

We thank *Representations* for permission to use a revised version of
Carlin Barton's article and Princeton University Press for permission to
reprint Lindsey Harlan's translations of poetry.

1 3 5 7 9 8 6 4 2
Printed in the United States of America
on acid-free paper

CONTENTS

CONTRIBUTORS

CARLIN BARTON is professor of history at the University of Massachusetts at Amherst. She received a Ph.D. in history from the University of California at Berkeley. Her primary field of interest is the physical, mental, and emotional lives of ancient peoples. Her first book, *The Sorrows of the Ancient Romans: The Gladiator and the Monster* (Princeton, N.J.: Princeton University Press, 1993), focused on the emotions of despair, desire, fascination, and envy. Other works include *Roman Honor: The Fire in the Bones* (Berkeley: University of California Press, 2001). She is currently working on a study of systems of sacrifice in the ancient world.

MARC BRETTLER received a Ph.D. in Near Eastern and Judaic Studies from Brandeis University, where he is Dora Golding Professor of Biblical Studies. He has published *God Is King: Understanding an Israelite Metaphor* (Sheffield: Journal for the Study of the Old Testament Press, 1989), *The Creation of History in Ancient Israel* (London: Routledge, 1995), *Biblical Hebrew for Students of Modern Israeli Hebrew* (New Haven: Yale University Press, 2001), and *The Book of Judges* (London: Routledge, 2001). He was associate editor of *The New Oxford Annotated Bible*, 3rd ed. (New York: Oxford University Press, 2001).

DANIEL BROWN holds a Ph.D. in Islamic Studies from the Department of Near Eastern Languages and Civilizations at the University of Chicago. His research and writing focus on modern trends in Islamic thought.

He is author of *Rethinking Tradition in Modern Islamic Thought* (Cambridge: Cambridge University Press, 1996), and his current research is on attitudes and approaches to violence in the Islamic tradition.

MARGARET CORMACK is associate professor in the Department of Philosophy and Religious Studies at the College of Charleston. She received a Ph.D. in Medieval Studies from Yale University. Her research interests include the history of Scandinavia and popular religion in the European Middle Ages. She is extending to the present the research published in her first book, *The Saints in Iceland: Their Veneration from the Conversion to 1400* (Brussels: Société des Bollandistes, 1994).

LAWRENCE FINE is Irene Kaplan Leiwant Professor of Jewish Studies at Mt. Holyoke College. He received a Ph.D. in Near Eastern and Judaic Studies from Brandeis University. His research and publications focus on mystical experience among the Safed kabbalists and include *Safed Spirituality* (New York: Paulist Press, 1984) and *Physician of the Soul, Healer of the Cosmos: Isaac Luria and His Kabbalistic Fellowship* (Stanford: Stanford University Press, in press). He has edited *Essential Papers on Kabbalah* (New York: New York University Press, 1995) and *Judaism in Practice* (Princeton, N.J.: Princeton University Press, 2001).

LINDSEY HARLAN is associate professor in Religious Studies at Connecticut College. She earned a Ph.D. from Harvard University in the history of religions and has published *Religion and Rajput Women: The Ethic of Protection in Contemporary Narratives* (Berkeley: University of California Press, 1992). With Paul Courtright she edited *From the Margins of Hindu Marriage: Essays on Gender, Culture, and Religion* (New York: Oxford University Press, 1995). Her most recent publication is *The Goddesses' Henchmen*, a book on Rajput hero veneration (New York: Oxford University Press, in press).

D. DENNIS HUDSON is professor emeritus of World Religions at Smith College. He received a Ph.D. in history of religions from the Claremont Graduate School. His research and publications focus on the religion and culture of Tamil India and include *Protestant Origins in India* (Grand Rapids, Mich.: Eerdmans, 2000). *The Body of God*, a study of an eighth-century temple, is forthcoming from Oxford University Press.

KEITH LEWINSTEIN is assistant professor in the Departments of History and Religion at Smith College and visiting scholar in the Center for

Middle Eastern Studies at Harvard University. He received a Ph.D. from the Department of Near Eastern Studies at Princeton University. He has published several studies in the field of early Islamic thought and is currently preparing a book entitled *Heresy and Dissent in Early Islam*.

CAROLE STRAW is professor of history at Mount Holyoke College. She received a Ph.D. in history at the University of California at Berkeley. In addition to numerous articles on martyrdom in the ancient world, she has published *Gregory the Great: Perfection in Imperfection* (Berkeley: University of California Press, 1988) and a volume on Gregory in the Variorum Authors of the Middle Ages series (1997). She is currently working on a volume entitled *Heroic Christianity*, which will examine free will and martyrdom in early Christianity.

INTRODUCTION

 The essays in this volume were originally presented as part of a series of lectures on the theme "Martyrdom: Past and Present" held at Smith College during the years 1993 and 1994. The aim of the lectures was to examine concepts of martyrdom in a variety of religions. The papers presented at Smith covered a period of four thousand years and a geographical span ranging from Iceland to India, with settings as varied as the arenas of Rome and the mystical journeys of the Kabbalah. Inevitably, there were gaps; for example, we would like to have included the Japanese practice of *seppuku* and the kamikaze pilots of World War II, as well as the Buddhist monks whose self-immolation was the most extreme form of political protest in the 1960s. Possible models and antecedents for the Buddhists are discussed by Hudson. In choosing the following selections for publication, we have narrowed the field even further, without prejudice to the other excellent papers that were presented. By limiting ourselves to two contributions on any single religious or cultural tradition, we hope to highlight not only the similarities between traditions but also the different interpretations of a single tradition to which changing historical circumstances can give rise.

Indeed, the essays in this volume were chosen not because they illustrate a generally accepted concept of "martyrdom," but rather because they challenge traditional ideas of what a "martyr" may be. Several chapters take as their starting point attitudes toward voluntary death in the ancient world examined recently by Arthur Droge and James Tabor (*A Noble Death* [San Francisco: HarperSanFrancisco, 1992]).

Droge and Tabor note that far from being condemned out of hand, a voluntary death might under certain circumstances be considered heroic or even obligatory. They conclude that the distinction between suicide and martyrdom is in the eye of the beholder and identify the following five characteristics of deaths characterized as martyrdom:

1. They reflect situations of opposition and persecution.
2. The choice to die, which these individuals make, is viewed by the authors as necessary, noble, and heroic.
3. These individuals are often eager to die; indeed, in several cases they end up directly *killing themselves*.
4. There is often the idea of vicarious benefit resulting from their suffering and death.
5. The expectation of vindication and reward beyond death, more often than not, is a prime motivation for the choice of death. (*A Noble Death*, p. 75)

These five characteristics are the point of departure for Brettler's examination of individuals in the Hebrew Bible who might be considered to merit the title of "martyr." None of the deaths analyzed by Brettler is condemned (all fulfill Droge and Tabor's second generalization), and a number of them prefigure ideas that are examined in detail by Barton and Straw: the concept that a voluntary death may, in some cases, be the only honorable death possible. However, other characteristics, notably the expectation of reward beyond death and of vicarious benefits (statements four and five) are absent in almost the entire Hebrew Bible. Brettler answers the question "Is there martyrdom in the Hebrew Bible?" in the negative.

Barton and Straw deal with two despised minorities made famous by the arenas of Rome: gladiators and Christians. As will be seen from their essays, which form a complementary pair, the vocabularies used in describing these groups are often identical. Both speak of vows—*devotiones*—in the one case to the gods of the underworld, in the other to the Christian God. A traditional vocabulary of honor and liberality is also shared. Both groups voluntarily undergo suffering and death. Here, however, the similarity ends. The gladiator, despised and dishonored, regains his lost honor by willing the very destruction he must undergo. Like Mucius Scaevola, who stands unmoved after putting his arm into the flames, the gladiator commits himself to a violent death *before* it can be imposed on him, thus escaping the degrading status of "victim." For Christians, however, the status of victim was not a degradation to be avoided but an honor to be sought. Christians believed that a humiliating death by torture, which imitated the death of Christ, would be rewarded in the next life. Christian martyrs embraced torments imposed by others rather than preempting them.

It is eagerness for death—Tabor and Droge's third requirement—that connects all but one of the remaining cultures in this volume. The exception is the group of Anglo-Saxon royal saints examined by Cormack. For this group, martyrdom entails not the will for death but rather death in dishonorable circumstances. For the Anglo-Saxons as for the Romans, honor was a warrior virtue; a warrior was expected to go down fighting, taking as many as possible of the enemy with him. A death in which the victim was deprived of such glory was the ultimate shame, not only for the victim himself, but also for the kinsmen who lived after him and who were duty-bound to avenge him. In ninth-century England, the victim of secret murder, deprived of a chance to fight back, was considered just as degraded as a Roman soldier or gladiator who pleaded for his life. As in ancient Rome, the Christian concept of the afterlife allowed for an inversion of the native norm. Divine signs indicating the sanctity of the victim turned his—and his kindred's—worldly disgrace into honor of the highest order, thus redressing their position in the political one-upmanship of the blood feud.

The Muslim ideal of martyrdom also originated in a warrior culture. As Lewinstein points out, the ideal is one of active struggle (*jihād*) in which the will to die in the way of God is decisive. So crucial is it that even those who die in shipwreck, childbirth, or pestilence may enjoy the rewards of the martyrs in paradise, while those who just happen to die in battle, but whose heart is on something other than God, may not. The Muslim scholars who thus defined marytrdom—and its reward—for the classical Islamic tradition were, on the whole, quietist, and their teachings were designed to discourage believers from fomenting rebellion.

Colonialism, however, brought a change to Muslim thinking about martyrs. Brown discusses how recent political events have led to a resurgence of the ideal of actually dying as part of the struggle in the way of God. Brown examines the ideologies of a number of contemporary Muslim groups and discusses contemporary justifications for martyrdom that do not rely on the expectation of a luxurious otherworld to make their point.

The ideology of *satī* immolation in contemporary Rajasthan fulfills all of Droge and Tabor's requirements for "martyrdom." In order to qualify as a *satī*, a woman must go to her death enthusiastically and voluntarily; her self-immolation is viewed as heroic, a femine parallel to death on the battlefield. It benefits not only the *satī* and her dead husband in after- (or future) lives but also their living descendants. Both Rajasthani legend and the current political situation reflect situations of "opposition or persecution." Legendary *satīs* died to preserve their honor, and that of their families, in times of military clashes between Hindus and Muslims; in the present day, the very concept of "*satī*" has become a rallying call for Hindu traditionalists against perceived persecution by a secular government. For them, the *satī* on the funeral pyre, like the Christian in the arena, bears witness to a higher truth in the midst of a corrupt world.

Gandhi, too, may be seen as having "died for Truth"; the concept of truth that motivated him and traditional mythic expressions of self-sacrifice for truth in the religions of South Asia are the subjects of Dennis Hudson's contribution to the volume. He examines analogues of the story of Harischandra, which had a profound influence on Gandhi. Using examples from Hindu and Buddhist texts, he shows how these stories illustrate a concept of the "person" as a collective whole. The result of such a concept is that the martyr may have to sacrifice others as well as himself before his "martyrdom" can be complete. His devotion parallels that of the *satī* to her husband. Hudson's material also contains striking parallels and inversions of the classical world. The *bodhisattva* who burns his arm as an offering to the Buddha reminds us of Mucius Scaevola, who holds his hand in the altar's flames, while the true statement that restores King Sibi's eyes is the mirror image of Papylus's death to defend the statement that "I am a Christian."

The deaths sought by medieval Kabbalists were not physical but mystical. Such "spiritual deaths" could bring great rewards but also entailed great dangers. Fine examines how this theme was developed in Jewish tradition. He shows how in the seventeenth century Kabbalistic conceptions of mystical redemption of the holy from the netherworld were interpreted so as to justify the apostasy of Sabbatai Sevi, whose violation of Jewish law was considered by his followers as a necessary "degradation" in the cause of the greater good. In the Jewish mystical tradition, as in the other religious traditions examined in this volume, we observe an overlapping among the concepts of martyrdom, asceticism, and purification. Fine also emphasizes an aspect of death that is implicit in the other essays: whether physical or spiritual, death functions as an initiation into another and better condition, with rewards at the very least for the initiate and in most cases for his earthly community as well.

In the religious traditions that have developed in the past two millennia, the ideal of martyrdom has had to be balanced carefully against the needs of a living (and not necessarily persecuted) tradition. Lewinstein's contribution most clearly traces the development of ways in which the rewards of martyrdom were made available to all in times of peace and prosperity. Just as medieval Muslims might value the life of the ascetic (or that of the scribe) as highly as that of the warrior, so also Christian, Jewish, and Buddhist texts present ascetic or pietistic alternatives to physical death, more suitable in times when heroic self-sacrifice is not a realistic possibility. However, as Brown has shown for the case of Islam and Harlan for Hinduism, changing political circumstances may lead to the revival and reinterpretation of older ideologies.

SACRIFICING THE SELF

ONE

IS THERE MARTYRDOM IN
THE HEBREW BIBLE?

Marc Brettler

 We can find almost anything in the Hebrew Bible, especially if we define the phenomenon we are seeking in a suitable fashion. For this reason, the definition we choose for martyrdom is of more than academic interest—it will determine whether or not martyrdom actually existed in ancient Israel. It is well known that the English word "martyr" ultimately derives from the Greek μάρτυς, "witness," which passed into Latin and from there to the Romance languages.[1] This is, for example, the predominant sense of the word in the Septuagint, the Greek translation of the Hebrew Bible, where it often appears in a juridical context, translating "witness" (*ᶜed*).[2] The more usual sense of martyr, however, developed within the Christian community in the second century C.E.;[3] it focuses on persecution, suffering, and death.

It is tempting to search for an equivalent Hebrew technical term for martyr. The term *kiddush hashem*, "sanctification of the name," closely identified with the crusades and even the holocaust,[4] immediately presents itself. Though this term is based on biblical usage, particularly on the prophet Ezekiel, it is not a suitable starting point for investigating martyrdom in the Hebrew Bible. In Ezekiel, it is typically God who sanctifies his name by saving Israel while the nations watch; see, for example, Ezekiel 36:22–23: "Say to the House of Israel: 'Thus said the Lord God; Not for your sake will I act, O House of Israel, but for my holy name, which you have caused to be profaned among the nations to which you have come. I will sanctify My great name which has been profaned among the nations—among whom you have caused it to be profaned. And the

3

nations shall know that I am the Lord—declares the Lord God—when I manifest My holiness before their eyes through you.'"[5]

In contrast to martyrdom, Israel here is a passive participant, while God is the active character.[6] The difference between the biblical *kiddush hashem* and the rabbinic *kiddush hashem*, which in some of its forms has many similarities to the predominant Christian notion of martyrdom, has been appreciated by Holtz, who notes that the rabbinic concept of "sanctification by death is a complete reversal of the biblical concept of the sanctification of the Name by miraculous but joyous, events in history."[7]

The absence of a term for martyr in the Hebrew Bible does not suggest that martyrs and martyrdom did not exist; after all, theodicy is a central issue of the Book of Job, but neither that book nor any other biblical work offers a Hebrew term for theodicy. Job is a particularly instructive example of how a text may assume a phenomenon without naming it. Readers of Job would agree that the first chapters of the book describe the testing or trial of Job as background to the poetic center, though any word related to the root "to try or test" (*nsh*) is absent. Job must be a central text in any serious discussion of theodicy or of how or why God tests people, even though it lacks the crucial Hebrew terminology for assigning it to these categories. Similarly, the Hebrew Bible belongs in the discussion of the development of the idea of martyr and martyrdom. Different scholars have proposed various definitions for the term martyr.[8] I will here adopt the defining characteristics proposed by Droge and Tabor in their study of Hebrew, Greek, and early Christian attitudes toward different types of suicide, *A Noble Death*.[9] This definition is useful in that it allows the biblical evidence to be incorporated into more general discussions of martyrdom. Droge and Tabor enumerate the following five characteristics of martyrs, placing special emphasis on the fifth:

1. They reflect situations of opposition and persecution.
2. The choice to die, which these individuals make, is viewed by the authors as necessary, noble, and heroic.
3. These individuals are often eager to die; indeed, in several cases they end up directly *killing themselves*.
4. There is often the idea of vicarious benefit resulting from their suffering and death.
5. The expectation of vindication and reward beyond death, more often than not, is a prime motivation for their choice of death.[10]

What is immediately striking once we begin to work with this conception of martyr is the general absence of martyrs in the Hebrew Bible. This point becomes quite clear once we examine the individuals who commit suicide in the Hebrew Bible. Certainly, suicide and martyrdom are closely related; as Droge and Tabor note, "One person's martyr was another person's suicide, and vice versa."[11] Six individuals commit suicide in the Bible: Abimelek, Saul, Saul's armor bearer, Samson, Ahitophel, and Zimri.[12] I will comment only on Saul and Samson, the best known of these individuals, whose deaths most closely approach those of martyrs.

The final chapter of First Samuel describes Saul's suicide in a single verse: "Saul said to his arms-bearer, 'Draw your sword and run me through, so that the uncircumcised may not run me through and make sport of me'" (31:4). Saul chose suicide in the middle of a losing battle against the Philistines; he was afraid that the Philistines would abuse his corpse, a fate which, according to the continuation of the chapter, befell him anyway. Yet, he was no martyr. He fulfills the first three criteria: he dies at a time of military opposition; the author seems to view his choice to die as noble and heroic; and he does (indirectly) kill himself. The last two criteria, however, that there would be some vicarious benefit from his death and that there would be some reward beyond death, are lacking.

Samson's death, though, approaches martyrdom. It fulfills all the criteria of Saul's death; in addition, there certainly is a vicarious benefit from his death: he killed many Philistines as he committed suicide, bringing down the Temple of Dagon on himself and the assembled celebrants. The text makes this quite clear, by claiming that Samson's final words were "Let me die with the Philistines!" (Judges 16:30aα) and by summarizing the episode "Those who were slain by him as he died outnumbered those who had been slain by him when he lived" (16:30b). Yet the final aspect, "the expectation of vindication and reward beyond death, more often than not, is a prime motivation for their choice of death," is absent. The Book of Judges makes it quite clear that Samson's vindication is the death of many Philistines, not some otherworldly reward. Additionally, many depictions of martyrs are typically paradigmatic, with the hero portrayed as an example of righteousness that others should follow. This is certainly not the case with Samson, whose behavior is so problematic that one scholar considers the Samson stories to be a type of allegory describing wayward Israel.[13]

I would like to turn briefly to resistance, a phenomenon which can turn into martyrdom, but, as we shall see, in ancient Israel typically did not do so. Several biblical texts from the Book of Kings reflect resistance to foreign political domination over the land of Israel in the preexilic period. A second, fundamentally different type of resistance may be seen in two of the latest biblical texts from the Persian and Greek periods, Esther and Daniel.

For much of the period during which the First Temple was standing, approximately 950–586 B.C.E., the Israelites did not enjoy political autonomy. Rather, they were a vassal state, often subjugated to one of the great Mesopotamian powers of Assyria or Babylon. This is not an arcane historical fact but rather an issue that is of fundamental importance for understanding the Bible and the ancient Israelite perception of self. Phrased differently, ancient Israel was a provincial country, situated between the great powers of Egypt and Mesopotamia, which had been flourishing for millennia before Israel arose. Ancient Israel found itself in the unenviable position of being a buffer state between these two great imperial powers—two high civilizations with old and sophisticated literatures, arts, and religions. It is certainly striking that under such circumstances, the people of the country could maintain their ethnic and religious identity to any degree, rather than becoming absorbed into the mainstream cultures. In fact, in various periods there was active resistance against these powers—against tremendous odds.

Our knowledge of much of the political, social, and religious history of biblical Israel is far from complete. There are few extrabiblical texts that offer knowledge concerning Israel; archeological evidence is often very difficult to interpret, and most biblical historical texts are written from a highly ideological perspective, making it difficult to use them to reconstruct the past. But it remains difficult to discount completely the many biblical texts that suggest extreme forms of acculturation to the surrounding societies.[14] The tendency toward accommodation in the biblical period may be seen most clearly in the stories in Kings concerning the prophet Elijah, whom I will examine later as a protomartyr. Elijah is presented as the lone remaining prophet to the God of Israel, fighting against an entire nation which had been swayed by the religion of the contiguous Phoenicians. Elijah states twice in the famous chapter in which God appears to him through "a small still voice": "I am moved by zeal for the Lord, the God of Hosts, for the Israelites have forsaken Your covenant, torn down your altars, and put your prophets to the sword. I alone am left, and they are out to take my life" (1 Kings 19:10, 14). Even once we factor in the exaggerated nature of this statement, it still likely reflects some reality of abandonment of native Israelite traditions to those of the surrounding cultures, especially given the political alliances between Israel and these city-states. In the words of a drier account in an earlier chapter of Kings: "Ahab son of Omri did what was displeasing to the Lord . . . he took as wife Jezebel Daughter of King Ethbaal of the Phoenicians, and he went and served Baal and worshipped him. He erected an altar to Baal in the temple of Baal which he erected in Samara . . . "[15] (17:30).

This account of northern Israelite religion in the ninth century B.C.E. is in no way unique. One of the most significant chapters for studying ancient biblical theology and the issues of exclusivity, acculturation, and assimilation is Jeremiah 44, which focuses on women's popular religion.[16] Jeremiah began prophesying while the First Temple was still standing, around the time of Josiah's reform—a reform which according to the Bible instituted strict Yahwism centered around Jerusalem and abolished the worship of other deities—and he continued to prophesy after the destruction of that Temple in 586 B.C.E. Chapter 44 is set after the fall of Jerusalem and the destruction of the Temple and is addressed to the community of exiles in Egypt. One of Jeremiah's most difficult tasks was to convince these exiles that their punishment was deserved, caused by the people's abandonment of God for other deities. The response of the Judean-Egyptian community to his harangue is quite significant:

> We will not listen to you in the matter about which you spoke to us in the name of the Lord. On the contrary, we will do everything that we have vowed—to make offerings to the Queen of Heaven and to pour libations to her, as we used to do, we and our fathers, our kings and our officials, in the towns of Judah and the streets of Jerusalem. For then we had plenty to eat, we were well off, and suffered no misfortune. But ever since we have stopped making offerings to the Queen of Heaven and pouring libations to her, we have lacked everything, and we have been consumed by the sword and by famine.[17]

The people here are saying that they have conducted an empirical experiment: before the days of the Josianic reform, when they worshiped the Queen of Heaven, almost certainly some form of the Mesopotamian high goddess Ishtar, all was well. However, after Josiah's reform, when exclusive Yahwism was instituted and the worship of Ishtar ceased, the nation's fate quickly declined—after all, the great reforming king, Josiah, was killed in battle by the Egyptian king a mere thirteen years after his religious reform, and several decades later, the Temple lay in ruins and much of the upper-class population was forcibly exiled to Babylonia. The results of the experiment are clear—avoid extreme nationalism, certainly on the religious level, but quite possibly on the political level as well. It is better to live a Babylonian lifestyle as a vassal of Babylon than to have Judah turned into a Babylonian province, depopulated of Judeans. Thus, this chapter reflects an early form of the argument that assimilation assures survival.

This was not, however, the only biblical view. In the late eighth century, Judah was a vassal of the mighty Assyrian empire. That culture had a tremendous influence on Judah: Assyrian loan words appear in the Bible,[18] and some of the prophecies of Isaiah reflect an intimate knowledge of Assyrian literary texts.[19] Assyrian religious practices also infiltrated into Judah. It was earlier felt that these were forced by the Assyrian overlords,[20] but more recent studies have debated this contention, noting that the Assyrians did not typically impose their religious beliefs on their vassals.[21] Most recently, a cogent middle position has developed: "Whether something is 'imposed' or 'voluntarily adopted' is a matter of perspective. To cite a modern illustration, an American visitor and an African national might have opposite views about the significance of an African bride wearing a very Western-looking white lace wedding gown. What the American might view as voluntary imitation, the African might consider cultural imperialism."[22]

Yet, what is decisive even in this new position is that the vassals were not punished if they maintained their native religious practices; just as Africans are not punished by Americans or Europeans for wearing traditional tribal garb during a wedding ceremony, the Judeans and Israelites who adhered to strict Yahwism were not punished by the Babylonians or the Assyrians. In the context of Judah as an Assyrian vassal, when Judah had adopted many Assyrian religious customs, the events of 701 B.C.E. are quite remarkable. The most accurate biblical account of that year's events reads: "Hezekiah son of King Ahaz became king . . . He abolished the shrines and smashed the pillars and cut down the sacred post . . . He trusted only in the Lord the God of Israel . . . He clung to the Lord; he did not turn away from following Him, but kept the commandments that the Lord had given to Moses . . . He rebelled against the king of Assyria and would not serve him" (2 Kings 18:1–7). Thus, rebellion against the Assyrian overlord and reintroduction of strict monotheistic practices and the rejection of Assyrian religious customs went hand in hand; the Bible depicts a political and religious rebellion. But what was the result of such a revolt? According to an Assyrian source, which is remarkably similar to one account found in 2 Kings 18:13–16: "As to Hezekiah, the Judean, he did not submit to my yoke, I laid siege to 46 of his strong cities, walled forts and to the countless small villages in their vicinity, and conquered them. . . . I drove out 200,150 people, young and old, male and female, horses, mules, donkeys, camels, big and small cattle beyond counting, and considered them booty. Himself I made a prisoner in Jerusalem, his royal city, like a bird in a cage."[23]

Hezekiah's attempt at gaining political freedom did not end well—the political situation of the Judeans was drastically reduced, and the following king, Manasseh, undid his father's reforms: "He rebuilt the shrines that his father Hezekiah had destroyed; he erected altars for Baal and made a sacred post . . . He bowed down to all the host of heaven and worshipped them, and . . . he built altars for all the hosts of heaven in the two courts of the House of the Lord" (2 Kings 21:3–5).

In sum, the evidence of Kings presents religious purists versus extreme assimilationists,[24] with all sorts of stripes in between. The more typical reaction then, as in more recent times, was accommodation. Hezekiah, at the very end of the eighth century, is an example of extreme resistance; he dared to oppose the mighty Assyrians, the great imperial power of his time that had overrun much of the ancient world. Though the Assyrians did not systematically slaughter the nations they conquered—these people were too valuable for forced labor—their extreme cruelty is evidenced in their literary texts, where they slay the enemy until their blood flows in rivers,[25] or in various reliefs, which show enemy men, naked and impaled,[26] reminiscent of more recent and contemporary horrors. The Bible depicts Hezekiah's religious and political idealism as highly positive, although it was political and military suicide—like the fighters in the Warsaw Ghetto, he believed in resistance at all costs.

Should Hezekiah be considered a martyr? Though a very broad definition of the term might view him as one, he does not fulfill certain crucial criteria of my understanding of the term. First, he is not killed; though his rebellion against the power of Assyria might be viewed as suicidal, it did not ultimately result in suicide. Though hindsight suggests that the attempt to rebel against "the might that was Assyria"[27] is quite foolhardy, there is no suggestion that Hezekiah was "eager to die" in this rebellion. More significant, the rebellion does not take place because of a situation of persecution. As noted before, the Assyrians did not enforce Assyrian religion or the worship of Assyrian gods on their vassals, though, much like today, many Israelites might have opted to incorporate elements of that religion in order to blend in with the politically dominant power. Most significantly, the rebellion was an attempt at gaining political (and economic) freedom. There is not the slightest hint that religious issues stood behind this rebellion or that through overthrowing his overlord, Hezekiah expected a "reward beyond death."

I have spent so much time discussing Hezekiah because a careful analysis of his rebellion and its failure helps to highlight why it is so difficult to discuss martyrdom within the context of preexilic Israel, namely, the absence of religious persecution in the ancient Near Eastern world. Oddly enough, Israel seems to be the only nation of that time that was, on occasion, fundamentally intolerant of other religions.[28] This is, of course, connected to the emergent monotheistic nature of some forms of Israelite religion, a long and complicated development which cannot be traced here.[29] Fundamental to this issue is the development of the notion of the *ḥerem*, translated as either "the ban" or "proscription," legislation that suggests that the autochthonous nations of Canaan must be exterminated because they will lead the radically monotheistic[30] Israelites astray.[31] This legislation, which may have reflected an ideal of religious purity rather than actual practice,[32] is a reflection of a type of religious intolerance of a group of people whom Morton Smith calls the "Yahweh-alone party."[33] This party was locked in fundamental conflict with those who practiced a syncretistic brand of Yahwism, the people whom Elijah alludes to in his famous words: "How long will you keep hopping between two opinions? If the Lord is God, follow him; and if Baal, follow him!" (1 Kings 18:21b).

The Book of Kings presents a picture of Elijah as the lone survivor of the conflict between the Yahweh-alone party, which he heads, and the syncretistic party, headed by Ahab and his wife Jezebel.[34] Should either Elijah or those who belonged to his party, whom the text suggests the king had killed, be considered martyrs?

Elijah fulfills several of the criteria for martyrdom. The entire Elijah cycle reflects "situations of opposition and persecution";[35] at one point, in 1 Kings 19, a chapter full of allusions to Moses,[36] Elijah is eager to die (1 Kings 19:4), and this choice seems to be viewed positively by the narrator, though God does not fulfill Elijah's will. Two Kings 9:7 suggests that various prophets contemporaneous with Elijah were actually killed.[37] There even is, to some extent, "the expectation of vindication and reward beyond death," as is made clear from Elijah's comment to his disciple (2 Kings 2:10), which suggests that Elijah knew that he would not die a natural death. Yet, there is no "idea of vicarious benefit resulting from [his] suffering and death." Additionally, the text presents the end of Elijah's life on earth as an extraordinary event; other Israelites could not expect to leave this world in "a fiery chariot with fiery horses" (v. 11). This absence of a widespread concept of "reward beyond death" is a decisive factor responsible for the lack of martyrdom in the preexilic period.

The analysis of Hezekiah's revolt and of the Elijah pericope highlights the fact that a full-blown ideology of martyrdom could not exist in preexilic Israel because that society typically lived in an era of religious tolerance and did not have a developed notion of a positive afterlife. In contrast to Elijah and Enoch, "whom God took" (Gen. 5:24), most Israelites expected to enter *sheol* upon their death.[38] *Sheol*, the underworld, was a rather unpleasant place, in which the individual lived a half-life of sorts. It was removed from the divine realm; various psalmists note that the dead do not praise God.[39] It is also the great equalizer; in the words of Job 3:19a, "Small and great alike are there." It would only be in the postexilic era, once the notions of the afterlife would begin to change and Israel would be confronted with extreme religious intolerance, that the notion of martyrdom could fully develop.

One of these elements, the confrontation with extreme religious intolerance, is first reflected in the Book of Esther.[40] The story of Esther is well known. It is set in the Persian empire, where Mordecai, a Jew, refuses to bow down to the king's vizier Haman the Agagite. As a result of this action, Haman decided to kill the entire Jewish population and had Mordecai not intervened with the help of his relative Esther, one of the king's wives, the Jews would have all been killed. Instead, "the opposite happened" (Esther 9:1); Haman was killed, the Jewish community was saved, many members of the non-Jewish community were massacred, and Mordecai the Jew was exalted, replacing his archenemy Haman.

The action that sets the problems into motion is quite obscure—Mordecai refuses to bow down to Haman. What is Mordecai's problem? The traditional Jewish position assimilates Mordecai into the martyr paradigm, claiming that it was forbidden to bow to a human being. However, bowing to a person is never prohibited in any biblical legislation, and people bow down to each other throughout the Bible—indeed, toward the end of the book (8:3), Esther bows down to Ahasuerus![41] In any case, as a result of Mordecai's actions, Haman decides that killing Mordecai alone is insufficient—all the Jews, Mordecai's coreligionists, must be killed (3:6). The verses in which Haman makes his request (3:8–9) are so significant that they are worth quoting: "Haman said to King Ahasuerus, 'There is a certain people, scattered and dispersed among the other peoples in all the provinces of your realms, whose laws are different from those of any other people and who do not obey the king's laws; and it in not in your majesty's interest to tolerate them.'"A major focus of these verses is that somehow difference is evil, a notion anticipated earlier when Mordecai took exception to the norm of bowing to Haman. Yet, this perception of difference was a minority opinion—according to the scroll, the city of Susa was dismayed when the edict concerning the destruction of the Jews was announced (3:15), and overjoyed at the eventual deliverance of the Jews (8:15). In fact, it is quite possible that Ahasuerus's edict was not at all motivated by what some would call anti-Semitism—Haman offers Ahasuerus an astronomical sum to pass the edict, computed by some to be over 60 percent of the annual tax revenues.[42] Haman is certainly motivated by fear of difference; Ahasuerus is motivated by monetary greed. Phrased differently, to the extent that ideology is central to the production of martyrs,[43] Haman's reasons, based on difference, are highly ideological and reflect issues connected to martyrdom, while the motivation attributed to Ahasuerus is economic and should not be connected to the ideology of martyrdom.

The Jews succeeded through physical resistance. Esther, jeopardizing her life, obtained permission for the Jews to fight back, and in typical biblical measure-for-measure fashion,[44] to do unto their enemies exactly what their enemies were intending to do to them.

Should Esther be considered a potential martyr? In some senses she is, for when Esther followed Mordecai's advice to go to the king and ask permission for the Jews to fight back, she risked death, since such unsolicited visits could result in death if the king did not show the visitor favor (4:11). The risk that she took saved the community as a whole. Yet, according to the definition proposed earlier, she could not be a martyr, for the central element of "the expectation of vindication and reward beyond death" is lacking.

Still, Esther is a fundamental text for understanding the development of martyrdom, for it is the earliest biblical text to suggest an ideological opposition to difference—in this case, practice of the Jewish religion. Though the Persians were not typically xenophobic,[45] ethnic strife could and did erupt in the vast Persian empire.[46] The Book of Esther must at least reflect the fear of such strife being directed against the Jewish community, if not an actual attempt to harm or to destroy that community. That book served as a significant myth of encouragement, telling the Jewish community that such attempts at destruction cannot, and will not, succeed.[47] Finally, the Jewish community, despite its fears of being so different, or perhaps because of those fears, could actually create as part of their story the idea that many of the people either converted or pretended to be Jews,[48] an inversion of the much later Conversos. Thus, although the Book of Esther introduces the element of national persecution, a fundamental element of martyrdom, this book is ultimately anti-martyrdom—the Jews of Esther redefine themselves as political victors rather than victims.

The themes of persecution and of the transformation of victim into victor also appear in the first six chapters of Daniel, which is similar to Esther in other significant aspects as well.[49] Daniel is an amazingly complex book, full of critical problems that have not been resolved.[50] All scholars agree that in terms of genre, the first six chapters, which are stories, should be distinguished from the last six chapters of the book, which are apocalyptic visions. There is, however, serious disagreement concerning the dating of the first part of the book. While there is a scholarly consensus that chapters 7–12 date from the period of persecution under Antiochus IV in the middle of the second pre-Christian century,[51] it is uncertain whether the first six chapters date from this period as well or whether they were written several centuries earlier.[52] In any case, these chapters show significant similarities to Esther.[53] They are both postexilic biblical texts set in the foreign court. Yet, it is not the mere placement of the Jew in the royal court that makes these stories relevant; in both, following certain well-established folk-tale patterns, a great danger—what folklorists call a "complication"—arises to either the Jewish individual or people, and through various unexpected twists, the problem is resolved, the situation of the Jews is improved, and they all live happily ever after.

Some of the stories from the first six chapters of Daniel are well known, at least from Western art—for example, Daniel in the lion's den from chapter 6 or the three friends of Daniel in the fiery furnace in chapter 3.[54] The book in its current form begins with the rather tame story of Daniel and his four friends succeeding in the royal court because they adhere to the Jewish dietary requirements (Dan. 1). This suggests that there is no need for Jews to be separate; divine intervention would assure that they could fully integrate. This story's author believed or hoped that God always intervenes to help his people.

The stories in Daniel get better and better. In chapter 3, Daniel's three friends refuse to bow down to an image, though failure to bow down was punishable by death in a fiery furnace.[55] The chapter is a literary masterpiece, including fine details—like the fact that the furnace was so hot, the people who threw the Jews into it were killed by the heat, and when Daniel's three friends emerged from the flames, they were totally unscathed, not even the odor of fire clung to them. The king, after viewing this "miracle," says that anyone who blasphemes this God "shall be torn limb from limb" (v. 29) and notes of the Jewish God: "His kingdom is an everlasting kingdom, and His dominion endures throughout the generations" (v. 33). Quite an amazing sentiment to come from the mouth of King Nebuchadnezzar, who destroyed the First Temple!

Daniel 6 is the most remarkable, and most fanciful, of these three stories. Various royal officials conspire against Daniel and get an edict passed that for the next thirty days prayers and petitions may only be addressed to the king, Darius. Yet, "When Daniel learned that [the decree] had been put in writing, he went to his house . . . knelt down, prayed and made confession to his God, as he had always done" (v. 11). The king, who loved Daniel, was beside himself, but had no choice—Daniel was thrown into the lions' den, which was closed with a rock and sealed with the royal signet ring. Yet, Daniel was saved by a divine angel "and no injury was found on him, for he had trusted in his God" (v. 24). The officials who wanted Daniel dead were then thrown into the lions' den along with their families, and "They had hardly reached the bottom of the den when the lions overpowered them and crushed all their bones" (v. 25). The chapter ends with a prayer by Darius to God, which is longer and more powerful than the earlier prayer of Nebuchadnezzar. The first part of Daniel concludes with a wonderful crescendo.

Like Esther, the stories of Daniel 1–6 all have as their basis the idea that "different is suspect."[56] Yet, this difference does not lead to genocide; it is only applied against powerful individuals, like Daniel and his friends, who are willing to die because of their beliefs. They do not eat the impure food; they do not bow to the statue; and they continue to pray to God. They feel that over the Jewish religion itself, there is no compromise.[57] And God hears their voices; such powerful and complete spiritual, nonviolent resistance is rewarded by God.

Here, too, we have a model of behavior that approaches martyrdom, of individuals willing to die at a time of persecution. But like Esther, these individuals should not be considered full-fledged martyrs, for they are not killed and, more fundamentally, they do not look forward to death as being better than life. The stories make it quite clear that the protagonists do not expect to die. They have great faith that God will intervene and save them; there is no sense that there will be a reward in the afterlife.

It is only in the final chapters of the Book of Daniel, representing the very latest of the canonical books of the Hebrew Bible, that all the necessary elements for martyrdom come together, as the notion of resurrection is first clearly seen in the Bible. The verses in question read, "Many of those that sleep in the dust of the earth will awake, some to eternal life, others to reproaches, to everlasting abhorrence. And the knowledgeable will be radiant like the bright expanse of sky, and those who lead the many to righteousness will be like the stars forever and ever" (12:2–3).[58] The origin of the idea of resurrection as it appears in Daniel is debated. Some see the text in Daniel as the culmination of a long biblical development, going back to the preexilic period.[59] Much more likely, however, is the possibility that this notion developed in the postexilic period, largely under Persian[60] or Greek influence.[61] This explains why, for example, none of the people who opt for death in the preexilic period ever expresses the notion that death is life.[62] Exactly when this idea entered Judaism, and the process through which it began to replace the earlier idea of *sheol*, is quite unclear. However, given the relative attractiveness of a positive afterlife to the half-life of *sheol,* it is quite easy to imagine this idea quickly winning acceptance, paving the way for a full-fledged concept of martyrdom.[63]

The last chapters of Daniel, with the idea of resurrection where the knowledgeable and/or righteous will be like stars, comes from the period of 167–164 B.C.E., during the persecution of the Jewish community under the Greek Seleucid King Antiochus IV Epiphanes, who, according to various traditions, desecrated the Second Temple and forbade central Jewish legal requirements, including circumcision and the study of Torah.[64] Antiochus was eventually defeated by the Maccabees, but for several years the community in Israel was terrorized by his decrees, decrees that were not at all normative for Seleucid rule, which was typically quite tolerant of non-Hellenistic religious practices. The reasons for Antiochus's extremism are unclear, though it is worth pointing out that several classical authors punned on his name Antiochus Epiphanes, "manifest (as god)," calling him Epimanes, "utterly mad," thus perhaps we need not look at the decrees of Antiochus as part of a fully conceived political or religious plan.

This shift to full-scale religious persecution is the last missing piece that allowed the idea of martyrdom to develop. The persecution is referred to in the typically difficult and obscure language of the concluding chapters of Daniel, which state concerning Antiochus: "He will have great strength, but not through his own strength. He will be extraordinarily destructive; he will prosper in what he does, and destroy the mighty and the people of holy ones" (8:24). The entire time period is conceived of as an era of "wrath" (8:19).[65]

The Book of Daniel sees the coalescence of these ideas of extreme religious persecution and immortality, leading, at the very end of what is considered the biblical period, to the only biblical example of true martyrdom. It is possible that the large-scale persecution of Jews for the observance of the Torah aided in fostering the notions of resurrection and immortality, but as noted above, these ideas probably did not develop *de novo* in this period. To the extent that they are Greek ideas, it is ironic that they should have been accepted by the extreme anti-Hellenistic community responsible for writing the second half of Daniel.

In sum, the question posed by this essay's title should largely be answered in the negative. There was no concept of martyrdom for most of the biblical period. Some of the preconditions for martyrdom developed, but the civilizations that ruled over ancient Israel were typically tolerant of this small religious minority, so that religious persecution, essential for the development of martyrdom, was absent. This began to change only with the writing of the Book of Esther. Even then, however, "the expectation of vindication and reward beyond death" as "a prime motivation for their choice of death" was absent.

It is only in Daniel, the very latest book of the Hebrew Bible, where we find the coalescence of all the factors necessary for true martyrdom, and the first descriptions of martyrdom as a religious ideal in Judaism. When embedded within a culture that is persecuted for its religious beliefs and believes in an afterlife, martyrdom becomes a very attractive idea and ideal, and thus it is no surprise that early Judaism continued to use and develop this idea. Various postbiblical historical figures were depicted as martyrs, sometimes by their contemporaries, at other times by later tradents; in this period even biblical figures could anachronistically be depicted as martyrs. An example of the latter is the treatment of Isaac as a prototypical martyr in some of the Targumim (Aramaic translations of the Bible).[66] There are many illustrations of the former. Prominent examples include the story told about a mother who martyred herself along with her seven children, either during the persecution of Antiochus or during the later Hadrianic persecutions and Bar Kochba Revolt (132–35 C.E.),[67] to the story, which exists in many forms and is historically impossible, of the ten sages put to death during the Hadrianic persecutions.[68] These stories would reach a new crescendo during the Crusades.[69]

A clear understanding of the biblical period, which rarely depicts martyrdom, is indispensable for understanding why this phenomenon only developed in the second century B.C.E., in the very latest part of the biblical period. Some scholars have argued recently for a strong discontinuity between the Bible and Hellenistic Judaism and have gone as far as suggesting that Judaism is a fundamentally Hellenistic phenomenon.[70] Though I disagree with the broad strokes of this picture,[71] for particular historical reasons, the observation is valid for the history of Jewish martyrdom, which is first evidenced during the Hellenistic period, perhaps under Hellenistic influence, and then becomes a fundamental element of Jewish religion.

Notes

I would like to thank Susie Tanchel of Brandeis University for her assistance in preparing this essay, which was last updated in 1997. The abbreviations follow the *Journal of Biblical Literature*.

1. On the etymology and early use, see Hermann B. Strathmann, "μάρτυς etc.," *TDNT* 4 (1967): 475–81; on the word in English, see *The Oxford English Dictionary*, 2nd ed., ed. J. A. Simpson and E. S. C. Weiner (Oxford: Clarendon Press, 1989), 9: 413–14.

2. Strathmann, "μάρτυς etc.," 482–83.

3. Ibid., 504–7; see especially N. Brox, *Zeuge und Märtyrer. Untersuchungen zur frühchristlichen Zeugnis-Terminologie* (Munich: Kösel, 1961).

4. Note the title of Shimon Huberband, *Kiddush Hashem: Jewish Religious and Cultural Life in Poland during the Holocaust*, trans. David E. Fishman (Hobokon, N.J.: Ktav, 1987).

5. Translations of the Hebrew Bible follow *Tanakh: A New Translation of the Holy Scriptures According to the Traditional Hebrew Text* (Philadelphia: Jewish Publication Society, 1985).

6. On God as holy in the Hebrew Bible, see John G. Gammie, *Holiness in Israel*, OBT (Minneapolis: Fortress, 1989), 45–51.

7. Avraham Holtz, "Kiddush and Hillul Hashem," *Judaism* 10 (1961): 360–67. According to n. 72*, this usage began with the Hadrianic persecutions.

8. For a survey, aside from the various studies in this volume, see the works in *Die Entstehung der Jüdischen Martyrologie*, ed. J. W. van Henten (Leiden: E. J. Brill, 1989), especially the discussion on 220–23.

9. Arthur J. Droge and James D. Tabor, *A Noble Death: Suicide and Martyrdom Among Christians and Jews in Antiquity* (New York: HarperSanFrancisco, 1992).

10. Ibid., 75.

11. Ibid., 188.

12. The most extensive discussion of these individuals is ibid., 53–60.

13. Edward L. Greenstein, "The Riddle of Samson," *Prooftexts* 1 (1981): 237–60. For an explanation of Samson's behavior based on folklore see Susan Niditch, "Samson as Culture Hero, Trickster, and Bandit: The Empowerment of the Weak," *CBQ* 52 (1990): 608–24.

14. For a different viewpoint which is deeply skeptical about the possibilities of using the Bible to reconstruct preexilic Israel, see Philip R. Davies, *In Search of "Ancient Israel,"* JSOTSup 148 (Sheffield: Sheffield Academic Press, 1992); Thomas L. Thompson, *Early History of the Israelite People from the Written and Archaeological Sources* (Leiden: E. J. Brill, 1992); and Niels Peter Lemche, "The Old Testament—A Hellenistic Book?" *Scandinavian Journal of the Old Testament* 7 (1993): 163–93. For a discussion of this new understanding of biblical history, see Hershel Shanks, moderator, "Face to Face: Biblical Minimalists Meet Their Challengers," *BARev* 23/4 (July/August 1997): 26–42, 66–67.

15. The clearest presentation of the religious parties of this period remains Morton Smith, *Palestinian Parties and Politics That Shaped the Old Testament* (New York: Columbia University Press, 1971): 15–56. On Ahab, see 34–35.

16. On this chapter see tentatively Susan Ackerman, "'And the Women Knead Dough': The Worship of the Queen of Heaven in Sixth-Century Judah," in *Gender and Difference,* ed. Peggy Day (Minneapolis: Fortress, 1989), 109–24, and more recently, Susan Ackerman, *Under Every Green Tree: Popular Religion in Sixth-Century Judah,* HSM 46 (Atlanta: Scholars Press, 1992), 5–35, especially 5–11 and 32–33.

17. Jeremiah 44:16–18.

18. See Édouard Lipiński, "Emprunts seméro-akkadiens en hébreu biblique," *ZAH* 1 (1988): 61–73 and Eduard Yechezkel Kutscher, *A History of the Hebrew Language* (Jerusalem: Magnes, 1982), 48–49 (with bibliography).

19. Peter Machinist, "Assyria and Its Image in the First Isaiah," *JAOS* 103 (1983): 719–37.

20. This view is especially associated with A. T. Olmstead; for a survey of its influence, see Morton Cogan, *Imperialism and Religion: Assyria, Judah and Israel in the Eighth and Seventh Centuries* B.C.E., SBLMS 19 (Missoula, Mont.: SBL and Scholars Press, 1974), 1–7.

21. See Cogan, *Imperialism and Religion,* and John William McKay, *Religion in Judah under the Assyrians 732–609 B.C.,* SBT² 26 (London: Alienson, 1973).

22. R. H. Lowery, *The Reforming Kings: Cults and Society in First Temple Judah,* JSOTSup 120 (Sheffield: Sheffield Academic Press, 1991); the quote is from p. 140.

23. *Ancient Near Eastern Texts Relating to the Old Testament,* 3rd ed. with Supplement, ed. James B. Pritchard (Princeton: Princeton University Press, 1969), 288. I have modified the translation slightly, correcting the translator's "Hezekiah the Jew" to "Hezekiah the Judean." The historicity of the various biblical accounts concerning 701 B.C.E. is one of the most debated issues of biblical scholarship. I favor the single campaign theory and am generally skeptical of the historicity of 2 Kings 18:13–20:19. For a discussion of the problem see especially Brevard Childs, *Isaiah and the Assyrian Crisis,* SBT² 3 (London: SCM, 1967); Mordechai Cogan and Hayim Tadmor, *II Kings,* AB 11 (New

York: Doubleday, 1988) 246–51; and Francolino J. Gonçalves, *L'expédition de Sennachérib en Palestine dans la littérature hébraïque ancienne*, Ebib n. s. 7 (Paris: Libraire Lecoffre J. Gabalda, 1986).

24. For this model, see Smith, *Palestinian Parties*.

25. See, e.g., the description from the Annals of Shalmaneser III, in *Ancient Near Eastern Texts Relating to the Old Testament*, 279.

26. See, e.g., the relief from the siege of Lachish, *The Ancient Near East in Pictures Relating to the Old Testament*, 2nd ed. with Supplement, ed. James B. Pritchard (Princeton: Princeton University Press, 1969), p. 131 #373.

27. The appropriateness of this epithet for Assyria is suggested by its use as a book title in H. W. F. Saggs, *The Might That Was Assyria* (London: Sidgwick and Jackson, 1984).

28. For various explorations for why this was so, see Mark G. Brett, ed., *Ethnicity and the Bible* (Leiden: E. J. Brill, 1996), especially 25–169.

29. For one reconstruction, see Baruch Halpern, "'Brisker Pipes than Poetry': The Development of Israelite Monotheism," in *Judaic Perspectives on Ancient Israel*, ed. Jacob Neusner et al. (Philadelphia: Fortress, 1989), 77–115.

30. The term is borrowed from Tikva Frymer-Kensky, *In the Wake of the Goddesses: Women, Culture, and the Biblical Transformation of Pagan Myth* (New York: Free Press, 1992).

31. On the *herem*, see Philip Stern, *The Biblical Ḥerem: A Window on Israel's Religious Experience*, BJS 211 (Atlanta: Scholars Press, 1991).

32. This is the position suggested by Moshe Greenberg, "Ḥerem," *EJ* 8 (1972): 349.

33. Smith, *Palestinian Parties*, especially 15–56.

34. See especially 1 Kings 18:22a and 19:10b. On Jezebel, see Duane L. Christensen, "Huldah and the Men of Anathoth: Women in Leadership in the Deuteronomistic History," *SBL Seminar Papers* 23 (1984): 399–404, and Claudia V. Camp, "1 and 2 Kings" in *The Women's Bible Commentary*, ed. Carol A. Newsom and Sharon H. Ringe (Louisville, Ky.: Westminster/John Knox, 1992), 103–4.

35. I emphasize the word "reflects." The Elijah cycle has gone through a long history of development and it is often difficult to determine the extent to which it contains factual information. On its history, see the relevant sections of Alexander Rofé, *The Prophetical Stories: The Narratives about the Prophets in the Hebrew Bible: Their Literary Types and History*, trans. D. Levy et al. (Jerusalem: Magnes Press, 1988). If the suggestion of Steven L. McKenzie, *The Trouble with Kings: The Composition of the Book of Kings in the Deuteronomistic History*, SVT 42 (Leiden: E. J. Brill, 1991), 81–100, that the Elijah pericope is post-Deuteronomistic, is correct, it is then especially distant from the events that it purports to describe and must be used with extreme caution in reconstructing history.

36. See, e.g., Robert R. Wilson, *Prophecy and Society in Ancient Israel* (Philadelphia: Fortress Press, 1980), 197–99.

37. For material on the death of the prophets, see Mitchell Glenn Reddish, "The Theme of Martyrdom in the Book of Revelation" (Ph.D. diss., Southern Baptist Theological Seminary, 1982), 21–25. For the assimilation of these messages into the martyr paradigm, see Alexander Rofé, *The Prophetical Stories*, 197–213 ("The Rise of Martyrology"). Though we use different definitions of martyrology, the following observation is especially apposite: "it is not surprising that martyrology is completely absent from early biblical historiography, and especially from the prophetic stories—the historical circumstances of those times simply did not lend themselves to the development of this type of literature" (p. 199).

38. For a summary of the Israelite concept of *sheol*, see Theodore J. Lewis, "Dead, Abode of the," *ABD* 2 (1992): 101–5. Cf. Klaas von Spronk, *Beatific Afterlife in Ancient Israel and in the Near East*, AOAT 219 (Kevelaer: Butzon & Bercker, 1986), 66–71.

39. See Psalms 6:6; 30:10; 88:11–12; 115:17.

40. My understanding of Esther is especially indebted to Michael V. Fox, *Character and Ideology in the Book of Esther* (Columbia: University of South Carolina Press, 1991) and Jon D. Levenson, *Esther*, OTL (Louisville, Ky.: Westminster/John Knox, 1997).

41. For various suggestions on this refusal to bow down, including sources for the predominant Hebrew school answer, see Fox, *Character and Ideology*, 42–45 and Levenson, *Esther*, 67–68.

42. Fox, *Character and Ideology*, 51–52.

43. The ideological aspect of martyrdom is stressed in Samuel Z. Klausner, "Martyrdom," in *The Encyclopedia of Religion*, ed. Mircea Eliade (New York: Macmillan, 1987), 9: 230–38.

44. On the predominance of this theme in the Hebrew Bible, see Patrick D. Miller, Jr., *Sin and Judgment in the Prophets: A Stylistic and Theological Analysis*, SBLMS 27 (Chico, Calif.: Scholars Press, 1982).

45. Fox, *Character and Ideology*, 49.

46. Robert Gordis, "Religion, Wisdom and History in the Book of Esther," *JBL* 100 (1981): 383–84.

47. I use "myth" in the sense developed by Walter Burkert, *Structure and History in Greek Mythology and Ritual* (Berkeley: University of California Press, 1979), which emphasizes the positive social role of myths, as well as their tendency to develop certain literary rather than historical features.

48. The key term *mtyhdym* (8:17) is ambiguous; see the commentaries.

49. On the links between Esther and Daniel, see W. Lee Humphreys, "A Life-style for Diaspora: A Study of the Tales of Esther and Daniel," *JBL* 92 (1973): 211–23; Susan Niditch and Robert Doran, "The Success Story of the Wise Courtier," *JBL* 96 (1977): 179–93; and Lawrence M. Wills, *The Jew in the Court of the Foreign King*, HDR 26 (Minneapolis: Fortress, 1990).

50. For a summary, see Otto Eissfeldt, *The Old Testament: An Introduction*, trans. P. R. Ackroyd (New York: Harper and Row, 1965), 512–29, and most recently, John J. Collins, *Daniel*, Hermeneia (Minneapolis: Fortress, 1993),

24–38. On martyrdom in Daniel, see most recently Ulrich Kellerman, "Das Danielbuch und die Märtyrertheologie der Auferstehung," in *Die Entstehung der Jüdischen Martyrologie*, 51–75.

51. For a summary of the history of this period, see Lee I. A. Levine, "The Age of Hellenism: Alexander the Great and the Rise and Fall of the Hasmonean Kingdom," in *Ancient Israel: A Short History from Abraham to the Roman Destruction of the Temple*, ed. Hershel Shanks (Washington, D.C.: Biblical Archaeology Society, 1988), 177–83; more detailed accounts may be found in *The Cambridge History of Judaism, The Hellenistic Age*, ed. W. D. Davies and Louis Finkelstein (Cambridge: Cambridge University Press, 1989), 278–91; Geza Vermes and Fergus Millar, *A History of the Jewish People in the Age of Jesus Christ (175 B.C.–A.D. 135)* by Emil Schürer (Edinburgh: T & T Clark, 1973), 1: 137–74; and Lester L. Grabbe, *Judaism from Cyrus to Hadrian* (Minneapolis: Fortress, 1992), 1: 221–85.

52. See Eissfeldt, *The Old Testament*, 521–22 for a defense of the unitary view. The view of two separate time-periods is closely associated with H. L. Ginsberg; for a summary, see his "Daniel, Book of," *EJ* 5: 1277–89. A middle position is advocated in Louis F. Hartman and Alexander A. Di Lella, *The Book of Daniel*, AB 23 (New York: Doubleday, 1978), 11–18.

53. See n. 50, above.

54. My discussion of these stories is especially indebted to Danna Nolan Fewell, *Circle of Sovereignty: A Story of Stories in Daniel 1–6*, JSOTSup 72 (Sheffield: Sheffield Academic Press, 1988).

55. On this chapter, see now E. Haag, "Die drei Männer im Feuer nach Dan. 3:1–30," in *Die Entstehung der Jüdischen Martyrologie*, 20–50.

56. Fewell, *Circle of Sovereignty*, 70.

57. P. R. Davies, *Daniel*, Old Testament Guides (Sheffield: JSOT Press, 1985), 54.

58. On these verses, in addition to the commentaries, see B. J. Alfrink, "L'idée de Résurrection d'après Dan., XII, 1.2," *Bib* 40 (1959): 355–71; George W. E. Nickelsburg, Jr., *Resurrection, Immortality, and Eternal Life in Intertestamental Judaism*, HTS 26 (Cambridge: Harvard University Press, 1972), especially 11–27; John J. Collins, "Apocalyptic Eschatology as the Transcendence of Death," *CBQ* 36 (1974): 21–43; Gerhard F. Hasel, "Resurrection in the Theology of Old Testament Apocalyptic," *ZAW* 92 (1980): 267–84; André LaCoque, *Daniel and His Time* (Columbia: University of South Carolina Press, 1988), 161–72; and Spronk, *Beatific Afterlife*.

59. Leonard J. Greenspoon, "The Origin of the Idea of Resurrection," in *Traditions in Transformation: Turning Points in Biblical Faith*, ed. Baruch Halpern and Jon D. Levenson (Winona Lake, Ind.: Eisenbrauns, 1981), 247–321 and Spronk, *Beatific Afterlife*.

60. This is considered a possibility by Shaul Shaked, "Iranian Influence on Judaism: First Century B.C.E. to Second Century C.E.," in *The Cambridge History of Judaism*, vol. 1, ed. Davies and Finkelstein, 323.

61. See Martin Hengel, *Judaism and Hellenism*, trans. John Bowden (Philadelphia: Fortress, 1974), 1: 196–202, and especially Warren Joel Heard, Jr.,

"Maccabean Martyr Theology: Its Genesis, Antecedents and Significance for the Earliest Soteriological Interpretation of the Death of Jesus" (Ph.D. diss., University of Aberdeen, 1987), 185–393, especially 333–93.

62. For this formulation of the key element of martyrdom, see Droge and Tabor, *A Noble Death*, 85, "Death was seen, paradoxically, as life."

63. See Jonathan A. Goldstein, "The Hasmonean Revolt and the Hasmonean Dynasty," in *The Cambridge History of Judaism*, vol. 2, ed. Davies and Finkelstein, 294, "Indeed, with the prospect of resurrection, such pious Jews faced extermination."

64. See the standard commentaries and n. 52, above.

65. The outlines of this persecution may be filled in with detail from much less esoteric writings, such as the First Book of Maccabees. For this work as a historical source, see *Jewish Writings of the Second Temple Period: Apocrypha, Pseudepigrapha, Qumran Sectarian Writings, Philo, Josephus*, Compendia Rerum Iudaicarum ad Novum Testamentum, section 2, ed. Michael E. Stone (Assen: Van Gorcum, 1984), 171–76 and Grabbe, *Judaism from Cyrus to Hadrian* 1: 222–24.

66. See Robert Haywood, "The Present State of Research into the Targumic Account of the Sacrifice of Isaac," *JJS* 32 (1981): 127–50.

67. For a summary, see Gerson D. Cohen, "Hannah and Her Seven Sons," *EJ* 7: 1270–72; see especially his study, "Hannah and Her Seven Sons in Hebrew Literature" in his *Studies in the Variety of Rabbinic Culture* (Philadelphia: Jewish Publication Society, 1991), 39–60.

68. For a summary, see Moshe David Herr, "Ten Martyrs, The," *EJ* 15: 1006–8; note especially his "Persecution and Martyrdom in Hadrian's Day," *ScrHier* 23 (1972): 85–125 and the new edition of these texts in Gottfried Reeg, *Die Geschichte von den Zehn Märtyren: Synoptische Edition mit Übersetzung und Einleitung*, Texte und Studien zum Antiken Judentum (Tübingen: J.C.B. Mohr [Paul Siebeck], 1985). For the historical background, see Grabbe, *Judaism from Cyrus to Hadrian*, 2: 599–606.

69. See discussion of the martyrological poetry produced during the Crusades in Shalom Spiegel, *The Last Trial: On the Legends and Lore of the Command to Abraham to Offer Isaac as a Sacrifice: The Akedah*, trans. Judah Goldin (Philadelphia: Jewish Publication Society, 1967). On martyrdom and the First Crusade, see Robert Chazan, *European Jewry and the First Crusade* (Berkeley: University of California Press, 1987) especially 99–136, and more recently, his *In the Year 1096: The First Crusade and the Jews* (Philadelphia: Jewish Publication Society, 1996).

70. S. D. Fraade, "Palestinian Judaism," *ABD* 3: 1054–61 and P. Schäfer, *The History of the Jews in Antiquity*, trans. D. Chowcat (Luxembourg: Harwood, 1995), xi.

71. See my "Judaism in the Hebrew Bible? An Exploration of the Transition from Ancient Israelite Religion to Judaism," *CBQ* 61 (1999): 429–47.

TWO

HONOR AND SACREDNESS IN
THE ROMAN AND CHRISTIAN WORLDS

Carlin Barton

I dedicate this chapter to Mark Bingham, Thomas
Burnett, Jeremy Glick, and to those heroes of flight
93 whose names I do not know.

The Romans in the late Republic and early Empire endured, for
the most part, a universe without salvation. The gladiator and
the Christian who eyed one another across the colored sands of the arena
were separated by a chasm as profound as that dividing mortal and
immortal in the *Iliad* of Homer. Perpetua would receive eternal life;
the gladiator who slew her would not. But when Perpetua guided the
gladiator's trembling hand to her throat, she was speaking to him in a
language he knew well, one expressing the ancient and adamantine bond
between honor and the sacred. The following essay will explore aspects
of Roman concepts of honor, sacrifice, and the sacred that linked the
condemned Roman to the imperishable Christian.

Livy's history of the besieged infant Roman Republic includes the
legend which describes how Mucius, the sworn would-be assassin of
the enemy king Lars Porsena, penetrated the enemy's lines in the hope
of avenging on Porsena the humiliation of being confined within the
walls of Rome.[1] Mistaking a scribe for the king, he murdered the wrong
man. Caught, he was led before king Porsena and threatened with torture by fire.[2] To the astonishment of his captors, he laid his sword
hand—the right hand, the hand of faith, of *fides*—on the flame of the
altar, and stood impassively while it burned. The enemy king, con-
founded by the miracle (*attonitus miraculo*), released the young Roman
and raised the siege.[3]

This event was commemorated a century later by the poet Martial.
Astonished by the dauntless self-mutilation of a condemned criminal

forced to reenact the role of Mucius Scaevola in the great new Flavian amphitheater, Martial composed this paean to the legendary Mucius Scaevola:

> The right hand that sought the king, cheated by his satellite, doomed, imposed itself upon the sacred hearth. But the pious enemy could not bear so cruel a spectacle [such a savage miracle, *tam saevum miraculum*] and demanded that the man, snatched from the flames, depart. The burning hand which Mucius, in contempt of the fire, could bear to watch, Porsena could not. The fame and glory of the cheated hand is the greater. Had it not erred it would have achieved less. (1.4)

In Martial's poem, the capture of the hero serves as the ground for his glory. His failure, his entrapment, allow for the *saeva miracula*. The enemy, moved by revulsion and sympathy so tremendous that he must avert his eyes, dismisses the man who would have murdered him, just as the crowd or the *editor* (the producer of a gladiatorial game) might grant a *missio*, a release or reprieve, to the exhausted or defeated gladiator whose death-defying valor had won for him their sympathy and admiration.[4]

Scipio and Caesar, Cicero and Virgil; these are the heroes of the modern classicist and historian. We honor the stupendous and "secular" successes of the Romans and choose our heroes from the emperors and empire builders, the warriors, artists, and lawgivers. But in the late Republic and early Empire the most popular of heroes and heroines represented in their persons and responded to what seem to us far less healthy and sober strains in the Roman psyche. Lucretia, Mucius, Decius, Regulus, and Cato the Younger were only the most conspicuous of the humiliated and defeated heroes who attempted to wring glory from their own bowels. There were many others: the gladiators, Spurius Postumius, Hostilius Mancinus, Horace's Cleopatra, Virgil's Dido, Lucius's Vulteius, Tacitus's Epicharis. What they shared was their disgrace and the pattern of their redemption.[5] By sacrificing their lives, they recovered their sacred honor.

A thing that was *sacer*, sacred, in ancient Rome was highly charged. It was sensitive and dangerous for good or for bad, something to be treated with elaborate care.[6] A human being, like a god, could be strongly or weakly charged, depending on how perilous, how respected he or she was. The charge within a person, the sacred thing within a person, was equivalent to the honor in which she or he was held.[7] *Virtus*, effective energy, was the manifestation of that charge. *Animus*, spirit or will, was its source. Honor for the Romans was a force-field, a sort of radioactive boundary whose existence was demonstrated only by the consequences of its breach.[8] The filament of a Roman's honor was preserved by a wall of inhibition, of etiquette, of *religio*, of *pudor*. Without the preservation of this charged boundary a Roman could have no being.[9] To be violated was to be prostrated, extinguished. For this reason, the person of honor was obliged to respond decisively to any threat to his or her boundaries. The ordeal could not be avoided.[10] The Roman proved his dangerousness in the ordeal (*agon, periculum, discrimen, certamen, contentio*)—that moment when, before the eyes of all, one exposed oneself to the perils of humiliation, pain, and annihilation against an equal or greater opponent. Honor needed to be gambled. In Dionysius of Halicarnassus's version of the Mucius Scaevola legend, the hero addressed the assembled senate: "Being about to encounter such great danger, I do not think it right that everyone should remain in ignorance of the high stakes for which I have played" (5.27.2).

It was hard to preserve one's honor. It was infinitely harder to regain it. "The linen of honor is only bleached with blood."[11] Preserving one's honor required vigilance and bravery. Redeeming one's honor required ferocity. In particular, redeeming one's honor required a contumacious commitment to one's own annihilation. The vindication of one's honor—when it did occur—was always a savage miracle.

The Roman paradigm of the redemption of honor through ferocious self-destruction is exemplified by an event that occurs between the supporters of Caesar and the supporters of Pompey in Book 4 of Lucan's epic *Bellum Civile* (447ff.), written in the time of Nero. According to Lucan, a group of six hundred Caesarian soldiers, under the commander Vulteius, was crossing the Adriatic on a raft when it was surrounded and trapped by many thousands of Pompeians. Despite the overwhelming odds, the Caesarians battled until darkness brought a truce. After night had fallen, Vulteius addressed his troops. I paraphrase: "No life is too short," he admonished his soldiers, "when it gives one time to kill oneself. And the glory of suicide is not lessened by the approach of a fated death. While it is praiseworthy to shorten your life when you still have years to look forward to, it is equally praiseworthy to shorten your life by a moment, provided you summon death by your own hand.[12] No one can be compelled to die who wishes to die."[13] He goes on: "There is no possibility of escape. We are in a trap. But if you choose death, fear will depart. Desire whatever is necessary. We are fortunate," Vulteius tells his fellows, "we will not die in the obscurity and haze of battle, we are on a raft exposed to the view of all. Sea and land and the heights of the cliffs will provide witnesses for our deaths.[14] Our deaths, furthermore, will be testimony of our love of Caesar. Would that our little children and our old folks were here to die with us. But at least our suicide will demonstrate to the witnesses that we are unconquered, *indomiti*. They will try to tempt us with offers of peace and offers of our lives. Let them go ahead and promise us pardon. Let them encourage us to anticipate salvation (*sperare salutem*). So that, when they see us pierce our vitals with the warm steel they will not think it is because we have despaired. Even if fate should now release me from her grasp," asserts Vulteius passionately, "I would not now spurn death. I am completely driven by the excitement of my coming death. I know only what those touched by this excitement know: It is a happy thing, a good fortune to die. The gods conceal this knowledge from men that they might go on living in duress." At dawn the devoted band of warriors, having rejected the light of life and consecrated themselves to the gods of the underworld, ferocious and secure, commit singularly bloody and joyous mutual suicide, each man thrusting his breast against the steel of his neighbor.

The Romans, like the Greeks, believed that a man possessed only what he gave away. Life was a treasure that gained value or power only when expended. The person who preserved his life at any cost was a miser, growing thin on his savings, living amid wealth with sunken, emaciated cheeks, like Telesphorus of Rhodes, Seneca's paradigm of the man caged, mutilated, and reduced to filth by his commitment to life. He was a thing of dirt, his spirit caged and contracted.[15] In contrast, the chosen, the voluntary, the generous death was the extreme renunciation that put a high charge on life.[16] It was the renunciation that enhanced life, that enhanced the value of a thing being renounced. Moreover, the chosen death sacralized, empowered the person or thing or value on which it was spent.[17]

A "potlatch" mentality characterized the Romans. Honor was connected with largess, wasting even to the point of destruction.[18] Like the generosity of the patron, it showed one's superiority.[19] What one could live without was proof of one's overflowing vitality and abundant wealth.

The sensation of volition was one of energy and enhanced existence, an experience often described by the Romans in terms of growth and expansion. The gladiator who contrived to slay himself on the way to the morning exhibition became the *vir magnus* for Seneca.[20] Cicero in discussing the advantages to be had from the endurance of pain talks in terms of the *amplitudo* and the *altitudo*, the lifting up, the exaltation of the spirit (*animus*).[21] According to Tertullian, the sublimity of Mucius's spirit, his *sublimitas animi*, was demonstrated by Mucius's voluntarily leaving his right hand in the flame (*Apologeticus* 50.5). Greatness of spirit, *magnanimitas* was revealed by the philosopher Anaxarchus jesting while being tortured to death (ibid. 50.6). Regulus's victory even in captivity was demonstrated by his submitting to torture with his entire being (*toto corpore*, ibid. 50.6). Destruction was a superior form of sacrifice. Self-destruction was the supreme form of munificence, the extremes of largesse and deprivation at once.[22]

The Romans rarely identified with or wanted to be seen as victims, even in the direst circumstances. And so their stories of the vindication of honor are designed not to elicit pity, not to reveal a victim, but to reveal an unconquered will. Lucan emphasizes the voluntarism of Vulteius's soldiers by describing them as *devoti*—as having consecrated themselves to the gods of the underworld—and by recalling the pleasure that they experienced in their suicide.[23] Indeed, the tales of the vindication of honor tend to be gleeful, if ghastly. Horace's Regulus returns to Carthage to be tortured to death "as if for a holiday" (*Carmina* 3.5). Seneca's Mucius Scaevola would rather burn his hand than warm it on his mistress's breast (*De providentia* 3.5). The hemlock was an elixir for Seneca's Socrates (ibid. 3.12). When Martial attributes honor to the condemned criminal playing Mucius Scaevola, he emphasizes the actor's voluntarism by emphasizing his pleasure. Such satisfaction had the hero experienced in burning his right hand that he had to be held back from destroying the other (8.30).

Another means of demonstrating will was the "unnatural" act. For example, the sanctity of the boundary in a culture that so valued the preservation of face made mutilation particularly horrible for the Romans. *Decus* was a synonym for beauty as well as honor, just as *dehonestamentum* was a synonym for both mutilation and dishonor. Therefore *voluntary* self-mutilation, the determined violation of one's own boundaries, like *seppuku* in Japan and for similar reasons, was a horrific and dramatically charged action. "It is a harsh thing to be burned," Seneca says, in praising Mucius Scaevola, "How much harsher to endure it self-inflicted" (*Epistulae* 24.5). Seneca says of Cato the Younger, "It is a weighty thing to lay a hand upon oneself. So may he do so!" (*De providentia* 3.14). Mutilation was added to torture in the story of the failed hero Regulus to demonstrate and heighten the power of the hero's will and faith in voluntarily returning to certain death at the hands of the Carthaginian enemy who had once already humiliated him.[24] The self-mutilation of Seneca's Oedipus or the self-inflicted burning of the captured Roman legate Pompeius in Valerius Maximus's account (3.3.2) were strong acts, as strong as suicide.

Unflinching eye contact was still another means of demonstrating will. The ability to meet the eye was the ability to respond to a challenge. Averting the eye was not only a sign of, but the very experience of, submission and defeat. Plutarch emphasizes the bold intensity and steadfastness of Mucius's gaze (*Publicola* 17.3). In Livy's account the contest in valor between Mucius and Porsena was decided by the eyes.[25]

To redeem one's honor, then, one must be fiercer in attacking oneself than those who would destroy you. Seneca remarks of Mucius, "See how much more zealous valor is to embrace peril than cruelty is to inflict it" (*Epistulae* 24.5). Livy's Mucius commands the king to observe his hand: "Behold! Know what little value is placed on the body by those who seek great glory" (2.12.13). Porsena could not threaten Mucius with death because, according to Dionysius, he had already condemned himself (5.29.1), like the philosopher Anaxarchus, who, when they pounded him like barley groats with a pestle, cried: "Pound away, pound away!" (Tertullian, *Apologeticus* 50.6). The dishonored general Spurius Postumius, when he submitted to be handed over naked and bound to the enemy Samnites (who had humiliated him at the Caudine Forks), bid the reluctant attendant, "draw the cords more tightly" (Livy 9.10.7). Having lost honor, one imposed the most severe and artificial restrictions on oneself, by the submission to which one demonstrated one's volition. Cato the Younger, defeated witness of a lost cause, plunged his sword into his "sacred breast" (*sacro pectori*) and drawing forth his most holy spirit (*sanctissimum animum*), becomes "the fiercest vindicator of himself" (*acerrimus sui vindex,* Seneca, *De providentia* 2.11),[26] like Livy's Lucretia, Virgil's Dido, or Puccini's Cio Cio San. Horace's despised Cleopatra, defeated by Octavian, "grew fiercer by her premeditated death." The *fatale monstrum,* however loathed and convicted, demonstrated by her calm and "generous" death that she was *non humilis mulier*—not a humiliated woman, not a humble woman. It is not possible to read Horace's famous ode without feeling the *saevum miraculum* working first on the author and then on his audience contemplating her death. By the end, she is not simply the hideous *virago,* she is also the vanquished and triumphant queen. In the words of Steele Commager, "Phoenix-like she rises from the ashes of her own defeat."[27]

It was in an attempt to consecrate his acts, to publicize and emphasize the voluntariness of his acts, that the enlisting gladiator proclaimed the fiercest of all ancient oaths of commitment, of sacralization, the *sacramentum gladiatorum.*[28] He swore, "to be burned, to be bound, to be beaten and to be slain by the sword."[29] No more ferocious commitment to one's own suffering could be made in the ancient world.[30] The *sacramentum gladiatorum* was simultaneously devotion, consecration, and execration, putting one's life on deposit to the infernal gods to be redeemed or sacrificed through an ordeal.[31] It formed the essential part of the gladiator's initiation, his *auctoramentum*, at once his investiture and his "augmentation."[32] The word that symbolized the initiation of the gladiator and the soldier, *auctoramentum* shared a penumbra of meanings with all the cognates of *augere*—to grow, to wax, to increase, to amplify, to exalt, to honor, including the English august, augment, author, authority, etc. "Augustus" meant sublime, lofty, great, grand, and could be used to describe the appearance of the voluntarily consecrated.[33] Statius's devoted Menoeceus, for example, in anticipation of his immediate self-immolation, is described by the poet as "already sacred in aspect" and having a visage "more august than commonly possessed" (*Thebais* 10.757). Livy's noble Publius Decius Mus, having devoted himself to the gods of the underworld, appeared to both armies with a "visage more august than human" (8.9.10). The *sacramentum* of the gladiator was, then, a public and solemn oath that voluntarized submission, that transformed servitude to service. The solemn oath with its self-curse, the *exsecratio*, reestablished the debased and humiliated as highly charged, as dangerous. Courage was not enough; valor was not enough; one needed and wanted desperately to demonstrate that one was not motivated by a desire to live.[34]

The soldier, having taken his oath, becomes sanctified—the *miles sacratus*. The gladiator, having taken his oath, was the *auctoratus*. By the oath, the *exsecratio* that Brutus the elder swore on the bloody knife with which the violated Lucretia had redeemed her honor, Brutus was changed. "He handed the knife to Collatinus and then to Lucretius and Valerius. They were stupefied by the miracle, for there was a new spirit in the breast of Brutus" (Livy 1.59.2). Brutus was no longer an object of ridicule.

The *sacramentum* erected a barrier that signaled and concentrated the power of the oath-taker: his or her *fides*.[35] *Fides*, faith, was the power of the oath, the force of the oath, the "*numen*" or "*mana*" of the oath.[36] It was also the charge on one, the sacredness resulting from the oath. The ordeal before witnesses then confirmed the oath, the shedding of blood putting an additional charge on the bond.[37] The agony proved the *fides*. Regulus, faithful to his oath even under torture, is, for Seneca, the living proof of faith, the ultimate witness of endurance (*documentum fidei*, *documentum patientiae* [*De providentia* 3.9]). Had he survived a little longer, Seneca might have included among his prodigies of fidelity Tacitus's freedwoman Epicharis, who alone of the conspirators (the *coniurati*, those who had sworn an oath together) did not break faith with the members of the "Pisonian conspiracy" against Nero. Epicharis endured the exquisite torments occasioned by her *fides*. Indeed, Nero's infuriated executioners interpreted her endurance (*patientia*) under torture as a humiliation and reproach to themselves. Like Mucius Scaevola, the envoy Pompeius, or the mother of *Maccabees*, she humiliated and defeated her enemies by her *patientia* (*Annales* 15.57). This is what Erving Goffman calls "cutting off the nose to destroy the other's face."[38]

We tend to draw a sharper border between the human and the divine, the sacred and profane, than the ancient Romans, and to think of the word sacrifice principally in terms of depriving or diminishing the sphere of the human to enlarge or augment the sphere of the sacred. What man takes away from himself he adds to God. Our notions of sacrifice tend to be altruistic and unidirectional. The thing sacrificed has merely the function of mediating this transfer of energy or vitality. In itself it is negligible. For us, the victim is the least important and most passive element in the process, a means to an end, at best an empty vessel serving as a vehicle for the desires of the sacrificer.

For the Roman, as for the early Christian, the victim was conspicuously central and active: the more actively voluntary, the more effective the sacrifice.[39] Sacrifice exalted the victim and rendered him or her divine. For the Roman, *sacrificare* still emphasized its root meaning, "holy making." The active rather than passive act of sacralizing is emphasized by the Roman words *sacrificare, sacramentum, exsecrare, devovere* etc. The forms of setting apart, of binding, were the forms of sacrifice. Notions of gift-giving implied in the transfer of energy were emphatically not absent from Roman forms of sacrifice, but the active and human agency predominated.

For Edward Gibbon as for Friedrich Nietzsche, the Romans were the strong and the noble. Both saw a sanguine, virile, joyfully predatory Rome, attacked by a mode of being foreign to the Roman spirit which subverted the valuation of the proud with the positive valuation of the humble. We might marvel or lament at the subversion of the victors by the victims, the masters by the martyrs, a mighty and worldly Rome mysteriously undermined by or converted to a view of the universe fundamentally at odds with that inhabited by the conquerors of Corinth and Carthage. If so, we fail to see the degree to which the proud Roman *animus* was already turned against itself. With the long civil wars and the establishment of the monarchy came the loss of the equal opponent and the erosion and collapse of the rules of the contest in which all honor was won. As a result, pride often exalted the Roman spirit less than humiliation weighed it down. Indeed, the apogee of Roman glory was often felt, by those who lived through it, to be concurrently its nadir, its victories hollow, its wealth an abyss, its victors enslaved as surely as the Gauls or the Greeks. The paradox of simultaneously heightened and spoiled honor bred its inverse, the paradox of spoiled, and simultaneously heightened, honor. Consequently, the Roman heroes and heroines of the civil war period and the early Empire were drawn often from the type of the disgraced and redeemed. The Roman gladiator could recognize the Christian Perpetua's gesture of baring her throat, *because it was his gesture*. And it was a Roman model that the Christian Tertullian recognized when he declared, "Mucius gladly left his right hand on the altar flames. Oh the sublimity of his spirit!" (Tertullian, *Apologeticus* 50.5).

Notes

This chapter is an abbreviated version of "Savage Miracles: The Redemption of Lost Honor in Roman Society and the Sacrament of the Gladiator and the Martyr," which appeared in the Winter 1994 edition of *Representations*.

1. For the story of Mucius, see also Cicero, *Pro Sestio* 21.48; Plutarch, *Publicola* 17; Valerius Maximus 3.3.1; Orosius, *Historiae adversus paganos* 2.5.3; Walter Otto, "Römische Sagen," *Wiener Studien* 34 (1912) 318–31, especially 320–21; Friedrich Münzer, art. "C. Mucius Cordus Scaevola," Pauly-Wissowa, *Real-Encyclopädie der klassischen Altertumswissenschaft*, vol. 16.1 (Stuttgart: J. B. Metzler, 1933), cols. 416–23; R. M. Ogilvie, *A Commentary on Livy, Books 1–5* (Oxford: Clarendon Press, 1965) 262–66.

2. In some versions of the story, Mucius's suffering is, simultaneously, a self-inflicted punishment—an expiation for having failed in his mission or for having broken his oath (Seneca, *De providentia* 3.5 [*erroris sui poena*], *Epistulae* 24.5; Valerius Maximus 3.3.1). Redemption and expiation could coincide in Roman thought as in Greek or in Japanese. Consider the deaths of Livy's Lucretia, Virgil's Dido, Sophocles' Ajax, and the self-mutilation of Oedipus the king.

3. Mucius, like the Roman hero Horatius Cocles and the heroine Cloelia, was a prodigy and miracle: *Illa tria Romani nominis prodigia atque miracula Horatius, Mucius, Cloelia* (Florus 1.4.3). The miracle, in Roman thought, like the prodigy, was something that was both a transgression and a revelation.

4. Porsena's murderous hostility is changed to astonishment and admiration (Plutarch *Publicola* 17.3–5; Valerius Maximus 3.3.1). Indeed, in Plutarch's account, Porsena personally restores to Mucius Scaevola his arms. Thus, one unarmed and defeated man is able to redeem the honor that whole armies were unable to preserve. Seneca remarks that Scaevola accomplished with his hand being burned what he could not with it armed—the rout of the enemy (*De providentia* 3.5).

5. See Carlin Barton, *The Sorrows of the Ancient Romans: The Gladiator and the Monster* (Princeton: Princeton University Press, 1993), part one.

6. The "sacred thing" was solemnly designated, set apart, charged with effective energy. *Sacer* implied both blessed and cursed, blessing and cursing. "*Sacer* designe celui ou ce qui ne peut être touché sans être souillé, ou sans souiller; de là le double sens de 'sacré' ou 'maudit'" (A. Ernout, A. Meillet, *Dictionnaire étymologique de la langue latine*,[4] Paris: Klincksieck, 1985, 586). "*Sacer*: es heisst nicht nur zugleich 'heilig' und 'verflucht', sondern ebenso aktivisch: 'segenbringend' und 'fluchbringend'" (Otto Seel, *Römertum und Latinitas* (Stuttgart: E. Klett, 1964), 114 n. 10, cf. 112–14, 450–51 n. 21). For the ambiguity of the sacred, see also Mircea Eliade, *Patterns in Comparative Religion*, trans. Rosemary Sheed (New York: Sheed and Ward, 1958), 14–19, 23–25; René Girard, *Violence and the Sacred*, trans. Patrick Gregory (Baltimore: Johns Hopkins University Press, 1972), 257–65; and Georges Bataille, *Erotism*, trans. Mary Dalwood (San Francisco: City Lights Books, 1986), 68, 124, 223. Transgression and transcendence were two closely related ideas for the Romans. In the compensatory (or retributory) physics of the Romans, every exalted person became a lightning-rod for the malice of gods and men. The extremely highly charged were liable to be ostracized, expelled, or sacrificed. The expression *sacer esto* that appears in the Twelve Tables was a declaration that someone (as a result of the crossing of boundaries) was too dangerous, too highly charged, and so constituted a condemnation as well as a consecration. (*homo sacer est quem populus iudicavit ob malefactum* [Festus p. 318, cf. Servius, *Ad Aeneida* 6.608].) "'The sinner, just like the criminal, is a sacred being" (Henri Hubert, Marcel Mauss, *Sacrifice: Its Nature and Function*, trans. W. D. Hall (Chicago: University of Chicago Press, 1969 [1898]), 53, cf. 3, 57–60, 98–99); Jean Bayet, *Histoire politique et psychologique de la religion romaine*[2] (Paris: Payot, 1969), 43, 60, 106. As Roger Caillois points out, to expiate was to rid oneself of the sacred (Cicero, *Leges* 2.9.21: one expiated the *sacrum commisum*), *Man and the Sacred*, trans. Meyer Barash (Glencoe, Ill.: Free Press of Glencoe, 1959 [1946]), 35; see the whole of the chapter entitled "The Ambiguity of the Sacred," 33–54 and 84; "La peine est avant tout une purification, et l'exécution de la peine, la supplicium, est une expiation religieuse" (Pierre Noailles, *Du Droit sacré au droit civil* [Paris: Recueil Sirey, 1949], 34–35).

7. For the relationship between honor and sacredness, see Erving Goffman: "One's face . . . is a sacred thing, and the expressive order required to sustain it is therefore a ritual one" ("On Face-Work: An Analysis of Ritual Elements in Social Interaction," in *Interaction Ritual: Essays on Face-to-Face Behavior* [New York: Doubleday, 1967] 5–45, especially 19). An individual, for Goffman, is a "ritually delicate object" (ibid., pp. 31–33. Cf. "The Nature of Deference and Demeanor," in *Interaction Ritual*, 47–95, especially p. 95). Émile Durkheim: "The sacred being is in a sense forbidden; it is a being which may not be violated. . . . The human personality is a sacred thing; one may not violate it nor infringe its bounds, while at the same time the greatest good is in commun-

ion with others" ("The Determination of Moral Facts," in *Sociology and Philosophy*, trans. D. F. Pocock [Glencoe, Ill.: Free Press, 1953] 36–37).

8. Compare Pierre Bourdieu on the Kabyle: "Honour in the sense of esteem is termed *esser*. *Esser* is the secret, the prestige, the radiance, the 'glory', the 'presence'" ("The Sentiment of Honour in Kabyle Society," in *Honour and Shame: The Values of Mediterranean Society*, ed. J. G. Peristiany [Chicago: University of Chicago Press, 1966], 217). "It is said of someone that '*esser* follows and radiates around him' or that he is protected by the barrier of *esser*. . . . *Esser*, that indefinable thing which makes a man of honour, is as fragile and vulnerable as it is imponderable" (ibid., 218; cf. 238, nn. 18–19). Honor energizes, dishonor enervates. Julian Pitt-Rivers, in his essay, "Honour and Social Status" (in *Honour and Shame*, 35), points to the identification made by early anthropologists between *mana* and honor. "Polynesian *mana* itself symbolizes not only the magical power of the person but also his honour, and one of the best translations of the word is 'authority' or 'wealth'" (Marcel Mauss, *The Gift: Forms and Functions of Exchange in Archaic Societies*, trans. Ian Cunnison (New York: Norton, 1967 [1925]), 36). See G. Van der Leeuw, *Religion in Essence and Manifestation* (New York: Harper and Row, 1963 [1933]), 336; W. Warde Fowler, *The Religious Experience of the Roman People* (New York: Cooper Square, 1971 [1911]), 118–19; and following him, Wilhelm Kroll ("Die Religiosität in der Zeit Ciceros," *Neue Jahrbücher für Wissenschaft und Jugendbildung* 4 [1928]: 524) interprets the Latin *numina* as "Äusserungen eines Willens," manifestations or expressions of a will.

9. Bataille talks about "the taboo without which we should not be human beings" (*Erotism*, 134).

10. Cf. H. Wagenvoort, *Roman Dynamism* (Oxford: B. Blackwell, 1947), 105 n. 1; Seneca, *De clementia* 1.7.3. "To leave an affront unavenged is to leave one's honor in a state of desecration. . . . Hence the popularity among the mottos of the aristocracy of *nemo me impune lacessit*" (Pitt-Rivers, "Honour and Social Status," 26). "Only the punctilious and active vigilance of the point of honour (*nif*) can guarantee the integrity of honour (*h'urma*) and procure the esteem and respectability conferred by society upon whoever possesses sufficient point of honour to protect his honour from all offences" (Bourdieu, "The Sentiment of Honour," 216–17). "The person who fails to take revenge ceases to exist for other people" (ibid., 211, cf. 214, 217). "Honor . . . that aspect of personal make-up that causes the individual dutifully to enjoin a character contest when his rights have been violated—a course he must follow in the very degree that its likely costs appear to be high" (Goffman, "Where the Action Is," in *Interaction Ritual*, 149–270, 242). "Le '*sacer*' est bien positivement pour les Latins l'"intouchable"" (Bayet, *Histoire*, 141). At the same time, the taboo creates the transgression. For Mary Douglas, the sacred is something "set apart," but this setting apart demands an opposition or inversion; the transgression is necessary for the existence of the boundary. See *Purity*

and Danger (London: Routledge and K. Paul, 1966), 160, and "The Social Control of Cognition," *Man* 3 (1968): 361–75; Bataille, *Erotism*, 218–19.

11. See Pitt-Rivers, "Honour and Social Status," 25.

12. Seneca's little Astyanax, confronted with death at the hands of the pitiless Achaeans after the defeat of Troy, leaps *by his own will* (*sponte sua*) from the tower a moment before he is thrown (*Troades* 1102–3).

13. Compare the Stoic formula, "Fate leads the willing; she drags the unwilling" (Seneca, *Epistulae* 107.11). A wonderful (and pathetic) statement of this strategy can be found in Seneca, *Epistulae* 105.

14. They are witnesses in the ancient sense.

15. Accumulation of wealth (like the hoarding of life), only had value if it resulted in expenditure. The accumulation of wealth for its own sake, without the intention of redistribution, was *avaritia* and impoverished one. *Semper avarus eget* (Horace, *Epistulae* 1.2.56–57). *Tam deest avaro quod habet quam quod non habet* (Publilius Syrus 694). *Desunt inopiae multos, avaritiae omnia* (Seneca, *Epistulae* 108.9; cf. 94.43). Telesphorus of Rhodes was Seneca's paradigm of the man caged, mutilated, and reduced to dirt by his hunger to live, by valuing life as an end and not a means (*De ira* 3.17.2–4; *Epistulae* 70.6–7).

16. As Bataille remarks, "renunciation enhances the value of the thing renounced" (*Erotism*, p. 218). Sacrifice is a deprivation by which one expands in power. "Asceticism is indeed the road to power . . . each renunciation redounds to his credit . . . what he disdained in the profane he recovers in the sacred" (Caillois, *Man and the Sacred*, 28–29). And so the Le Gros Ventre Indians, Caillois adds, tortured themselves on the eve of a military expedition to intensify their power. Karen Blixen's story "Babette's Feast" and Gabriel Axel's exquisite realization of it on film are brilliant allegories of the "physics" of deprivation and redemption. "The only things which we may take with us from our life on earth are those which we have given away!" ("Babette's Feast," *Anecdotes of Destiny* [New York: Random House, 1958]).

17. "Le sang répandu sauve, et sauve d'abord celui qui est sacrifié" (Aline Rousselle, *Porneia; De la maîtrise du corps à la privation sensorielle, IIe–IVe siècle de l'ère chrétienne* [Paris: Presses Universitaires de France, 1983], 154). Choosing to die for something or risking your life for something imprinted that object on one's culture as "something worth dying for." The Chosen Death was (and is) the chief means of affirming existing values or of sanctifying new ones. In the absence of the Chosen Death nothing was sacred, including life. The Romans, like the Greeks, looked with regret on the premature, the accidental, or the sickly death as a wasted death.

18. Mauss explains the relationship of honor to the extravagance of the "potlatch," a form of *agon* which is also a form of sacrifice. "Consumption and destruction are virtually unlimited. In some potlatch systems one is constrained to expend everything one possesses and to keep nothing" (*The Gift*, 35). For the "potlatch" aspect of Roman life, see Paul Veyne's discussions of Roman euergetism in *Le pain et le cirque* (Paris: Seuil, 1976) and *A History of Private Life* (Cambridge, Mass.: Belknap Press, 1987) vol. 1, 113–15. Bayet

interprets Roman *vota* as provocations to a "potlatch": "un sorte de contrainte sacrée exercée sur le dieu que l'on provoque, comme dans le potlatch, à rendre plus qu'il ne reçoit" (*Histoire*, 131; cf. 141). The tales of Roman youths recklessly spending or gambling away their resources in the late Republic and early Empire recount attempts to restore lost honor. Sallust complains: "Such habits have now become prevalent, that young men think it highly honorable to squander their own property and those of others, and to refuse nothing either to their own passions or to the requests of their friends, imagining such extravagance to be greatness and nobleness of spirit . . . " (*Ad Caesarem* 2.5).

19. "In the old days the glory of giving was deemed greater than titles or *fasces*." (*Namque et titulis et fascibus olim maior habebatur donandi gloria* [Juvenal 5.110].) See Leon Festinger, "A Theory of Social Comparison Processes," *Human Relations* 7 (1954), especially 128 (generosity establishes superiority). Mauss: "The rich man who shows his wealth by spending recklessly is the man who wins prestige" (*The Gift*, 35). The "potlatch," like other forms of liberality, did not even or necessarily indicate benevolence. For the hostility behind ritual competitions in generosity, see Goffman, "On Face-Work," 39–40.

20. Cf. Seneca, *Epistulae* 70.25, cf. 24.6–7, 78.14–15.

21. Cicero, when discussing the advantages to be had from the endurance of pain, talks in terms of the *amplitudo* and the *altitudo*, the *exaggeratio* (lifting up, exaltation) of the spirit (*Tusculanae disputationes* 2.26.64). See H. S. Versnel, "Self-Sacrifice, Compensation and the Anonymous Gods," in *Le Sacrifice dans l'antiquité* (Geneva: Fondation Hardt, 1980), 135–85, especially 152, 158. The reverse, humiliation or enslavement, is often experienced as a physical diminution. We say, "She made him look small," or "She felt small."

22. Mauss, *The Gift*, 102 n. 122. Bataille discusses at length the sanctity of wasting in his *Erotism*, and his brilliant meditation on Aztec sacrifice and the potlatch in *The Accursed Share* (trans. Robert Hurley [New York: Zone Books, 1988], 45–77). The Powers That Be waste everything in exuberant destruction; hence, to waste is divine.

23. See Barton, *The Sorrows of the Ancient Romans*, chap. 1, for a discussion of the *devotio*, a model of redemptive self-sacrifice.

24. Cicero, *In Pisonem* 43; Valerius Maximus 9.2, ex. 1; Aulus Gellius, *Noctes Atticae* 7.4.3. See H. C. Nutting, "*Oculos Effodere*," *Classical Philology* 17 (1922): 313–18.

25. Compare the description of the Christian martyr Perpetua's portentous entry into the arena: "Perpetua advanced with shining countenance and calm step . . . casting down the stare of the crowd with the power of her gaze" (*vigore oculorum deicens omnium conspectum* [*Passio Perpetuae* 18.2, Musurillo ed.]). The ability to maintain eye contact was the ability to respond to a challenge with one's eyes. For averting the eyes as submission or defeat, see Livy 9.6.8 (the Roman soldiers reaching Capua after their disgrace at the Caudine Forks cannot lift their gaze even when treated well); cf. Livy 9.8.3; Propertius 1.1.4. There were 20,000 gladiators in the *ludus* of Caligula, according to Pliny the

Elder, and of these there were only two who could refrain from blinking when threatened. These two were, consequently, invincible (Pliny, *Naturalis historia* 11.54.114).

26. For Seneca, death "consecrated" Cato and others who availed themselves of a similar means of vindication (*De providentia* 2.12). Compare the suicide of the gladiator in Howard Fast's *Spartacus* (New York: 1951) with that of Mr. Klein in Joseph Losey's powerful film of the same name (1977).

27. *The Odes of Horace* (New Haven: Yale University Press, 1962), 94.

28. On the gladiator's *sacramentum*, see Edouard Cuq, art. "*Sacramentum*," in *Dictionnaire des antiquités grecques et romains*, ed. Charles Daremberg and Edmond Saglio (Paris: Librarie Hachette, 1873–1884), vol. 4.2; Cesare Sanfilippo, "Gli auctorati," *Studi in onore di Arnaldo Biscardi* (Milan: Istituto Editoriale Cisalpino, La Goliardica, 1982), 181–82; Antonio Guarino "I gladiatores et l'*auctoramentum*," *Labeo* 29 (1983): 7–28. For the Roman oath in general, see Ernst von Lasaulx, *Der Eid bei den Römern* (Würzburg: Thein, 1844).

29. For variant forms of the gladiator's oath, see Horace, *Satirae* 2.7.58–59; Pseudacron, *Scholia in Horatium vetustiora* ad. loc.; K. Schneider, "*Gladiatores*," Pauly-Wissowa, *Real-Encyclopädie*, Supplement vol. 3 (1918); Ludwig Friedländer, *Darstellung aus der Sittengeschichte Roms*,[10] ed. Georg Wissowa (Aalen: Scientia Verlag, 1964), vol. 2, p. 60; Keith Hopkins, "Murderous Games," in *Death and Renewal: Sociological Studies in Roman History*, vol. 2 (Cambridge: Cambridge Unviersity Press, 1963), 24; Georges Ville, *La Gladiature en Occident des origines à la mort de Domitien* (Rome: École Française de Rome, 1981), 471.

30. The Roman soldier's oath was not so fierce or unconditional. He vowed to obey his officers and the regulations of the camp and not to abandon the standards; he consecrated himself, his family and his possessions to the god(s) in case of his failure to uphold the oath. After having sworn his oath, the soldier was *sacratus*. See Polybius 6.21; Dionysius 10.18, 11.43; Livy 28.27. In the Empire the soldier swore to respect no man above Caesar (Arrian, *Epicteti dissertationes* 1.14). Nevertheless, without the oath it was not possible to be a true soldier (cf. Cicero, *De officiis* 1.11.36–37). In addition, the oath put a sacred charge on the soldier: *pro solemni et sacrata militia sit* (Livy 8.34.10). See von Lasaulx, *Der Eid*, 18.

31. "Le *vir iuratus* est celui qui, par son serment, s'est mis dans la main des dieux" (Pierre Noailles, *Du Droit sacré au droit civil*, 23). "[L]'atto di auctoramentum può consistere in una consacrazione agli dei di un proprio sottoposto, libero o schiavo, ed a quindi natura sacrale" (Guarino, "I gladiatores," 14; J. de Ghellinck, *Pour l'histoire du mot "sacramentum*," Spicilegium Sacrum Lovaniense, Études et Documents, fasc. 3 [Paris/Louvain: E. Champion, 1924], especially 45, 49, 70–77. The consecration of the gladiator was something like what Hubert and Mauss call the "Entry Sacrifice" (the consecration which renders the *sacrifiant* sacred in anticipation of the completion of the sacrifice) (*Sacrifice*, 20–22).

32. For the sacral aspects of the *auctoramentum*, see Guarino, "I gladiatores," 7, 14–17, 20, 24; Sanfilippo "Gli *auctorati*," pp. 184, 187. "[L]e rite par lequel

il est initié, *sacramentum* . . . l'initiation des 'soldats' de Mithra s'apelle aussi *sacramentum* . . . au fond le serment et l'initiation sont les moyens de consecration" (de Ghellinck, *Pour l'histoire du mot "sacramentum,"* p. 75). De Ghellinck equates *sacratus* with "initiated" (71–72).

33. See H. S. Versnel, "Self-Sacrifice," 151. For Wagenvoort, *augustus* is all but synonymous with *sacratus/consecratus* (*Roman Dynamism*, 3). The title "*Augustus*" was bestowed on Octavian in 27 B.C.E. as a result of his voluntary assumption of limitations, specifically, his surrender of control of the state to the senate and people of Rome *(Res Gestae Divi Augustae* 34.1; cf. Velleius Paterculus 2.89). The renunciation augmented him. Although the result of binding, *auctoritas* gave Octavian "unbound" power.

34. For Seneca, the gladiator's fierce oath, provided it is taken willingly and freely (*volens* and *libens*) liberates the man who takes it from being a victim, under compulsion. He may be compelled to suffer and die, but he does so *invictus*. It is both the strongest bond of the good man to his suffering and the means to transform that suffering. Nevertheless, Seneca anticipates the possible hostile evaluation of the witnesses: "You have enlisted [in life] under oath. If any man should say that this is a soft or easy form of soldiering it will only be because he wishes to mock you. But I do not want you to be deceived: the words of this most honorable of contracts are the very same as those of the most foulest of compacts: 'to be burned, to be bound, to be slain by the sword'." "You must die," he continues, "erect and invincible" (*Epistulae* 37, cf. 72.21–2). See Barton, *The Sorrows of the Ancient Romans*, chap. 1.

35. Cicero: "Our ancestors considered there to be no more narrow constraint on *fides* than the oath." (*Nullum enim vinculum ad astringendam fidem iure iurando maiores artius voluerunt* [*De officiis* 3.31.111].) Ammianus Marcellinus: *Romanorum exercituum fides et religionibus firmis iuramenta constricta* (26.7.16).

36. Maximinus apud Herodianus: The oath of her soldiers was the *semnon mysterion* of Roman rule (8.7.4); cf. Caecilius in Aulus Gellius, *Noctes Atticae* 20.1.39.

37. Cf. Livy 1.24–26: The "striking" of the treaty (at the time of the battle between the Horatii and the Curiatii) is quite literally the "striking" of the sacrificial animal. Boyancé: "Paroles du serment, sacrifice qui le rend opérant" ("Fides et le serment," 97). The degree of sacredness of a thing or a person was often the result of a cumulation of acts. Just as we "charge" a marriage bond with a license, an oath, a ceremony, a public kiss, prayers, a communal meal, sexual "consummation," etc., so Jupiter might charge a treaty with his lightning (*Jupiter qui foedera fulmine sancit* [Virgil, *Aeneid*, 12.176ff.]), and the Romans might contribute a blood sacrifice and a handshake. It is not a matter of one rite doing the sacralizing and the others having different functions; they all contributed to the heightening of the sanction on the bond. The fierceness with which the Christians insisted on their *sacramentum* led to the Romans' assumption (attested by Minucius Felix) that the "conspiracy" (*coniuratio*, literally, "swearing together") of the Christians was cemented with the sacrifice of infants, the drinking of their blood, sexual couplings, etc. These are not

merely calumnies; they were all very ancient ways of putting tremendously high charges on a commitment. (See Hubert and Mauss, *Sacrifice* 17.) Wherever the Romans saw ferocious commitments, they saw "unnatural acts" (e.g., the Catilinarian conspiracy), for the reason that it was, above all, "unnatural" acts (transgressions against the *mos maiorum*) that were required to demonstrate that one had will, that one had power over oneself, that one was sacred. (See Roger Caillois, *Man and the Sacred*, 39.)

38. "Where the Action Is," 222.

39. On the singular importance of voluntarism both for transforming slaughter to sacrifice and for the effectiveness of sacrifice, see H. S. Versnel, "Self-Sacrifice," especially 145–48. The *hostis* in a Roman sacrifice was led to the altar by a slack rope, in order that it might not seem to be dragged by force (Petronius, fragment 1: Pliny, *Naturalis historia* 8.183; Servius, *In Vergiliam Commentarius* 2.104 and 140; Macrobius, *Saturnalia* 3.5.8). As Hubert and Mauss explain, the spirit of the unwilling victim would seek vengeance; the sacrifice, instead of promoting the health of the community, would threaten it (*Sacrifice*, 30–33). "Il ne suffit pas que l'animal soit, d'un bout à l'autre, conduit sans violence, sans lien, sans coercition, de plein gré; la bête est aussi censée donner par un mouvement de tête ou un frisson du corps son assentiment au coup qui va l'atteindre; à la limite elle se précipite elle-même dans le feu sacrificiel" (Jean-Paul Vernant, "Théorie générale du sacrifice et mise à mort dans la *thusia* grecque," in *Le Sacrifice dans l'antiquité* [Geneva: Foundation Hardt, 1981], 1–39, especially 7). "The sacred animal, already half divinized, had to be free, had to choose, designate itself" (Jane Ellen Harrison, *Themis: A Study of the Social Origins of Greek Religion* [Cleveland: World Publishing Company, 1962 (1912)], 152 and n. 2, 154); Aline Rouselle, *Porneia*, pp. 154–56, 162. The importance of the voluntarism of the sacrificial victim is still to be found in Christian thought. Paulinus of Nola recounts the miracle of a pig devoted to Saint Felix who, being too big to fit on the cart, and compelled to remain behind, arrived by itself at the festival in order to be eaten by the celebrants. Paulinus also tells us of the cow who refused to be bound to the carriage but who walked alone to the sacrifice and then extended her neck to receive the knife (Aline Rouselle, "Paulin de Nole et Sulpice Sévère, hagiographes, et la culture populaire," in *Les Saints et les stars*, ed. Jean-Claude Schmitt (Paris: Beauchesne, 1983), 27–40, especially 38).

THREE

"A VERY SPECIAL DEATH":
CHRISTIAN MARTYRDOM IN ITS
CLASSICAL CONTEXT

Carole Straw

Clement of Alexandria wrote from experience. In 202–203, during the persecution of Septimius Severus, he had been forced to flee to Asia Minor. In his *Miscellanies* (*Stromata,* 4.4), he discusses the perfection of martyrdom that had eluded him and compares martyrdom to the valiant death of classical heroes: "And the ancients laud the death of those among the Greeks who died in war, not that they advised people to die a violent death, but because he who ends his life in war is released without the dread of dying." Just like the heroes of epics and the arena, the Christian martyrs displayed a contempt of death that allowed them to face the end with unnerving self-control. "We conquer death and are not conquered by it," boasted the martyr Flavian.[1] And Cyprian proclaimed that martyrs could be killed, but they could never be harmed.[2]

Yet, while pagans might die *invicti,* unconquered by the fear of death, Christians did more—they conquered death itself. They had no need whatsoever to fear. Death was only of the body (and even that was temporary), never of the soul; for the martyr's heroic death recapitulated Christ's paradoxical victory on the Cross and anticipated the resurrection: "O, death, where is thy sting? O, grave, where is thy victory?" (1 Cor 15:56). "What is more glorious," Cyprian asks, than "by dying to have overcome death itself, which is feared by all?"[3] Because of this supernatural conquest of death, the Christian martyr could become invincible in a way the classical hero could never be.

Defenders of Christianity such as Tertullian, Minucius Felix, Justin Martyr, Clement of Alexandria, and Augustine[4] conceded that the classical heroes of redeemed honor, such as Mucius Scaevola, Curtius, Regulus, the Decii, had valiantly "despised death and all sorts of savage treatment"; but they were far outshone by the Christian martyrs.[5] "These martyrs," Augustine writes, "far surpassed the Scaevolae, and the Curtii, and the Decii, both in virtue, because they possessed true piety, and also in the greatness of their number."[6] With such indomitable witnesses, surely Christianity had surpassed paganism! This was the point Christian apologists belabored, and it was not to be forgotten.

Such "one-upmanship" arguments were the core of a rhetorical strategy by which early Christians hoped to crush their pagan opponents. Christian writers would utilize the language of honor and the heroic death,[7] even as they modified the meanings and rejected the most fundamental pagan attitudes toward death and the supernatural. They labored to establish a rivalry between the pagan practices and their own in order to defeat the pagans on their own terms. Their arguments were straightforward: Christians were the better fighters; theirs was the true cause; theirs the crown of victory, the only real crown of glory. To some extent, their "one-upmanship" arguments reveal an identity with their adversaries' cultural values, as well as a transcending of them: by necessity, apologists had to accept the outline of the same classical values that they claimed only they could realize—honor, courage, glory, etc. At issue, however, is exactly how deeply this cultural mimesis went: Was it anything more than a strategy of meeting pagans on common ground? Or are deeper continuities and more radical differences discernible?

Consonant with the classical honor code and its ideal of the good death, a martyr's confrontation with death distilled the essence of his or her actions and worth. A martyr's feelings of control over death and torture—the voluntary, even eager acceptance of condemnation—transformed the sordid ordeals one suffered into a most honorable vindication. In the Christian mind, this fall and rise embodied the familiar Pauline and Johannine dialectic of the slave who in suffering an ignominious death ascended to the heights (Phil 2:5–11) and the seed that must die to bear fruit (Jn 12:24). Yet this dialectic was also a counterpart to that of the repugnant, yet prized, Roman gladiator.[8] Precisely, and paradoxically, because suffering was so contemptible when imposed against one's will, it became all the more glorious and stunning when embraced actively with the will. In this case, the "charge" or valence reverses. For, by definition, whatever one willed freely was honorable— even, and *especially*, degradation—because that self-abnegation was the

ultimate and most solemn of sacrifices: one could give no more than
the offering of one's own life. This was Lucan's lesson with Vulteius.
Hedged in by Pompey's troops and facing extermination (cf. *Bellum
Civile* 4.441–581), Vulteius exhorted his men before their imminent
death by making clear that no one could force suffering upon anyone
who *chose* to suffer: "No one is forced to die, who dies voluntarily."
Volition was always the trump card for both pagans and Christians. We
have then parallel and congruent traditions. Yet nuances and differences
move us into another world.

Granted, both the pagan gladiator and the Christian martyr rise to
glory by embracing and thus conquering degradation. Both act for themselves and the greater community. To some extent, one may draw
parallels between martyrs like Polycarp and Zachary, who died as scape-
goats,[9] and heroes such as Curtius and the Decii, who vowed their lives
to the gods of the underworld so that the Roman people might win
victory. But the meanings of those ultimate goals differ. As Tertullian
put it: Romans have their statues, Christians their resurrection.[10]
Romans sacrificed their lives to win honor, immortal fame, and the
prosperity of their earthly community. In the Christian's eyes, this was
a sorry substitute for the true glory of eternal life and the beatitude of
the transcendent city of God. Unlike the pagans, Christians had trans-
valued life and death.

These very ends in turn reshape the means employed, for the Christians went a step further. They redefined heroic behavior, in effect
"pouring new wine" into the proverbial "old wineskins." A Christian
gloried in suffering for its own sake, for this sacrifice imitated the passion of Christ, which had redeemed humanity from the dreadful damnation of hell. Passivity itself became the ideal, for it replicated Christ's
teaching to "turn the other cheek" (Mt 5:39), his prayer that the Father
forgive his enemies (Lk 23:34), and his assurance that "the meek will
inherit the earth" (Mt 5:5). The aristocratic Cyprian taught these humble
lessons and lived them out in his own martyrdom as well. Even when
persecuted, Cyprian warned, "It is not permitted the innocent to kill
even the aggressor, but promptly to deliver up their souls and blood."[11]
Other Christians, however, crossed this line of gentle self-control. The
homeless Euplus knocked on the Roman governor's door and announced recklessly, "I want to die; I am a Christian."[12]

We moderns acknowledge that martyrdom encompassed varying
expressions in the early Church, but this only made such bravado more
comprehensible—attractive or reprehensible—to pagan audiences sharing a common vocabulary of histrionic, if gruesome, valor. Only in the

early fifth century would Augustine differentiate proper immolation from those types which sought to storm heaven by force. Until then (and sometimes even after) lines between suicide and martyrdom could be vexing and blurred.[13] Clarification on this issue emerges only when one realizes the fundamental distinction between the ways pagans and Christians valued human self-assertion. If Christians esteemed passivity and self-sacrifice in imitation of Christ's death, Romans cherished victorious activity and aggression. To state the obvious, Romans were encouraged to fight and glory in the triumph over their enemy. As we know from Appian, conquering generals were painted vermilion in the likeness of Mars; their captives were chained, humiliated, and paraded in front of them in triumphal processions celebrating their victories.[14] The confession of defeat and surrender were anathema.[15] To mention Vulteius again, only when suffering became Necessity, the inescapable lot of fate, would he and other Romans assert their power to the extreme and reverse defeat by an act of sheer will. At that moment violence toward oneself became active, and an effective revenge, for it deprived the victor of his glory. To the Christian, suicide could never be a cure for the life without honor, for true honor could never bless this earthly life. Violence against oneself was homicide—the murder of a creature God had created; and only God could take away a life.[16] To pagans, to confess being the victim and suppliant was to be thoroughly despised. To Christians, such status was potentially the highest holiness.

The Christian martyr strove for purity, for clean, distinct categories. As pagans did, Christians probably found a certain intoxicating power in violence directed at themselves, but their immolations were only executed through the indirect—and thus safe—agency of Divine Providence. Since Christian ends were transcendent—and eschatological—they could freely invoke divine vengeance and believe that the ultimate vindication of their convictions would occur at the Second Coming, when their persecutors would tremble.[17] Vengeance was postponed; only postponed—but safely postponed. Christians had willingly renounced earthly power, believing that God would act supernally on their behalf. And with the possible pollution of human agency removed, divine agency ruled all.

This realignment of agency transforms the classical values. The salient point is that Christians staked a claim to a new moral high ground that represented true heavenly values, and that the new precepts commanded mercy and sympathy for—not domination over—innocent victims. Could this approach ever appeal to the pagan Romans steeped in the tradition of imperial success? Such pitiful supplication would most likely have seemed disgusting to many and would have won few admirers. In response, Christians could demonize their opponents as depraved and cruel. They could present the Romans as exulting in novel and ingenious tortures, making sadistic jokes at the expense of their victim.[18] As Christians strove to characterize pagans as inhumane brutes, at the same time they offered themselves as champions of compassion and charity. The moral choice for any civilized person was meant to be fully obvious. (Even here Christians play to a growing unease in classical sensibilities.) The Christian victim gained a hallowed status: he was purified of the sordid ambiguities that troubled the classical *piaculum* (sin offering), both hated and cherished, damned and honored. The Christian cherished the victim *qua* victim as a blameless sacrifice to their God. In evaluating patience, Christians went further than the Stoics (and all other classical philosophers as well), for they gloried in suffering for its own sake. Suffering was an imitation of the passion of Christ, which had redeemed humanity from damnation, and it earned one the crown of martyrdom: "for a martyr cannot be crowned unless he pours out his blood and sanctifies his body through the power of suffering."[19] Indeed, the martyr Justin exulted when the Prefect Rusticus threatened punishment: "This is exactly what we pray for: to contrive our salvation through punishment."[20] In this Justin and other Christians followed the model of Christ, who "willed to have his fill of joy in suffering."[21] Patience was "the very nature of God."[22] Thus, redefining this quality of heroism also meant rewriting its history.

Christians validated their tradition further with a genealogy that challenged the sanguinary pagan rulers who traced their ancestors back to Romulus and Remus and Mars. In Christian tradition, purity and innocence had reigned, starting with the pure and righteous Abel, Isaac, and Christ. And in this the lesson was clear: the good had always suffered; it was part of their identity. Suffering bravely, not fighting valiantly, became the sine qua non of the Christian heroic ideal; and this new and true fortitude would ultimately win converts (or so Christians hoped). Their possession of the truth would necessarily generate a greater power and ability by bearing witness in this terrible new style of "active" suffering. The brave martyrs would astonish even the torturers themselves as "cruelty was overcome by patience."[23] Suffering one's own death, not killing the enemy, won the cause.[24]

Action was everything, and the very truth of Christianity fueled the engine of martyrdom. Tertullian compared the simple but adamantine Christians to the jejune and feckless classical philosophers. Seneca, Diogenes, Pyrrho, and Callinicus may have "preached the endurance of pain and of death," "but their words never found so many disciples as have Christians, who teach by deeds. That very obstinacy (*obstinatio*) you condemn is your teacher. For who that sees it is not stirred to inquire what lies within it? Who, on inquiry, does not join us; and joining us, does not hope to suffer?"[25]

Like Roman heroes, the martyrs in their suffering and death demonstrated a defiant will and the highest courage; thus, it was true honor. But the end of the Christian's display was not vain; it was meant to persuade the audience to acknowledge the sanctity of suffering itself. This was not a proposition which critics such as Lucian of Samosata or Marcus Aurelius were likely to applaud. To them it was madness, folly, and ignorance.[26]

Yet, like the Roman gladiator or hero, the martyr also had a "chosen death." And pagans and Christians would fight for their respective gods on the common ground of the arena. To stress volition, Christians, like pagans, trumpeted their heroic virtues: courage, fortitude, reckless enthusiasm, and blithe contempt of death. In this high profile of sheer vitality and self-actualization, Christians equated honor with volition, just as their classical rivals did. Their language of honor and self-determination comes through strikingly in the exhortations to martyrdom and in the *Acta* themselves. Origen's *To the Martyrs* (22) is the cynosure. The martyr loves honor (*philotimea*). He has generosity (*liberalitas*), freedom (*libertas, eleutheria*), self-control (*sophrosyne*), and the confidence of speaking freely (*parrhesia*). His acts are freely chosen— voluntarily and deliberately (*proaieresis, autoproairetos, thelesis*). The martyrs' deeds become noble examples of courage and manliness (*andreia, virtus, fortitudo*).

Why this parallelism? Christians were very much a part of the ancient dialogue on freedom and the will.[27] Self-determination and self-control, the power to live as one's own master, separated the free citizen from the slave and the wise man from the victim of passion.[28] Even Paul addressed this freedom of will, complaining of the conflict between his spirit and his rebellious members (Rm 7:15ff.). Free will was further exalted in the philosophical debate against the determinism of fate and astrology. Only with free will could there be moral responsibility, and the praise or blame of ethical choices.[29] Free will separated men from beasts and inanimate creation.[30] It was the image linking humanity with God; and it was through free will (and grace) that one could imitate God and attain to his likeness.[31]

For Christian martyrs, as for their classical counterparts, the *voluntary* assumption of peril demonstrated free agency. The martyrs did not passively "tell the truth." In their *obstinatio* and *contumacia* (disobedience to a judicial order), they actively "gave witness," putting their lives on the line to guarantee their testimony. As Tertullian argues above, words without deeds are nothing, for action proves, forges, and creates truth. By choosing to face the ordeal, martyrs proved both their own honor—that is, their free will—and the honor, truth, and validity of their cause. Speech without corroborating evidence was useless.

Like the oaths of the pagan Romans, the oaths of the Christians were also the means of codifying and formalizing their commitment to face the ordeal. Like their counterparts, Christians consecrated themselves to their God, pledging their lives in fidelity. So it was with Justin Martyr's vow (devotio): "now through Jesus Christ, even under the threat of death, [we] hold these [pagan gods] in contempt, while we consecrate ourselves to the unbegotten and impassible God."[32] This binding act had several descriptions among Christians. One might die to honor one's oath (sacramentum), confession of faith (confessio fidei), pledge (pignus), or covenant (diatheke) with God. One might take a stand to die for Christ, share the cup of His suffering, die for the sake of His name (a Hebraic tradition, kiddush hashem);[33] or like Justin and the Roman hero, one might consecrate oneself to God in a devotio. The standard symbols of this commitment are not only the cup but also the ring (a familiar symbol to the Romans of fidelity), the seal (signaculum), and the ensign (signum), both of military origin; even pieces of cloth could serve as the seal of one's complete consecration.[34]

While the various confessions of faith found in the martyrs' lives often echo baptismal or liturgical creeds,[35] they also often strikingly employ Roman military imagery for expressing Christian loyalty. As de Ghellinck and others have noted, the Latin word sacramentum (oath) has its origins in the Roman military oath.[36] (The Greek word for sacrament, mysterion, on the other hand, emphasizes the privilege of partaking in sacred events.) Tertullian explains the Latin word, "We were called to be soldiers of the living God already when we responded to the words of the sacramental oath (sacramentum)."[37] "I shall appeal to the prime and principal authority of our seal (signaculum) itself. When we step into the water [of baptism] and profess the Christian faith in the terms prescribed by its law, we bear public witness that we have renounced the devil and his pomp and his angels."[38] As the Roman soldier owed fides, fidelity or faith to his oath, so too the Christian must be bound. Cyprian's devotio echoes this Roman military language;[39] Ignatius of Antioch, on the other hand, employs as the model for his oath the more terrible oath of the gladiator: "Come fire, cross, battling with wild bears, wrenching of bones, mangling of limbs, crushing of my whole body, cruel torture of the devil—only let me get to Jesus Christ."[40] One must appreciate the blurred lines between the gladiator and the soldier to grasp the dire intensity of the Christian's oath, now modeled on these pagan actions. One must imagine, too, the possible appeal or repugnance the martyr held for his pagan audience.

However it was cast, the oath, confession, or covenant set up "contractual" terms, defining all action as volitional. It established boundaries that the faithful honored and defended with their lives: "I am a Christian, and you have no more to hear from me than this, for there is nothing greater or nobler I can say," Papylus said, dying to honor that statement.[41] Shaped by apocalyptic urgency, these terse pledges equated the willingness to die with simply *being* a Christian—here is the consequence of the baptismal oath.[42] Justin's pledge was typical: "One must fulfill the commandment of our Lord . . . here I take my stand, and in it I wish to die for Christ."[43] Ignatius of Antioch believed that the only way to prove himself an authentic Christian was to die to honor his oath: "I shall be a convincing Christian only when the world sees me no more."[44]

In all these expressions of ultimate commitment, a series of equations exists: volition = honor = death = proof of authenticity. This chain is as true for classical heroes making a *devotio* as it is for Christian martyrs. Yet the *telos* for which each gave witness was distinctly different. In the Christian's mind, the earthly (and diabolical) ambitions of the pagans were fiercely opposed to their own heavenly aspirations: they were set in opposition as realms of darkness and light, flesh and spirit, deceit and truth.

A crucial difference also exists between the oath of the Roman heroes and that of the Christian martyrs. For the Christian, a reciprocity lay at the core of his "contract" with God. God would reciprocate for service or defection: "He will save the life that has been lost for His name's sake, but will destroy the one that has been gained against His name," Tertullian wrote, echoing the Gospels (cf. Mt 10:39; Mk 8:35; Lk 9:24).[45] The fires of hell threatened those who lapsed, but Christ will recognize in heaven those who confess him on earth, just as he will deny those who have denied him.[46] If the Roman hero tried to strike a bargain with the gods of the underworld *before* his sacrificial act, he could still never be certain that the invidious gods would play by the rules and help their *devoté*. The gladiator was even a more desperate case, because his contract was one-sided: the gods were to punish him if he *failed* to redeem his besmirched honor; but they were not obliged to help or to reward him if he did indeed succeed. The gladiator's pledge was explicitly to his trainer to fight and die valiantly; the gods were simply enforcers of his desperate contract. Here there was no question of salvation—it did not exist. At issue, rather, was that ephemeral substitute, immortal fame. This may have made the gladiators' deaths even more glorious in the sheer extravagant and gratuitous expenditure of life, but it was a perverse and foolish glory, at least in the Christian's eyes.

In contrast with Roman heroes and gladiators, Christian martyrdom was grounded in the belief about God and his universe, which differed fundamentally from the Roman perspective. Christians could not accept callous or whimsical behavior as worthy of a god any more than they could believe the licentious escapades of Jupiter or Venus.[47] Christians, such as Tertullian, could be appalled that the cruelties and obscenities of the gods could be mocked in the theater,[48] or worse, reenacted by gladiators in the arena.[49] The somber majesty of any real god would be defiled by human laughter and applause.[50] The Christian's willingness for martyrdom was founded in a profound trust in a providential, just God—a God who behaved as a true God, and not a piece of clay hawked at the Capitol as if at a vegetable market,[51] or turned into a cooking pot or ladle as household necessity dictated.[52] These are Tertullian's complaints, but he speaks for others equally bent on separating the sacred from the profane.

When Christians viewed the world of the Romans, they were deeply troubled by its indeterminacy and ambiguity. The Christian demanded an orderly world of crisp boundaries and certainties. Minucius Felix complained that for Romans "in human affairs, everything is doubtful, uncertain, unsettled; everything a matter of probability rather than truth."[53] Fortune ruled the world and the misguided Romans felt that "chance, unrestrained by laws, rule[d] supreme by capricious and hazardous whims."[54] Minucius Felix insisted on clarity and unequivocal order, manifest in the existence of Divine Providence; other apologists affirmed this, as well. The Christian believed in a neat, orderly universe governed by Providence. For him, the sacred became the purely good—no joking, no obscene divinities here. Evil was assigned to the devil alone, whose realm included the profane domain of the secular world. For the Christian, order was not only maintained by this sharp division between sacred and profane, with a just, providential God replacing chance and ambiguity, but also consisted of reciprocity and balance, a kind of justice (*dike*) governing the cosmos that all must obey. Consequently, a pattern of reciprocity structures Christian martyrdom at all levels.[55] The Gospel dictated a "potlatch" reciprocity of mutual gain by expenditure: "whosoever would save his soul will lose it, and whoever loses his soul for my sake will save it" (Mt 16:24–25);[56] and it stated, "The measure you give will be the measure you get back" (cf. Lk 6:38; Mt 7:2; Mk 4:24). Man owed God his life, because God became incarnate and gave his life for man. "You are not your own," Cyprian warned, "for you have been bought at a great price. Glorify God and bear him in your body" (1 Cor 6:19–20).[57] Yet, if a Christian is obliged to reciprocate the sacrifice of Christ, how could it be voluntary? And does it not render the pagan's vow consecrating him to death (*devotio*) even more splendidly extravagant and glorious because his was potentially a futile offering to a capricious and indifferent universe? Arguably, here is the expansive magnanimity of classical heroes!

At this point we may detect a warm shift from the Roman world. Origen answers by emphasizing the generosity and the mutual love and energy of this sacrificial exchange. One simply wanted and burned with all the passion of Solomon's bride to recompense the glory bestowed on the soul. Since Origen perceived a munificent God who did not "quibble about trifles"[58] but even "reward[ed] more than the contestant deserve[d],"[59] Christians, he believed, were therefore bound to prove their love with equal lavishness. Thus, love and sacrifice would be mutual exchanges. The love of God was a powerful antidote against the deepest tortures, more compelling than any love spell, Origen wrote.[60] This overwhelming love for God should then culminate in self-immolation through free will:

> Such is martyrdom, and so great the freedom and confidence (*parrhesia*) before God produced, that we should ponder it deeply. Since a saint loves honor and is generous (*philotimos*) and wishes to repay the benefits bestowed upon him from God, he searches out what he can do for the Lord in return for everything he has received from Him. And he finds that nothing can be given to God from one rightly intentioned that will so equally balance His benefits as perfection in martyrdom.[61]

Paradoxically, by destruction Christians are restored, by immolation they are exalted, by dying they live. Origen returns the reader to a certain hope, if not security, in mapping out the structure of this transformation. We see here another chain of connections between munificence, reciprocity, honor, free will, love, and self-immolation. Commerce and mutual exchanges balance the world as surely as any classical notion of *dike*. Furthermore, by casting the obligation of self-immolation in terms of generosity and love, Origen utilizes the familiar vocabulary of volition and honor that connects him to the pagan, classical world.[62] But the Christian martyr will always be distinguished from the pagan on at least one essential issue: unlike the classical hero, the Christian martyr could trust the guarantor of the contract. The Christian by definition believed in the transformations promised him, and it is important to recognize the logic in the two-way nature of these transforming activities. God became man so that man could become godlike. And if the martyrs were honored with a sanctity excelling the glory of Roman heroes, God was honored as well. The obedient deaths of the martyrs therefore amplified God's stature on this earth; they bore witness to his heavenly grandeur as Creator, and they sanctified his name. As Origen urged, "Let us then glorify God, exalting him by our own death, since the martyr will glorify God in his death."[63] In self-sacrifice then, humanity held the power of praising and honoring God, of returning to God some of that vital force that originates from the Creator himself—light, life, *virtus*, manna, or *numen*—whatever that powerful energy is called that stands in opposition to death, disorder, and the devil. God's rewarding his faithful witnesses with honor and glory at their deaths in turn maintained this cycle in its dynamic, yet balanced state—continuous and stable, paradoxically eternal through reciprocal exchanges.

We tend to think of God in static, Platonic terms, as eternal and immutable, beyond the realm of change. But in practice the Judeo-Christian Yahweh gained and lost honor just like the pagan gods, whose very statues might be defaced to insult the god inside. The status of gods, therefore, was not static but continually changing and in need of defenders. The Christian apologists understood this and argued hotly to expose the naked impotence and immorality of pagan deities. We moderns often forget this competition, but the early Christians grasped the superiority of their belief in its very ability to summon martyrs to defend and indeed glorify it. Socrates may have been a good philosopher, Christians conceded, but no one was willing to die for Socrates or for what he taught.[64] But the martyrs' deaths exalted and magnified God's name, so augmenting his people. Tertullian welcomed these deaths that would expand the Church: "Crucify us, torture us, condemn us, rub us out, but your tortures accomplish nothing. We become more numerous the more you mow us down."[65]

In so praising, glorifying, and honoring God, martyrdom became a "special kind of death," an "exaltation."[66] Origen quotes Jn 12:32, "When I am exalted from the earth, I will draw all men to myself"; and Jn 21:19, "This He said to show by what death He was to glorify God" to argue that the martyrs' deaths will glorify God and are thus exalted, "Christian," "pious," and "holy."[67] The reciprocal world of the Christian is therefore a cycle of transforming energy and change. Honor and sacredness flow from God to humanity and return in praise and glory. In this divine scheme, God and humanity participate in a dynamic balance. At the same time, we must also recall that the age of the martyrs was in many ways continuous with Roman values, too: the Christian writers located honor in volition and identified the will with the sacred power of the omnipotent God; volition was expressed in deeds of courage and fortitude. And both Romans and Christians shared the model of the failed hero, who redeems his honor through bold acts of the will, be it the disgraced general, the despised gladiator, or the tormented martyr.

As modern scholars, we need to pay more attention to the common cultural context that pagan and Christian Romans shared if we are to understand the religious changes of late antiquity. Christians were scrupulous about cleansing the world and establishing sharp categories of good and evil, sacred and profane. But if we return to the pagan world before this watershed, we may learn much when we explore the ambiguities confounding the conventional categories of pagan and Christian, sacred and profane, victim and victor. Knowing better the commonalities of pagans and Christians, we can become more sensitive to the most critical differences. We must, for example, ask why the Christian's universe could even offer salvation and successfully elicit trust and hope. Or how Virgil's observation, that "one salvation remains to the defeated—to hope for none" (Aeneid 2.354), can be displaced by Paul's gracious consolation: "We were so unbearably crushed that we despaired of life itself. He who rescued us from so deadly a peril will continue to rescue us, and on Him we must set our hope" (2 Cor 1:8). As historians of late antiquity, we must continue to seek answers to that dramatic change.

Notes

Abbreviations follow *L'Année Philologique*.

1. *M. Mont. et Luc.* 19.6 in Herbert Musurillo, *The Acts of the Christian Martyrs* (Oxford: Clarendon Press, 1972), 232; hereafter ACM: "uiuere nos etiam cum occidimur; nec uinci morte sed uincere." "[Martyrs] cannot be conquered . . . they are able to die, and . . . they are invincible because they do not fear to die," Cypr. *ep.* 60.2.3 (CCL 3C, 376). The passage exemplifies the use of military imagery common in martyrologies: "Sed retusus adunati exercitus fide pariter et uigore intellexit milites Christi uigilare iam sobrios at armatos ad proelium stare, uinci non posse, mori posse et hoc ipso inuictos esse quia mori non timent,

nec repugare contra inpugnantes, cum occidere innocentibus nec nocentes liceat, sed prompte et animas et sanguinem tradere, ut cum tanta in saeculo malitia et saeuitia grassetur, a malis et saeuis uelocius recedatur. Quale illud fuit sub oculis dei spectaculum gloriosum, quale in conspectu Christi eius ecclesiae suae gaudium, ad pugnam quam temptauerat hostis inferre, non singulos milites, sed tota simul castra prodisse." For Cyprian's use of such imagery, see Edelhard L. Hummel, *The Concept of Martyrdom according to St. Cyprian of Carthage* (Washington, D.C.: Catholic University Press, 1946).

2. Cf. Just. *1 apol.* 45 (SQ, 138); an echo of Socrates, Pl. *apol.* 30d.

3. Cypr. *ep.* 31.3.1 (CCL 3B, 153–4): "Quid enim gloriosius . . . quam ipsam quae ab omnibus metuatur moriendo mortem subegisse. . . . " See also Or. *Cel.* 3.8, tr. Henry Chadwick (Cambridge: Cambridge University Press, 1965), 133: "For a few [martyrs] . . . have died occasionally for the sake of the Christian religion by way of reminder to men that when they see a few striving for piety they may become more steadfast and may despise death. . . . that the weaker men might recover from anxiety about death, God's providence has cared for believers; for by His will alone He has dispersed all the opposition to them, so that kings and local governors and the common people were unable to be too violently inflamed against them."

4. See Tert. *apol.* 50.5–16 (CCL 1, 170–1), who also mentions Dido, Regulus, Anaxarchus, Attica, Zeno, and the Spartan boys undergoing ritual flagellation; Tert. *anim.* 4.9 (CCL 1, 180) notes Regulus and Curtius. In *mart.* 4.1.4–9 (CCL 1, 6–7), written about 197–202 C.E., that is, before Tertullian's Montanist period, he adds honorable suicides to the list of heroic self-sacrifice: Lucretia, Scaevola, Heraclitus, Peregrinus, Dido, the wife of Hasdrubal, Regulus, even Cleopatra! Cf. also Clement of Alexandria, who mentions courageous women: Leaena, Telesilla, Alcestis, Theano, along with women philosophers, in *Strom.* 4.19 (GCS 15, 300–303); M. Felix, *Oct.* 37.3–6 (CSEL 2, 52), who discusses Scaevola, Aquilius, and Regulus. Augustine mentions Regulus, Scaevola, the Decii, Cato, Lucretia, etc. in *civ.* 5.18 (CCL 47, 151ff.); cf. also *civ.* 15–24 (CCL 47, 16–59). On the shared examples of courage, see Mary Louise Carlson, "Pagan Examples of Fortitude in the Latin Christian Apologists," *CPh* 43 (1948): 93–104.

5. Tert. *apol.* 50.10 (CCL 1, 170).

6. Aug. *civ.* 5.14 (CCL 47, 144).

7. By focusing on those pre-Constantinian lives deemed most reliable historically, and by choosing Christian writers of the same period, a reasonable model of comparison emerges between the Christian martyr and the pagan soldier or gladiator. A certain number of these early martyrs' *Acta* are considered "authentic" (i.e., reasonably close to the communities whose members were martyred), although even these lives carry a "message" that may be set against the models of heroism found in Roman generals and gladiators. A watershed exists with the conversion of Constantine: later martyrs' *Acta* are more didactic and less reflections of historical truth; they are part of a literary and theological tradition whose primary aim is to teach ideals of Christian perfection. The objection can be made that these lives were not designed to

address the conversion of the pagan community. The aim for writing these early lives clearly is to encourage and console those facing martyrdom, particularly by stressing the doctrines of the final judgment and the resurrection. The *Acta* also reinforce the power of the bishop vis-à-vis the confessors and help to solidify a community undergoing persecution, etc. Christians, however, were sensitive to the pagans' critique of Christianity but could internalize the terms of the debate, thereby transforming their meanings and so advance the Christian cause.

8. See Carlin Barton's contribution in this volume. For the Smith Conference, our presentations were coordinated to demonstrate continuities and differences; as the conference was taped, original transcripts are available. Barton's version of our panel has since been published as "Savage Miracles: The Redemption of Lost Honor in Roman Society and the Sacrament of the Gladiator and the Martyr," *Representations* 45 (1994): 41–71, see note 1. Some of my work appears in "Martyrdom and Christian Identity: Gregory I and Tradition," in *The Limits of Ancient Christianity: Essays on Late Antique Thought and Culture in Honor of R. A. Markus,* ed. William Klingshorn and Mark Vessey (Ann Arbor: University of Michigan Press, 1999); and "Settling Scores: Eschatology in the Church of the Martyrs," in *The Last Things: Death and the Apocalypse in the Later Middle Ages,* ed. Caroline Bynum and Paul Freedman (Philadelphia: University of Pennsylvania Press, 2000).

9. *M. Poly.* 14.1 (ACM, 12); *M. Lyons* 1.10 (ACM, 4); cf. also Tert. *apol.* 40.1 (CCL 1, 153).

10. Tert. *apol.* 50.11 (CCL 1, 170–71).

11. Cypr. *ep.* 60.2.3 (CCL 3A, 37).

12. *M. Eupl.* 1.1 (ACM, 310).

13. G.E.M. de Ste. Croix notes that volunteering is condemned by Clement of Alexandria, Origen, Lactantius, and by at least three bishops: Cyprian and Mensurius of Carthage, and Peter of Alexandria. The canons of the Council of Elvira and *M. Poly.* similarly condemn the practice. See G.E.M. de Ste. Croix, "Why Were the Early Christians Persecuted?" *Past and Present* 25 (1963): 21–2; documentation is supplied in "Aspects of the 'Great Persecution,'" *HTR* 47 (1954): 83, n. 63. One must also consider the implicit desire to avoid martyrdom if possible. One may infer from the apologies of Justin, Tatian, and Minucius Felix, who defend Christianity against unjust persecution. Even Tertullian, who is enthusiastic about martyrdom, especially in his Montanist years, argues only that one must not flee from persecution, not that one should actively volunteer for it. See now Arthur J. Droge and James D. Tabor, *A Noble Death: Suicide and Martyrdom Among Christians and Jews in Antiquity* (New York: HarperCollins, 1992), who emphasize traditions of voluntary death.

14. App. *Pun.* 9.66. See especially H. S. Versnel, *Triumphus: An Inquiry into the Origin, Development and Meaning of the Roman Triumph* (Leiden: Brill, 1970).

15. Cf. Livy 9.4.14: "foeda atque ignominiosa deditio est." S. Wirnstock, "Victor and Invictus," *HTR* 50 (1957): 211–47, notes the change from the

cult of the noble failure of the Republic to the cult of victory in the period beginning with Marius and Sulla.

16. See Darrel W. Amundsen, "Suicide and Early Christian Values," in *Suicide and Euthanasia: Historical and Contemporary Themes*, ed. Baruch A. Brody (Dordrecht: Kluwer Academic Publishers, 1989); and Alexander Murray, *Suicide in the Early Middle Ages* (Oxford: Oxford University Press, 1997).

17. *M. Carp.* 4.4 (ACM, 32); Tert. *orat.* 5.3 (CCL 1, 260).

18. Cf. *M. Mar. et Iam.* 5.4–8 (ACM, 200); Tert. *cult. fem.* 1.8.5 (CCL 1, 250–51).

19. *De Centesima* 18, cited by Jan Den Boeft and Jan Bremmer "Notiunculae Martyrologicae," *VigChr* 35 (1981): 42–56, at 44. They conclude: "Although the Church strongly disapproved of those who voluntarily were seeking martyrdom and death, the real martyr's wish to reach his salvation through suffering was deemed completely normal."

20. *M. Just.* 5.8. Translation by Den Boeft and Bremmer, "Notiunculae," 44, following G. Rauschen and G. Lanata using recension B.

21. Tert. *patien.* 3.9 (CCL 1, 301).

22. Tert. *patien.* 3.11 (CCL 1, 302).

23. Lact. *instit.* 6.17 (CSEL 19, 549).

24. In this mentality of self-sacrifice, which extends to modern civil disobedience, the governing logic includes the assumption that a higher courage is manifest when one endures an injury to oneself rather than killing the enemy or stranger.

25. Tert. *apol.* 50.14–15 (CCL 1, 171): "Multi apud uos ad tolerantiam doloris et mortis hortantur, ut Cicero in *Tusculanis*, ut Seneca in *Fortuitis*, ut Diogenes, ut Pyrrhon, ut Callinicus; nec tamen tantos inueniunt uerba discipulos, quantos Christiani factis docendo. [15] Ipsa illa obstinatio, quam exprobratis, magistra est. Quis enim non contemplatione eius concutitur ad requirendum, quid intus in re sit? Quis non, ubi requisiuit, accedit, ubi accessit, pati exoptat, ut totam Dei gratiam redimat, ut omnem ueniam ab eo compensatione sanguinis sui expediat?"

26. *M. Aur. Med.* 11.3, ed. and trans. A.S.L. Farquharson, 2 vols. (Oxford: Clarendon Press, 1968), 1:217; Lucian, *Pereg.* 13 (LCL, 14). The *Acta* reveal pagan derision; see *M. Pion.* 20.6 (ACM, 162); *M. Phileas* from Papyrus Bodmer (ACM, 342).

27. Albrecht Dihle has contrasted the Greek definition of moral freedom arising from the intellect with the Hebraic notion of will, which is best defined when seen as the manifestation of God's absolute power by which the universe exists. See Albrecht Dihle, *The Theory of Will in Classical Antiquity* (Berkeley: University of California Press, 1982), especially 1–19. But the political freedom of the Greeks and Romans is central: Hector laments the thought of Andromache spending her life toiling at the loom of another, "a helpless drudge with no will of [her] own" (Homer, *Iliad* 6.498). Achilles thinks the lot of a helot (a kind of serf) is about the worst fate on earth: only the life of a shade in Hades is more miserable (Homer, *Odyssey*, 9.487f). Examples of

such desires for self-determination could be multiplied: Herodotus's contrast between the slavish Persians and the free Greeks; Thucydides' Melian Dialogue, etc. For the Roman world, one should consider especially the heroes and heroines of Livy's *Histories*, who imperil themselves or sacrifice themselves for the sake of freedom: Horatio, Mucius Scaevola, Cloelia, etc.

28. See especially Helen North, *Sophrosyne: Self-Knowledge and Self-Restraint in Greek Literature* (Ithaca: Cornell University Press, 1966); Pierre Hadot, *Exercises spirituels et Philosophie antique* (Paris: Études Augustiniennes, 1981); Michel Foucault, *Histoire de la sexualité*, 3 vols. (Paris: Gallimard, 1976); Jackie Pigeaud, *La Maladie de l'âme* (Paris: Société d'édition "Les Belles Lettres," 1981).

29. Cf. Just. *1 apol.* 43 (SQ 1, 35).

30. Just. *1 apol.* 43 (SQ 1, 36); cf. Or. *princ.* 3.1.1f (GCS 5:578).

31. Or. *princ.* 3.6.1. (GCS 5:580): (An exegesis of Gn 1:26–27): "Hoc ergo quod dixit 'ad imaginem Dei fecit eum' et de similitudine siluit, non aliud indicat nisi quod imaginis quidem dignitatem in prima conditione percepit, similitudinis vero ei perfectio in consummatione servata est: scilicet, ut ipse sibi eam propriae industriae studiis ex Dei imitatione consciceret, quo possibilitate sibi perfectionis in initiis data per imaginis dignitatem in fine demum per operum expletionem perfectatam sibi ipse similitudinem consummaret." See also, Or. *Cel.* 4.30 (GCS, 1:299); *comm. in Rom.* 4.5 (PL 14:978); *princ.* 3.6.1 (GCS, 5:281): (An exegesis of Jn 17:24 and 21): "In quo iam videtur ipsa similitudo, si dici potest, proficere et ex simili unum iam fieri, pro eo sine dubio quod in consummatione vel fine omnia et in omnibus Deus est" (cf. 1 Cor 15:28). Quoted by Gerhard B. Ladner, *The Idea of Reform* (New York: Harper and Row, 1967), 88. In addition to Ladner, see especially Henri Crouzel, *Théologie de l'image de Dieu chez Origène* (Aubier: Éditions Montaigne, 1956).

32. Just. *1 apol.* 25.1–22 (SQ 1, 20).

33. See especially Aharon (Ronald E.) Agus, *The Binding of Isaac and Messiah: Law, Martyrdom and Deliverance in Early Rabbinic Religiosity* (Albany: State University of New York Press, 1988).

34. Saturus dips in his own blood the ring of the soldier Pudens and gives it back to him as a pledge (*pignus*), M. *Perp.* 10.5 (ACM, 130). Prudentius also sees the smoke from the pyre of Emeterius and Chelidonius wafting up as a ring that is a "sign of the faith" of the one, while a linen kerchief is caught by the wind and raised, the "pledge" of the other. Prud. *Peri.* 1.84–86 (CCL 126, 254).

35. While redactors of the martyrs' lives may have deliberately expanded such statements of faith for apologetic purposes, the point remains that the confession of faith is perceived as worth dying for. See Adalbert Hamman, "La Confession de la Foi dans les Premiers Actes des Martyrs," in *Epektasis; mélanges patristiques offerts au cardinal Jean Daniélou*, ed. Jacques Fontaine and Charles Kannengiesser (Paris: Beauchesne, 1972), 99–105. Hamman notes the diverse formulations of such confessions. Some arise from the recitation of

the Creed at the liturgy, others from baptismal vows. Formulas also vary for eastern and western churches. See also Giuliana Lanata, *Confessione o Professione? Il Dossier degli atti dei martiri* (Roma: Collection de L'École Française de Rome, 1988).

36. For the *sacramentum*, see J. de Ghellinck, S.J., *Pour l'histoire du mot "sacramentum"* (Louvain: Spicilegium Sacrum Lovaniense, 1924); Christine Mohrmann, "Sacramentum dans le plus anciens textes Chrétiens," in *Études sur le Latin des Chrétiens*, 2nd ed. (Rome: Edizioni di Storia e Letteratura, 1961), 233–44.

37. Tert. *mart.* 3.1 (CCL 1, 5): "Vocati sumus ad militiam Dei uiui iam tunc, cum in sacramenti uerba respondimus." See also *scorp.* 4.5 (CCL 2, 1076), where Tertullian emphasizes the relationship of the soldier to the commander who orders his fighting: "Huic sacramento militans ab hostibus prouocor. Par sum illis, nisi illis manus dedero. Hoc defendendo depugno in acie, uulneror, concidor, occidor. Quis hunc militi suo exitum uoluit, nisi qui tali sacramento eum consignauit?" The idea of a covenant is also strong in Or. *mart.* 12 (CGS 1, 11–12).

38. Tert. *spect.* 4.1 (CCL 1, 231): "ad principalem auctoritatem conuertar ipsius signaculi nostri. Cum aquam ingressi Christianam fidem in legis suae uerba profitemur, renuntiasse nos diabolo et pompae et angelis eius ore nostro contestamur." For *signaculum*, see also Tert. *spect.* 24.3 (CCL 1, 248).

39. Cypr. *ep.* 58.4.2 (CCL 3C, 325): "spectat militem suum Christus ubicumque pugnantem et persecutionis causa pro nominis sui honore morienti praemium reddit quod daturum se in resurrectione promisit." For the *devotio* and *sacramentum* in Cyprian, see also *ep.* 10.2; 15.1; 28.1–2; 54.1; 58.4; 60.2; 76.4; 76.6; 77.2.

40. Ign. *Rom.* 3.3 (SC 10, 128); cf. *Smyrn.* 4.2 (SC 10, 158).

41. *M. Carp.* 35 (ACM, 26).

42. Such strictness of identity is also seen in Perpetua's explanation to her father why she cannot recant: "'[D]o you see that vessel lying here to be a little pitcher, or something else?' And he said, 'I see it to be so.' And I replied to him, 'Can it be called by any other name than what it is?' And he said, 'No.' 'Neither can I call myself anything else than what I am, a Christian,'" *M. Perp.* 3.3.1–2 (ACM, 108).

43. *M. Just.* 2.1–2 (ACM, 55–56).

44. Ign. *Rom.* 3.2 (SC 10, 128).

45. Tert. *coron.* 11.5 (CCL 2, 1057): "Nec enim delictorum impunitatem aut martyriorum immunitatem militia promittit. Nusquam Christiano alius est unum euangelium et idem: Iesus negaturus omnen negatorem et confessurus omnen confessorem et saluam facturus animam pro nomine eius amissam, perditurus autem de contrario aduersus nomen eius lucri habitam."

46. Or. *mart.* 10 (SQ 1, 10).

47. Min. Felix, *Oct.* 23.7 (CSEL 33).

48. Tert. *apol.* 15.1ff. (CCL 1, 240).

49. Tert. *apol.* 15.4 (CCL 1, 240).

50. Tert. *apol.* 15.3 (CCL 1, 240).

51. Tert. *apol.* 13.5 (CCL 1, 111).

52. Tert. *apol.* 13.4 (CCL 1, 239). On the fashioning of idols, Tertullian remarks that if one can make gods (idols)—and if by hanging something on a gibbet, scraping, and baking one can make something constituting divinity—then those who threaten Christians with torture consecrate them. See also Tert. *apol.* 12.3–5 (CCL 1, 238).

53. Min. Fel. *Oct.* 5.2 (CSEL 2, 6–7): "nullum negotium est patefacere, omnia in rebus humanis dubia, incerta, suspensa, magisque omnia uerisimilia quam uera." Several works are useful for Minucius Felix's attitude to classical culture: Carl Becker, *Der 'Octavius' des M. Felix: Heidnische Philosophie und frühchristliche Apologetik*, in *Sitzungsberichte der bayerischen Akademie der Wissenschaften, philosophisch-historische Klasse* 2 (1967); Franz Xavier Burger, *Minucius Felix und Seneca* (Munich: C. H. Beck'sche Verlagsbuchhandlung, 1906); Mauriz Schuster, "Minucius Felix und die christlichen Popularphilosophen," *Wiener Studien* 52 (1934): 163–67.

54. Min. Fel. *Oct.* 5.13 (CSEL 2, 9): "adeo aut incerta nobis veritas occultatur et premitur, aut quod magis credendum est, variis et lubricis casibus soluta legibus fortuna dominatur"; cf. also 6.1: "fortuna caeca aut incerta natura sit" (CSEL 2, 9).

55. Georges Dumézil briefly discusses the equilibrium of Roman religion in *La religion romaine archaïque* (Paris: Payot, 1974), 131–41. Patterns of reciprocity in Roman religion need to be studied. The *do-ut-des* quality of Roman religion implies reciprocity. See J. van Baal, "Offering, Sacrifice, and Gift," *Numen* 23 (1975): 11–178, which stresses the need to reciprocate for the gift (of sacrifice) given. Claude Lévi-Strauss has identified reciprocity as one of the fundamental structures of the human mind; see *Les structures élémentaires de la parenté,* 2nd ed. (Paris: La Haye, Mouton et Co., 1967), 98.

56. Or. *mart.* 12 (GCS 1, 11–12). Origen continues: "If we wish to save our soul in order to get it back better than a soul, let us lose it by our martyrdom. For if we lose it for Christ's sake, casting it at His feet in a death for Him, we shall gain possession of true salvation for it. But if we do the contrary, we shall hear that it profits in no way the one who has gained the entire perceptible world by losing or forfeiting himself." The Christian must give his soul in martyrdom in order to get it back in salvation. If he is miserly and resists this giving, he gains nothing of worth, even if it be the material world.

57. Cypr. *fort.* 6 (CCL 3, 194).

58. Or. *mart.* 2 (GCS 1, 4).

59. Or. *mart.* 2 (GCS 1, 4).

60. Or. *mart.* 27 (GCS 1, 23–24).

61. Or. *mart.* 28 (GCS 1, 24).

62. Scholars such as Robert Daly have emphasized the spiritual side of Origen's attitude toward sacrifice; see his "Sacrificial Soteriology in Origen," *StPat* 17 (1982): 872–78; and "Sacrifice in Origen," *StPat* 11 (1972): 125–29.

Frances M. Young argues that the martyr's sacrifice, like that of Christ, is an aversion sacrifice (277ff.); see *The Use of Sacrificial Ideas in Greek Christian Writers from the New Testament to John Chrysostom* (Cambridge, Mass.: Philadelphia Patristic Foundation, 1979).

63. Or. *mart.* 50 (GCS 1, 47).

64. Just. *1 apol.* 10 (SQ 1, 8–9).

65. Tert. *apol.* 50.13 (CCL 1, 171).

66. Or. *mart.* 50 (GCS 1, 47).

67. Or. *mart.* 29 (GCS 1, 26).

FOUR

MURDER AND MARTYRS IN
ANGLO-SAXON ENGLAND

Margaret Cormack

The arenas of Rome left an indelible imprint on Christianity. Christians believed that the martyrs who voluntarily gave up their lives for Christ were rewarded by joining Him immediately in heaven. Since they had proved their faith by making the ultimate sacrifice, the Last Judgment would find them among the judges, not the judged. In the meantime, they were able to aid those still on earth in all manner of ways, from curing sickness or changing the weather to afflicting tyrants with loathsome diseases. Their relics were sources of healing and power and became objects of pilgrimage.[1]

As Christianity developed, such powers became associated not only with martyrs but also with other types of saints, whose devotion to Christ took forms such as asceticism or leadership of the Church. Such saints, known as "confessors," were venerated in the communities in which they had lived, in religious houses which they had led, and in churches where their relics were found. In the early Middle Ages, the development of such a cult reflected the efforts of local monks or clergy, whose authority was sufficient to establish it. Formal canonization procedures under the control of the papacy did not emerge until the thirteenth century.[2]

Saints qualified for their status by being, in one way or another, imitators of Christ. Martyrs were perceived to have imitated Jesus most closely by giving their lives for Him, as He had given His for them. Martyrdom was thus the ultimate standard against which other saints were judged and to which accounts of their lives were assimilated. The *vitae* of paradigmatic ascetics such as Antony or Symeon the Stylite include episodes in which self-imposed austerities and/or the attacks of demons clearly function as equivalents to the tortures of the arenas. Both these saints undergo a symbolic "death" at an early stage in their careers.

The martyrdom of the living did not, however, have to be as spectacular as that of Antony or Symeon. Gregory of Tours comments that "the confessors of Christ . . . have become their own persecutors, in order to be thought worthy of God. They have charged themselves with various crosses of abstinence, and in order to live with Jesus Christ they have mortified their flesh."[3] Or as expressed by Gregory the Great: "There are two kinds of martyrdom . . . one that is secret and one that is public. Martyrdom is secret or hidden whenever the soul is eager and ready for suffering even if there is no open persecution. . . . [John and James both "drink of the cup" of martyrdom, though one dies violently, one not]. . . . From this we can conclude with full assurance that there is a martyrdom without *external* suffering [italics mine]."[4] According to Gregory the Great, anyone could be a martyr, if only the soul was ready.[5]

In spite of such teachings on "martyrdom by intent," saints who died in their beds never achieved the same spiritual status as those who had been persecuted for their faith. Theologians to the contrary, in the popular mind a "real" martyr was one who had suffered a violent death, and such was the status of martyrdom that a tendency developed to call any saint who died violently a "martyr," whether or not his death resulted from persecution.[6] Among the saints who benefited by this tendency were a number of bishops who were "martyred" in the seventh century during the political struggles of Merovingian Gaul.[7] Another such group consists of murdered members of Anglo-Saxon royal families, whose cults as martyrs developed in the seventh through the tenth centuries.

The two groups of martyrs may not be unrelated. The ruling families of the Anglo-Saxon kingdoms had been in contact with their Christian counterparts in Gaul long before the arrival of Augustine's mission in 597; indeed, the success of that mission undoubtedly owed much to the fact that the pagan king Æthelbert had a Christian Frankish queen. It is therefore quite likely that the model for calling victims of a political struggle "martyrs" arrived in England from Gaul. There was a significant difference, however. The Merovingian martyrs were almost uniformly bishops, who represented Christianity by virtue of their office. The Anglo-Saxon royal martyrs had taken neither holy orders nor monastic vows; their deaths are not even connected with defense of the Church. Why should the mere fact of a violent death—a not uncommon event in early medieval England—cause them to be classified as martyrs?

The historical and hagiographical sources pertaining to the eleven murdered royal saints who were venerated as martyrs have been the subject of an article by David Rollason (1983) that forms the point of departure for the present study. Rollason's article contains a detailed analysis of the political, social, and ecclesiastical circumstances under which the cults developed. In what follows, I will speculate about the ideological factors that inform the cults, and why the deaths of these saints, which correspond so poorly with any recognized ideal of martyrdom, developed into a "type" in England.

First, however, it will be necessary to discuss the theories that have been put forth to explain the phenomenon. Most scholars who have considered the problem have focused on the martyrs' royal blood and assumed that the cults that developed had something to do with kingship. There are two camps: those who derive the ideology of the royal martyrs from pre-Christian beliefs and practices, and those who see it as a development of Christian kingship by the grace of God. There are, however, flaws in both hypotheses.

The theory that cults of royal martyrs derive from a form of pre-Christian sacral kingship is based on very fragmentary evidence. Knowledge of the beliefs of the Germanic peoples in pre-Christian times is based primarily on the writings of Roman or medieval Christian authors. The first detailed description of the mythology of a Germanic people dates from the thirteenth century, when traditional poetry was recorded and speculated about by Icelanders who were at least two centuries removed from the religious beliefs and practices of their ancestors.

These sources do provide strong evidence for a pre-Christian belief in the king's "luck," which ensured victory in battle and the fertility of the land.[8] References to such a belief survived the conversion to Christianity, and are recorded in Sweden as late as the sixteenth century.[9] The earliest evidence for such a belief is provided by Ammianus Marcellinus (c. 330–395), who informs us that rulers who were not successful in battle could be deposed.[10] It has been concluded by scholars of prehistoric European culture that these kings, as well as kings held responsible for bad harvests, were sacrificed to the gods. In 1970, William Chaney argued that memories of the sacrifice of kings provided the basis for the cults of royal martyrs.

As has been pointed out by Janet Nelson and Susan Ridyard,[11] such "sacral kings" embody qualities diametrically opposite to those required of Christian saints: on the one hand, fertility and military might; on the other, chastity and pacifism. Against this it could be argued that precisely the lack of Christian virtues accounts for the emphasis on the violent deaths of the saints—their lives did not bear examination. To my mind, it is not arguments based on Christianity that undermine the theory of continuity between pagan sacral kingship and martyr cults, but the evidence of the very descriptions of pagan practices usually cited in defense of the theory. Ammianus Marcellinus mentions no fate worse than deposition; the assumption that this is a diluted form of sacrifice relies primarily on a verse in a ninth-century Scandinavian poem and the commentary supplied for it by a thirteenth-century Christian author, Snorri Sturluson.[12] The poem purports to describe the Swedish ancestors of the historical line of Norwegian kings. The verse in question informs us that the Swedes sacrificed their king, Dómaldi; Snorri explains that this was the result of a famine, not failure in war. Dómaldi himself belongs not to any historically accessible period of Swedish history, but to the mythic past—a past so distant that, unlike the known Scandinavian gods, he has no cult associated with him. In an article on Scandinavian sacral kingship, McTurk refers to the Dómaldi episode as containing "the belief, or the memory of a belief" in such a ritual.[13] Indeed, if the verse does reflect the actual practice of any society, there is no way of determining when and where that society existed and left its traces in the mythology. Given the fact that Irish sources are often adduced in support of the Germanic practice, it could have originated at any time between the ninth century and the murky antiquity of the Indo-European past. The relationship between myths and the societies that believe the myths is complex; how much more so is the relationship of myths to a society that has ceased to believe them? Patrick Wormald's warnings about the use of mythological material for the study of early Irish kingship apply equally well to Scandinavia.[14]

Even if we assume that kings were sacrificed at some point in the common past of the Germanic tribes, there is no evidence that those kings were worshiped after their deaths. This is not to say that kings could not be deified. A ninth-century missionary to Sweden, St. Ansgar, is said to have met with an unusual obstacle in his attempts to spread the faith. He was informed that the Swedes had recently received a message from their gods to the effect that, if the Swedes wanted an additional deity, the gods would be happy to accept the deceased king Eric among their number. On no account, however, should the Swedes accept the cult of the "foreign god," Christ.[15]

We know absolutely nothing about King Eric, but it is unlikely that he had lost many battles or been sacrificed after a crop failure. What reason could there be for venerating such an individual? When Snorri Sturluson does give an example of a man who became a god, the situation is the opposite of Dómaldi's. Snorri informs us that the god Freyr was once a human king who was subsequently worshipped because of the *abundant* harvests that occurred during his reign.[16] There is no sacrifice in Snorri's story—Freyr's death is, in fact, carefully hidden from the population, who continue to pay taxes to their deceased ruler. Snorri's euhemeristic interpretation reflects his Christian background, but his comments agree with my intuition; gods can be created from successful human beings, not from failures.

Finally, as has frequently been pointed out,[17] when information about their origins is available, saints' cults are found to originate in ecclesiastical communities, often royal foundations connected with the saint's family. There is no evidence whatsoever for the takeover of cults of pagan gods. While Christian saints undoubtedly came to fulfill the functions once filled by the gods, this does not mean that a god changed into a saint overnight.

A stronger argument can be made for the Christian version of sacral kingship. That the medieval church promoted kings as Christ's representatives on earth is too well known to need repeating here.[18] In the Anglo-Saxon context, Rollason has pointed out that cults of royal murder victims appear most frequently in the late eighth and early ninth century. He sees this development as a direct result of the visit in 786 of papal legates who emphasized the position of kings as the "Lord's anointed" and condemned those who killed them in no uncertain terms.[19] Although Rollason argues that the condemnation of the killing of kings would apply, by extension, to all members of the royal family, I am not convinced that this would have been the case. The purpose of the council was to limit the number of individuals who might be recognized as kings—and there were undoubtedly enough deposed kings in Northumbria at this time that it was unnecessary to take uncrowned claimants into consideration.[20]

In order to understand what was at stake in the stories of murdered kings and princes, it will be necessary to consider some features of the society and ideology of the Anglo-Saxon world of the seventh through the tenth centuries. During this period in England—and indeed, throughout the Christianized Germanic world—royal and aristocratic families produced large numbers of high-ranking churchmen, who were in a position either to be venerated as saints or to support claims to sanctity on behalf of deceased relatives.[21] The royal families of the Anglo-Saxon kingdoms, like those of the Franks, produced their share of saintly ascetics, bishops, and virgins of noble or royal blood, as well as the requisite number of abbots and abbesses capable of fostering the cults of their kinsmen.[22]

The number of legitimate candidates for sanctity makes the designation of political victims as "martyrs" even more striking. The key to the popularity of this type of martyr in England must be sought in the hagiographic narratives that describe their deaths.

Rollason has outlined the common features of the hagiography of such saints as follows. The victim, who is the member of a royal family if not a reigning king, is typically slain by an agent of his enemy and the body secretly disposed of. (It may be added that the agent is commonly someone trusted by the victim.) The crime is revealed by a divine manifestation, usually a column of light shining over the corpse or the place of the crime. Recognition of the saintly status of the victim follows, often including the foundation or dedication of a church or monastery to him.[23] Although the hagiographers may try to provide a rationale for the crime that would give it a religious significance, it is clear that the real cause for the elimination of the victims was their status as potential rivals to a throne.

In the following I will argue that the features in the stories of the murdered royal saints that clash so jarringly with the traditional model of Christian martyrdom resonate with the ideology of pre-Christian culture. However, what is at issue is not some special charisma pertaining to kingship, but more basic attitudes toward death, honor, and kinship that existed throughout Anglo-Saxon society. If these attitudes are embodied in the stories of royal murder victims, it is because it was precisely at the royal level that the ideals pertaining to them were severely strained.

The basic value of Germanic societies was honor. Its most important features are that (1) it was demonstrated largely, if not exclusively, by means of physical courage; (2) it was a communal possession—the honor of an individual contributed to, and was influenced by, that of any group to which he belonged; (3) it depended on public valuation. These were shame, not guilt, cultures.

Taking these points one by one, what counted most in establishing honor was physical courage, in particular, bravery in battle or in the face of certain death. Tacitus comments of the Germanic tribes that "To throw away one's shield is the supreme disgrace, and the man who has thus dishonored himself is debarred from attendance at sacrifice or assembly. Many such survivors from the battlefield have ended their shame by hanging themselves."[24] The author of a Latin saint's life composed c. 975–1025 expressed the same ideal: "One of our men, a valiant soldier called Stremwold, was killed along with several others who chose to end their lives in death by battle rather than to live on in shame."[25]

The state of his honor was not the exclusive concern of an individual; it also redounded on any group with which he was associated, such as the military association consisting of a lord and his retainers (his *comitatus*) or the kindred. Tacitus comments on the former case:

> On the field of battle it is a disgrace to a chief to be surpassed in courage by his followers, and to the followers not to equal the courage of their chief. And to leave a battle alive after their chief has fallen means lifelong infamy and shame. To defend and protect him, and to let him get the credit for their own acts of heroism, are the most solemn obligations of their allegiance. The chiefs fight for victory, the followers for their chief . . . the Germans have no taste for peace; renown is more easily won among perils, and a large body of retainers cannot be kept together except by means of violence and war. . . . A German is not so easily prevailed upon to plough the land and wait patiently for harvest as to challenge a foe and earn wounds for his reward. He thinks it tame and spiritless to accumulate slowly by the sweat of his brow what can be got quickly by the loss of a little blood.[26]

This ideal is also reflected in Anglo-Saxon legislation, which considers fighting on behalf of one's lord a legitimate activity[27] and specifies sanctions to punish those who fail to do so.[28]

The honor of the kindred was also shared and depended on the honor of its members. This is reflected in the practice of the bloodfeud, which defined the balance of power in early Germanic societies. According to the ethics of the feud, harm done to any member of a given group had to be avenged—with interest, if possible—on the group to which the aggressor belonged. Tacitus remarks that "heirs are under an obligation to take up both the feuds and the friendships of a father or kinsman."[29] Only thus could the honor of the victim's family be maintained. The Anglo-Saxon poem "Beowulf" contains the following exhortation to action: "Do not, as a man of reason, give yourself up to grief. It is a finer thing in any man that he should avenge his friend than that he should unduly mourn. Each one of us must live in expectation of an end of life in this world: Let him who can gain good repute before death—that is the finest thing thereafter for the lifeless man."[30] Slaying for vengeance was not a crime; it was a duty, recognized as such in the early codes of Anglo-Saxon law.[31]

Slaying in return for slaying need not, however, result in an unending cycle of violence. Under favorable circumstances, the feud could be brought to an end by means of a money payment: "But feuds do not continue forever unreconciled. Even homicide can be atoned for by a fixed number of cattle or sheep, the compensation being received by the whole family."[32]

Intrinsic to the feud is the fact that slayings and compensation are public; publicity was what defined the honor of the parties in a conflict. To be effective, justice must be seen to have been carried out. To conceal a slaying would imply fear of retaliation and was at least as shameful as leaving a kinsman unavenged.

As stated in the passage of "Beowulf" quoted above, what counted in this world was reputation, and for the Germans, as for the gladiators and early Christians, what put the final touch on one's reputation was the way one met one's death. The best one could do was to die defending one's lord or fighting on against unsurmountable odds— vikings at Maldon, a dragon in "Beowulf." Honorable burial was a corollary to honorable death; it, too, reflected the life one had led and was denied to the unworthy. The castigation of those who run away from battle has already been mentioned, and Tacitus informs us concerning criminals: "The mode of execution varies according to the offence. Traitors and deserters are hanged in trees; cowards, shirkers, and sodomites are pressed down under a wicker hurdle into the slimy mud of a bog. This distinction in punishments is based on the idea that offenders against the state should be made a public example of, whereas deeds of shame should be buried out of men's sight."[33]

The way in which an individual died reflected not only on him but also on his family. One gloried in the accomplishments of one's kinsmen, past or present; one was shamed by the failure of honor on the part of any one of them. The dishonorable death of a relative was a breach in the honor of his kindred. If it was deserved, this is obvious; but it was equally the case if the slain individual was an innocent victim. Quality of death, good or bad, was a commentary on life. On the general principle of "no smoke without a fire," someone who died a dishonorable death was assumed to have deserved it. The Anglo-Saxons would have appreciated in their own way the biblical statement that "a hanged man is accursed by God."[34]

Killings committed in secret or by treachery (two categories that often overlap) deprived both the victim and his surviving kin of honor. The victim was deprived of witnesses to his "last stand" (in fact, he might be deprived of a "last stand"), and his kin were left in the position of being unable to take vengeance—of having to live with a stain on their honor that it was impossible to wipe out.[35]

If there was anything worse than not knowing who the killer was, it was knowing—and being unable to do anything about it. This could happen in the case of criminals, executed by the authority of a king.[36] The worst-case scenario, however, was a killing that took place within the kindred itself. In such a case, stained honor could not be cleansed because to do so would either compound the crime by further slaying of kindred, or leave it unatoned for because those responsible for taking revenge were themselves the guilty parties. The Beowulf poet expresses his opinion of such slayings in several passages. An accidental death at the hand of a kinsman is tragic, "wearying to mind and to spirit."[37] Words addressed by the hero of the poem to one guilty of such a crime are quite explicit: "you did become the killer of your brothers, your chief kindred; and for that you must endure damnation in hell."[38] In the face of his own death, Beowulf reflects: "I have bided the decrees of Providence in their own good time, at home; I have ruled well over my own, I have not gone looking for contrived quarrels nor have I sworn lots of oaths perjuriously. Sick as I am with a mortal wound, I can take comfort in all this, for the Ruler of men will have no cause to accuse me of the violent killing of kinsmen when my life slips away from my body."[39] We are informed that his soul departs to heaven.[40]

Odd though it may seem to us, for a king like Beowulf to live out his life and keep his hands free from the blood of kinsmen was a major accomplishment. In the royal families of the Germanic world, internecine strife was endemic. With kingship at stake, the tension between the ideal of family solidarity and the realities of power politics became intense, and it was generally political considerations that won out.[41] When kinsman kills kinsman—and the slayer is a king—the victim must by double necessity lie unavenged.[42]

It is precisely such dishonorable, unavengeable deaths that are suffered by the "royal martyrs." They die at the instigation of claimants to the throne who are, as often as not, their relations. The martyr is *always* the victim of treachery, being slain either by a family member or by someone from whom he had a right to expect protection and support.

The cult of saints provided a solution to such "crises of honor" that was impossible in pre-Christian times, when the way one met one's death was the ultimate comment on one's life. Abandoned (if not actually murdered) by his human family, the victim is recognized by a divine one; God himself prosecutes the feud, striking down the aggressors if they fail to make proper amends. As Rollason points out, the compensation could take the form of the foundation of a church or monastery in which the deceased was honorably buried; in such cases, development of a cult was

only a matter of time. Even more than the actual compensation, however, the victim's new status as a martyr restored the lost honor of both
the victim and his kinsmen—indeed, it put the supporters of his cause
one move ahead in the game of one-upmanship that was the feud.

A classic account of a death that illustrates the traditional motifs and
resultant sanctification is contained in the entries of the *Anglo-Saxon
Chronicle* describing the death of King Edward the Martyr, killed in 978
or 979 while visiting his half-brother, Æthelred. The D/E version of
the *Anglo-Saxon Chronicle* presents us first with the bare facts, then with
a commentary that breaks into verse:

> In this year King Edward was killed at the gap of Corfe on 18 March in
> the evening, and he was buried at Wareham without any royal honors.
> And no worse deed than this for the English people was committed
> since first they came to Britain. Men murdered him, but God honoured
> him. In life he was an earthly king; he is now after death a heavenly
> saint. His earthly kinsmen would not avenge him, but his heavenly
> Father has greatly avenged him. The earthly slayers wished to blot out
> his memory on earth, but the heavenly Avenger has spread abroad his
> memory in heaven and in earth. Those who would not bow to his liv-
> ing body, now bend humbly on their knees to his dead bones. Now
> we can perceive that the wisdom and contrivance of men and their
> plans are worthless against God's purpose.

A year later "Ealdorman Ælfhere fetched the holy king's body from
Wareham and bore it with great honour to Shaftesbury."[43]

According to the legend that developed within a few years of his
death, Edward had been slain at the instigation of his stepmother, stabbed
by a servant as he gave him the kiss of peace. The corpse was disposed
of in a bog and subsequently revealed (in one version, uncorrupt) by a
column of light from heaven, indicating Edward's sanctity.

It should be emphasized that in order for a cult to be successful, all
the circumstances had to be right. The power relations between those
promoting the martyr and those responsible for his death could not be
too one-sided, and the Church had to be supportive. This was easy
enough when churchmen were also kinsmen, but a royal murder victim was unlikely to be declared a martyr if there was significant tension
between throne and church.

In this context, a brief comparison between Anglo-Saxon England
and Merovingian Gaul may prove valuable. As noted above, Merovingian
Gaul produced martyred bishops rather than martyred kings—with one
interesting exception, King Sigismund of Burgundy.[44] Gregory of Tours
describes his death in two works, *The History of the Franks* and *Glory of*

the Martyrs. The latter, composed c. 590, describes Sigismund's fate as follows:

> For the Lord often suppresses the arrogance of a stubborn mind with his rod of correction so that he might restore the same mind to respect for his worship. As clear confirmation there is the behavior of King Sigismund in the past. His heart was filled with remorse after he had killed his own son at the urging of his evil wife. He went to St. Maurice d'Agaune, and there he knelt before the tombs of the most blessed martyrs of the propitious [Theban] Legion. He performed penance and prayed that divine vengeance would punish him for his misdeeds in this world, so that he might be considered absolved in judgment if he repaid the evils he had committed before he departed from the world. He instituted there the daily recitation of psalms, and he most generously enriched the place with new lands and with other endowments. Later he and his sons were captured by King Chlodomer at whose order he was killed. His body was brought to [the monastery of St. Maurice d'Agaune] and buried in a tomb. This [following] event indicates that he was received into the company of the saints. For wherever people suffering from chills piously celebrate a mass in his honor and make an offering to God for the king's repose, immediately their tremors cease, their fevers disappear, and they are restored to their earlier health.[45]

In his *History of the Franks,* Gregory informs us that Chlodomer had also slain Sigismund's wife and children and ordered all the bodies thrown into a well.[46]

Gregory of Tours was a Gallo-Roman bishop whose aristocratic family had a long tradition of ecclesiastical service. For him a violent death was *not* sufficient to account for Sigismund's sanctity, which is instead justified in terms of the king's remorse. According to Gregory, this remorse was demonstrated by Sigismund's support of the monastery of St. Maurice at Agaune—whose monks were responsible for his burial there.[47] Sigismund's death at the hands of his kinsman, Chlodomer, is deserved punishment for the slaying of his own son. However, as in the case of the Roman gladiators and martyrs, the punishment and humiliation are voluntarily undergone—in fact, prayed for. The ensuing miracles are signs, not of God's wrath at Chlodomer's act, but that Sigismund has been forgiven. The message of Gregory's story— a message that he surely would wish to be heard by the Frankish kings of his own day—is that even the greatest of sinners, a slayer of his own son, can attain salvation through repentance and appropriate penance.

Also implicit in Gregory's account is the importance of the Church. Indeed, Gregory's statement that Sigismund has been received "into the company of saints" is to a certain degree subverted by the information that people are still celebrating masses "for the king's repose." One prayed *to*, not *for*, a saint. Since he included Sigismund in his volume *Glory of the Martyrs*, Gregory can have no doubts about his powers of intercession; his description of the mass, however, serves as a not-so-subtle reminder to his readers that it is only through the Church that one can gain entry into heaven.

As Paxton has noted, the masses themselves reflect a certain degree of uneasiness concerning Sigismund's saintly status.[48] By the early ninth century, however, the author of his *passio* had produced a narrative that left no room for doubt. Sigismund's murder of his son is omitted, and instead of being captured and killed by an enemy king, Sigismund is betrayed to that king by his own people. Learning of the betrayal, he enters the monastic life and is slain shortly thereafter. His body, and those of his family, are thrown into a well. Three years later, the column of light appears, and an angel informs the abbot of St. Maurice d'Agaune that the sacred bodies, whose souls are in heaven with the Theban Legion, should be associated with the relics of the Legion in the church. Reburial of the remains is now interpreted as a translation.[49] All the elements familiar from the Anglo-Saxon narratives are there: betrayal by those who owe loyalty, disposal of the body in a well, divine revelation of sanctity. The only difference is that Sigismund is a monk, not a king, when he is martyred. Frankish churchmen were apparently not willing to go quite as far as Anglo-Saxon ones.

The historical Sigismund was not a monk. As Paxton points out,[50] his initial burial and subsequent veneration at St. Maurice reflect a period of cooperation between Sigismund and local bishops, which had been cemented by the foundation of the monastery and continued until shortly after the king's death. Sigismund's life and cult correspond to a brief moment of Merovingian history, in which ecclesiastics and kings were allies rather than adversaries—a set of circumstances that would not recur before the emergence of the Carolingian dynasty.

Changes in the relationship between secular and religious authorities may also account for the periods at which the cults of Anglo-Saxon royal martyrs develop. Catherine Cubitt has pointed out that in eighth-century England there was considerable tension between the laity and the Church.[51] This could explain the chronological gap between the earliest cults of royal martyrs, which date from the seventh century, and the large number that date from the late eighth and early ninth centuries. As noted by Rollason, these decades saw a renewed interest in kingship on the part of the Church, which included a greater willingness to present royal murder victims as saints.

I have tried to explain the phenomenon of "murdered royal martyrs" in terms that would have been comprehensible to the martyrs' contemporaries. Modern theologians may shake their heads and ask, "But how could churchmen possibly have approved anything so bizarre?" It must be remembered that the churchmen themselves were children of their times, and although more learned than their lay contemporaries, shared their culture without perceiving any conflict with their Christian faith.

When Anglo-Saxons read in Romans 12:19: "Vengeance is mine, I will repay, says the Lord" what could this mean but that God would take up the feud on behalf of His own? Nor were they the first to assume this; Wallace-Hadrill has discussed in detail the attitudes toward (and participation in) the feud on the part of Merovingian ecclesiastics, who considered it only natural that God would avenge those who had no other avengers.[52] Our prime source for this period, Gregory of Tours, objected to the feud only when it led to killings within the kindred—but, as we have seen above, he did not go so far as to claim that royal deaths justified the divine feud.

On one issue, Christians and pagans saw eye to eye: the way in which one met one's death was extremely important, and unexpected death was a disaster. The warrior ideal of the Germanic tribes called for a heroic death on the battlefield. Christians were concerned with the need to make confession and receive extreme unction; a sudden death deprived the victim of his chance to prepare his soul for the next world. When due to natural causes, such deaths were often seen by Christians as a judgment on the victim's life—as a judgment of God.[53]

Unexpected deaths at the hands of other human beings fell into a different category. I have tried to show why a treacherous betrayal was the ultimate dishonor in secular terms; Rosalind Hill has pointed out that for the Venerable Bede, the most learned monk of his time, loyalty was the highest possible expression of lay virtue, treachery the ultimate crime.[54] Churchmen could find biblical models to support this attitude; the worst crime in the Bible—the slaying of Jesus himself—involves a betrayal of not *a* lord, but *the* Lord by one of his "men." The "kisses of peace" with which several of the martyrs are betrayed are surely meant to echo that of Judas, and their deaths that of Christ. Even older than the sin of betraying one's lord was that of betraying one's kin. According to the Venerable Bede, it was not Stephen, nor even Christ, but Abel, slain by his brother Cain, who was the first martyr.

Notes

1. The classic work on the subject is Brown, *Cult of the Saints*.

2. Papal approval of canonization procedures was not required until the thirteenth century. This did not, however, mark an end to popular cults, which flourished even without papal approval. Indeed, popular veneration necessarily preceded canonization because it produced the miracles that were required for the establishment of an individual's sanctity.

3. Gregory of Tours, *Life of the Fathers*, Book 2, ch. 1, p. 35.

4. Gregory the Great, *Dialogues*, 160–61.

5. For the equation of monasticism with martyrdom, see Malone, *The Monk and the Martyr*.

6. The standard dictionary of Medieval Latin begins its entry for "martyr" with a definition that would be accepted by most: "one who suffers death for Christ and the Christian faith," but goes on to inform us that the term is also used for those who did not die for confessing the name of Christ, but received death in some other way, "from brigands or impious men." DuCange, *Glossarium Mediæ et Infimæ Latinitatis* 4.291–92.

7. See most recently Scheibelreiter; also Wallace-Hadrill, *The Frankish Church*, 89ff.

8. See most recently Kienast; also Folz and McTurk.

9. McTurk, 139.

10. Ammianus Marcellinus, with an English translation by John Rolfe (Cambridge: Harvard University Press, 1935–39), 3 vols., 3.168–69, = lib. 28.5.14.

11. Janet Nelson, "Royal Saints and Early Medieval Kingship" and Susan Ridyard, *The Royal Saints of Anglo-Saxon England*, ch. 3.

12. Snorri Sturluson, *Heimskringla*, Ynglinga saga, ch. 15.

13. McTurk, 157.

14. Patrick Wormald, "Celtic and Anglo-Saxon Kingship."

15. Rimbert, *Vita Anskarii*, ch. 26.

16. *Heimskringla*, Ynglinga saga, ch. 10.

17. See works by Ridyard, Rollason, and Thacker.

18. See Ridyard, ch. 3, Nelson, and Hill.

19. Rollason (1983), 17; *Councils and Ecclesiastical Documents*, ed. Hadden and Stubbs, 3.447–62.

20. See John, *Orbis Britanniae*, 34.

21. Rollason (1983), especially 13. There were in addition royal "martyrs," such as Oswald, who died in battle; they do not concern me here.

22. These families of saints have been the subject of much scholarship, most recently that of Folz. For England, see most recently Ridyard (1988) and Rollason (1982).

23. For details of the promotion of murdered royal saints in monasteries associated with royal houses, see Ridyard, Rollason, and Thacker.

24. Tacitus, *The Agricola and the Germania*, ch. 6, 106–7. All translations from Tacitus are from this edition. "Scutum reliquisse praecipuum flagitium,

nec aut sacris adesse aut concilium inire ignominioso fas, multique superstites bellorum infamiam laqueo finierunt." Tacitus, *Germania*, ch. 6, in *Cornelii Taciti Opera Minora.* In quoting Tacitus, I am not unaware of the difficulties attached to using as evidence a text that purports to describe the barbarian enemies of Rome but in fact presents a not-so-subtle criticism of the author's "civilized" contemporaries. While Tacitus was far from being an accurate anthropological observer of the Germanic tribes of his time, the passages I have quoted nonetheless provide an apt and concise summary of ideals and values reflected in the literatures of several Germanic peoples. It should be kept in mind that the ideals portrayed in literature are not necessarily exemplified in the day-to-day life of society. As Roberta Frank (1991) has pointed out, the ideals themselves may even be mutually exclusive.

25. "Nam occisus est ex nostris miles fortissimus nomine Stremwold, cum aliis nonnullis—qui bellica morte magis elegerunt uitam finere quam ignobiliter uiuere." "The *Life of St. Oswald,*" ed. Michael Lapidge, in *The Battle of Maldon AD 991*, 52, 54.

26. Tacitus, *The Agricola and the Germania*, 113–14. "Cum ventum in aciem, turpe principe virtute vinci, turpe comitatui virtutem principis non adaequare, iam vero infame in omnem vitam ac probosum superstitem principi suo ex acie recessisse; illum defendere tueri, sua quoque fortia facta gloriae eius adsignare, praecipuum sacramentum est: principes pro victoria pugnant, comites pro principe . . . ingrata genti quies et facilius inter ancipitia clarescunt magnumque comitatum non nisi vi belloque tueare . . . nec arare terram aut expectare annum tam facile persuaseris quam vocare hostem et vulnera mereri; pigrum quin immo et iners videtur sudore adquirere quod possis sanguine parare." *Germania*, ch. 14.

27. Liebermann, *Die Gesetze der Angelsachsen*, 1.76–77.

28. Discussed by Roberta Frank in "The Ideal of Men Dying with their Lord in the *Battle of Maldon*," 100. See also Liebermann, *Die Gesetze der Angelsachsen*, 1.364–65. While I agree with Frank's emphasis on the fluidity and adaptability of the "men dying for their lord" theme, I am not convinced that this reflects a specifically Christian ethos. Without claiming that the ideal was always lived up to, it seems to me that the Christian teaching of self-sacrifice was grafted on to a value system with which it was consistent.

29. *The Agricola and the Germania*, 119. "Suscipere tam inimicitias seu patris seu propinqui quam amicitias necesse est." *Germania*, ch. 21.

30. *Anglo-Saxon Poetry*, trans. S. A. J. Bradley, 448.

> Ne sorga, snotor guma! Selre bið æghwæm
> þæt he his freond wrece, þonne he fela murne.
> Ure æghwylc sceal ende gebidan
> worolde lifes; wyrce se þe mote
> domes ær deaþe; þæt bið drihtguman
> unlifgendum æfter selest.

Beowulf and the Fight at Finnsburg 1384–9.

31. The Laws of Alfred the Great (849–99) permitted a man to fight without incurring the feud on behalf of his lord (or the lord on behalf of his man) 42.5; on behalf of a kinsman who is being wrongfully attacked, except against his lord 42.6; he may also fight if he finds a man seducing his wife, daughter, sister, or mother 42.7. Liebermann, *Die Gesetze der Angelsachsen*, 1.76–77.

32. Tacitus, *The Agricola and the Germania*, 119. "nec inplacabiles durant; luitur enim etiam homicidium certo armentorum ac pecorum numero recepitque satisfactionem universa domus, utiliter in publicum, quia periculosiores sunt inimicitae iuxta libertatem." *Germania*, ch. 21.

33. Ibid., 111. "distinctio poenarum ex delicto: proditores et transfugas arboribus suspendunt, ignavos et inbelles et corpore infames caeno ac palude, iniecta insuper crate, mergunt, diversitas supplicii illuc respicit, tamquam scelera ostendi oporteat dum puniuntur, flagitia abscondi." *Germania*, ch. 12. It goes without saying that for Tacitus's Germans and their descendants, the Anglo-Saxons, the concept of the state did not exist.

34. Deut. 21:23.

35. It has recently been argued by Bruce O'Brien that the essential meaning of Anglo-Saxon *morðor*, ancestor of modern English "murder," was that of an unatonable slaying. See his "From *Morðor* to *Murdrum*" at 343ff.

36. *Beowulf* 2444ff., translated in *Anglo-Saxon Poetry*, 475–76, describes the agony of a father whose son hangs on the gallows, presented as a comparison to the (accidental) slaying of one brother by another in the preceding passage.

37. *hygemeðe*, *Beowulf* 2442, *Anglo-Saxon Poetry*, 475.

38. *Anglo-Saxon Poetry*, 427.

> ðu þinum broðrum to banan wurde
> heafodmægum; þæs þu in helle scealt
> werhðo dreogan.

Beowulf 587–9

39. *Anglo-Saxon Poetry*, 483.

. . .

> forðam me witan ne ðearf Waldend fira
> morðorbealo maga, þonne min sceaceð
> lif of lice.

Beowulf 2741–3

40. *Anglo-Saxon Poetry*, 485 "But the soul departed from him to seek the glory of those steadfast in truth."

> him of hræðre gewat
> sawol secean soðfæstra dom.

Beowulf 2819–20

41. In "Feud in Medieval England," Paul Hyams argues that there is "a strong *prima facie* case that feud was a genuine and recurrent feature of life at the top of Anglo-Saxon society, in competition for the greatest prize of the

royal crown" (p. 8). For the political realities behind the feuds, which led to the elimination of possible rivals to the throne, see David Dumville, "The ætheling," especially 19–20.

42. It has recently been argued by Craig Davis (1996) that in "Beowulf" the figure of Grendel—a descendant of the first murderer and kin-slayer, Cain—is in fact meant to symbolize this very horror.

43. *The Anglo-Saxon Chronicle*, trans. Dorothy Whitelock et al., 79–80.

44. For discussion of the cult of St. Sigismund, see articles by Paxton.

45. Gregory of Tours, *Glory of the Martyrs*, ch. 74, 96–97.

46. Gregory of Tours, *History of the Franks*, Book 3, ch. 6, 166.

47. In c. 535–36, abbot Venerandus of St. Maurice placed the remains of Sigismund and his family in a church near the Abbey at Agaune, which had been founded by Sigismund. I accept Paxton's opinion (1993, n. 5, p. 96) that this is more likely to represent an honorable burial for the monastery's founder than a translation of relics.

48. Paxton (1994), 29–31.

49. *Passio Sancti Sigismundi Regis*, 337–39. Paxton points out that the use of the plural may reflect the beginnings of association of Sigismund's "companions" with him, as found in later masses (1994, 37).

50. Paxton (1993), 101.

51. Cubitt, *Anglo-Saxon Church Councils*, 110ff.

52. Wallace-Hadrill, *The Long-Haired Kings*, ch. 6, "The Blood-feud of the Franks."

53. See Scheibelreiter, "The Death of the Bishop in the Early Middle Ages," 32–43, for the specific case of bishops.

54. Rosalind Hill points out that for the Venerable Bede, "loyalty was the highest possible expression of a layman's virtue," while treachery was the sole crime condemned by Bede as *detestanda* (1975, 40).

Select Bibliography

Primary Sources

Bradley, S. A. J., trans. *Anglo-Saxon Poetry*. London, Dent: Everyman's Library, 1982.

Gregory the Great, *Dialogues*. Trans. Odo John Zimmerman, O. S. B. Fathers of the Church, no. 39. Washington, D.C.: Catholic University of America Press, 1959.

Gregoire le grand. *Dialogues*. 3 vols. Introduction, bibliographie et cartes par Adalbert de Vogüé. Sources chrétiennes nos. 251, 260, 265. Paris: Éditions du Cerf, 1978.

Gregory of Tours. *Life of the Fathers*. 2nd ed. Trans. Edward James. Translated Texts for Historians, Latin Series 1. Liverpool: Liverpool University Press, 1985.

Gregory of Tours. *Glory of the Martyrs*. Trans. Raymond van Dam. Translated Texts for Historians, Latin Series 3. Liverpool: Liverpool University Press, 1988.

Gregory of Tours. *The History of The Franks*. Trans. Lewis Thorpe. Harmondsworth: Penguin, 1974.

Hadden, A. W. and Stubbs, W., eds. *Councils and Ecclesiastical Documents Relating to Great Britain and Ireland*. 3 vols. Oxford: 1869–71.

Klaeber, Fr., ed. *Beowulf and the Fight at Finnsburg*. 3rd ed. Boston: D. C. Heath and Co., 1950.

Krusch, Bruno, ed. *Passio Sancti Sigismundi Regis* in *Monumenta Germaniae Historica. Scriptorum Rervm Merovingicarvm*, vol. 2. 329–340. Hannover: Hahn, 1888.

Liebermann, Felix. *Die Gesetze der Angelsachsen*. 3 vols. Halle a. S.: M. Niemeyer, 1898–1912.

Rimbert. *Vita Anskarii*. Ed. W. Trillmich. in *Quellen des 9. und 11. Jahrhunderts zur Geschichte der Hamburgischen Kirche und des Reiches*, ed. Werner Trillmich and Rudolf Buchner. Ausgewählte Quellen zur deutschen Geschichte des Mittelalters. Darmstadt: Wissenschaftliche Buchgesellschaft, 1961.

Snorri Sturluson. *Heimskringla: A History of the Kings of Norway*. Trans. Lee M. Hollander. Austin: University of Texas Press for the American Scandinavian Foundation, 1964.

Snorri Sturluson. *Heimskringla*. 3 vols. Ed. Bjarni Aðalbjarnarson. Íslenzk fornrit, 26–28. Reykjavík: Hið íslenzka fornritafélag, 1941–51.

Tacitus. *The Agricola and the Germania*. Trans. H. Mattingly, translation revised by S. A. Handford. Harmondsworth: Penguin, 1970.

———. *Germania* in *Cornelii Taciti Opera Minora*. Ed. M. Winterbottom and R. M. Ogilvie. Oxford: Clarendon Press, 1975.

Whitelock, Dorothy, David C. Douglas and Susie I. Tucker, trans. *The Anglo-Saxon Chronicle*. 2nd ed. London: Eyre and Spottiswoode, 1965.

Secondary Works

Brown, Peter. *The Cult of Saints: Its Rise and Function in Latin Christianity*. Chicago: University of Chicago Press, 1981.

Chaney, William A. *The Cult of Kingship in Anglo-Saxon England: The Transition from Paganism to Christianity*. Manchester: Manchester University Press, 1970.

Cubitt, Catherine. *Anglo-Saxon Church Councils c. 650–850*. London: Leicester University Press, 1995.

Davis, Craig. *Beowulf and the Demise of Germanic Legend in England*. Albert Bates Lord Studies in Oral Tradition 17. New York: Garland, 1996.

DuCange, C. *Glossarium Mediæ et Infimæ Latinitatis*. Rpt. of 1883–87 edition. Graz: Akademische Druck- und Verlagsanstalt, 1954.

Dumville, David. "The ætheling: A Study in Anglo-Saxon Constitutional History." *Anglo-Saxon England* 8 (1979): 1–33.

Fell, Christine E. "Edward King and Martyr and the Anglo-Saxon Hagiographic Tradition." In *Ethelred the Unready: Papers from the Millenary Conference,* ed. David Hill, 1–13. BAR British Series no. 59. Oxford: British Archaeological Reports, 1978.

Folz, Robert. *Les Saints Rois du Moyen Age en Occident (Vie–XIIe siècles).* Subsidia Hagiographica no. 68. Bruxelles: Société des Bollandistes, 1984.

———. "Zur Frage der heiligen Könige: Heiligkeit und Nachleben in der Geschichte des burgundischen Königtums." *Deutsches Archiv für Erforschung des Mittelalters* 14, no. 2 (1958): 317–344.

Fouracre, Paul. "Merovingian History and Merovingian Hagiography." *Past and Present* 127 (May 1990): 3–38.

Frank, Roberta. "The Ideal of Men Dying with their Lord in the *Battle of Maldon*: Anachronism or *Nouvelle Vague*." In *People and Places in Northern Europe,* ed. Ian Wood and Niels Lund, 95–106. Woodbridge and Rochester, N.Y.: Boydell Press, 1991.

Gorski, Karol. "Le roi-saint: Un problème d'idéologie féodale." *Annales: Économies, Sociétés, Civilisations* 24 (1969): 370–76.

Graus, František. "La sanctification du souverain dans l'Europe centrale des Xe et XIe siècles." In *Hagiographie Cultures et Sociétés IVe–XIIe siècles.* Actes du Colloque organisé à Nanterre et à Paris (2–5 mai 1979). Centre de Recherches sur l'Antiquité et le haut Moyen Age Université de Paris X. 559–572. Paris: Études augustiniennes, 1981.

Hill, Rosalind. "Holy Kings—the Bane of Seventh-century Society." In *Church, Society and Politics,* ed. Derek Baker, 39–43. Studies in Church History no. 12. Oxford: Basil Blackwell, 1975.

Hoffmann, Erich. *Die heiligen Könige bei den Angelsachsen und den skandinavischen Völkern.* Neumünster: K. Wachholtz, 1975.

Hyams, Paul. "Feud in Medieval England." *Haskins Society Journal* 3 (1991): 1–21.

John, Eric. *Orbis Britanniae and Other Studies.* Leicester: Leicester University Press, 1966.

Kienast, Walther. "Germanische Treue und 'Königsheil'." *Historische Zeitschrift* 227, no. 2 (Oct. 1978): 265–324.

Lapidge, Michael, ed. "The *Life of St. Oswald.*" In *The Battle of Maldon AD 991,* ed. Donald Scragg. Oxford: Basil Blackwell in association with the Manchester Centre for Anglo-Saxon Studies, 1991.

Liebermann, Felix. *Die Heiligen Englands.* Hannover: Hahn, 1889.

Malone, Edward. *The Monk and the Martyr: The Monk as Successor of the Martyr.* Catholic University of America Studies in Classical Antiquity 12. Washington: 1950.

McTurk, R. W. "Sacral Kingship in Ancient Scandinavia: A Review of Some Recent Writings." *Saga-Book of the Viking Society* 19, parts 2–3 (1975–76): 139–69.

Nelson, Janet. "Royal Saints and Early Medieval Kingship." In *Sanctity and Secularity: The Church and the World,* ed. Derek Baker, 39–44. Studies in

Church History no. 10. Oxford: Basil Blackwell, 1973. Rpt. in Nelson, Janet. *Politics and Ritual in Early Medieval Europe*, 69–74. London and Ronceverte, W.Va.: Hambledon Press, 1986.

O'Brien, Bruce. "From *Morðor* to *Murdrum*: The Preconquest Origin and Norman Revival of the Murder Fine." *Speculum* 71 (April 1996): 321–57.

Paxton, Frederick. "Power and the Power to Heal: The Cult of St. Sigismund of Burgundy." *Early Medieval Europe* 2 (1993): 95–110.

———. "Liturgy and Healing in an Early Medieval Saint's Cult: the Mass *in honore sancti sigismundi* for the Cure of Fevers." *Traditio* 49 (1994): 23–43.

Ridyard, Susan. *The Royal Saints of Anglo-Saxon England. A Study of West Saxon and East Anglian Cults*. Cambridge Studies in Medieval Life and Thought 4th Series no. 9. Cambridge: Cambridge University Press, 1988.

Riley-Smith, Jonathan. "Death on the First Crusade." In *The End of Strife*, ed. David Loades, 14–31. Edinburgh: T. and T. Clark, 1984.

Rollason, David. "Lists of Saints' Resting-places in Anglo-Saxon England." *Anglo-Saxon England* 7 (1978): 61–95.

———. *The Search for St. Wigstan*. Vaughan Paper no. 27. Leicester: University of Leicester, Dept. of Adult Education, 1981.

———. *The Mildrith Legend: A Study in Early Medieval Hagiography in England*. Leicester: Leicester University Press, 1982.

———. "The Cults of Murdered Royal Saints in Anglo-Saxon England." *Anglo-Saxon England* 11 (1983): 1–22.

Scheibelreiter, Georg. "The Death of the Bishop in the Early Middle Ages." In *The End of Strife*, ed. David Loades, 32–43. Edinburgh: T. and T. Clark, 1984.

Thacker, Alan. "Kings, Saints, and Monasteries in Pre-Viking Mercia." *Midland History* 10 (1985): 1–25.

Wallace-Hadrill, J. M. *The Long-Haired Kings*. [London: Methuen, c. 1962] Medieval Academy Reprints for Teaching 11. Toronto: University of Toronto Press in association with the Medieval Academy of America, 1982.

———. *The Frankish Church*. Oxford History of the Christian Church. Oxford: Clarendon Press, 1983.

Wolpers, Theodor. *Die englische Heiligenlegenden des Mittelalters*. Tübingen: M. Niemeyer, 1964.

Wormald, Patrick. "Celtic and Anglo-Saxon Kingship: Some Further Thoughts." In *Sources of Anglo-Saxon Culture*, ed. Paul Szarmach, 151–83. Studies in Medieval Culture 20. Kalamazoo: Medieval Institute Publications, 1986.

FIVE

THE REVALUATION OF MARTYRDOM
IN EARLY ISLAM

Keith Lewinstein

Small philological observations can sometimes introduce us to larger historical problems. No one familiar with Christian martyrdom will be surprised to learn that the Arabic words which Muslims use for "martyr" and "witness" are identical. The terminology is unmistakably Christian. By the fourth century, the Greek *martys* (witness) had acquired a technical sense and had come to denote one whose suffering and death bore witness to the truth of Jesus' passion and resurrection. Witnessing, suffering, death, and heavenly reward have since been intimately connected in Christian life and thought.

Given the parallel terminology, one might expect to find a similar understanding of martyrdom in Islam. At the level of reward, Muslim martyrs are not far from their Christian counterparts. Both are promised remission of sin and immediate life in Paradise; the souls of both reside at the highest level of Paradise, near the Throne of God; both are given the privilege of interceding with God on behalf of their coreligionists. Overall, the benefits accorded Muslim martyrs closely resemble those in Syriac Christianity.[1]

Whatever the similarities, there is one major difference in conception between Muslim and Christian martyrdom: for Muslims, one earns the title of martyr (*shahīd*; pl. *shuhadā'*) without any apparent act of witnessing. The martyr's sacrifice does not generally attest to anything specific, nor does it symbolize much beyond the obvious sense of death in the service of God's plan.[2] The Qur'an, our earliest Muslim testimony, does not know the term *shahīd* in its technical sense, although the later exegetical tradition has sought to read "martyr" into a few passages where the word appears.[3] Generally, Muslim scripture conveys the notion of martyrdom not through the root sh-h-d, but with circumlocutions such as "those slain in the path of God" (e.g., Q.2:154, 3:169, and elsewhere). *Shahīd* itself likely acquired its classical sense of "martyr" not because of any intrinsic connection in Muslim minds between witnessing and self-sacrifice, but as a reflex of late antique Christian usage (Greek *martys* = Syriac *sāhdā* = Arabic *shahīd*).[4]

This awkward fit between witnessing and martyrdom is further suggested by the strained attempts of some Muslim authorities to make sense of the word. We are told in one tradition, for example, that the martyr is called "witness" because his soul is alive and able to behold directly the Abode of Peace, while the souls of others see Paradise only on the Day of Resurrection. Elsewhere, we learn that the martyr is a "witness" because his death is "witnessed" by the angels; or because God and the angels bear witness to his place in Paradise; or because he undertook to testify to the truth until his death; or because he will serve as a witness against the ancient communities who rejected God's prophets; or because (echoing Qur'an 2:143) the Prophet will be a witness on the Day of Judgement for those of his followers slain in the way of God.[5] With respect to their burial, there are suggestions that one reason for not washing the bodies of martyrs is so that their wounds might continue to testify to their status in the afterlife.[6] In short, the Muslim tradition had to invent for itself a connection between witnessing and martyrdom, since none was immediately apparent.

All this is more than an isolated philological problem. It points up the distinctive attitude toward sacrifice and struggle among Muslims, an attitude forged by a political experience quite different from that of the early Christians. Martyrdom achieved its religious significance for Christians in the period before the faith had enjoyed any political success. Asserting an ultimate, heavenly victory was at least in part a way for Christians to face down political failure, represented in the first instance by the career of Jesus himself. Islam, by contrast, had more success from the beginning; it emerged not as a persecuted sect, but in the course of military conquest and political victory. While there had been persecutions in Mecca during Muhammad's early career, and no shortage of martyrs created in the battles against the Meccan Quraysh and the conquests of the Near East, early Muslim martyrs, such as Sumayya and Ḥamza, did not enjoy any special cultic visibility in the later tradition.[7] The religious value of suffering and death was never the obvious lesson to draw from the career of the Prophet or from the experience of the early Muslim community. What struck Muslims more naturally was the Prophet's call for active struggle against injustice and idolatry. Even the dramatic accounts of Ḥusayn's martyrdom at Karbala', an event that would become central to Shī'ite sectarian identity, tend to emphasize righteous struggle against worldly injustice more than patient endurance of suffering and death.

Where the early Christians mourned, the Muslims strove. As one historian put it almost forty years ago, Muslims sought not so much consolation as guidance from their faith.[8] The ideal was less to die for the faith than to struggle actively for it, and to enjoy the fruits of victory here on earth. However ambiguous its use of the term "witness," the Qur'an is absolutely clear on the Muslim's duty to struggle in the service of God, and on the rewards enjoyed by those slain in the course of that struggle (jihād): "And those slain in the way of God, He will not send their works astray. He will guide them, and dispose their minds aright, and He will admit them to Paradise, that He has made known to them" (Q.47:4–6). While the element of active struggle (or at least endurance) is certainly not absent on the Christian side,[9] it is the martyr's death rather than his fighting that carries ultimate religious significance. The opposite is true for Muslims.[10]

The Muslim ideal of active struggle was just that: an ideal, and one tempered for many by a pragmatic quietism which evolved throughout the ninth and tenth centuries. The end of the conquests, the disbanding of the Arab tribal armies, the rise of post-conquest urban societies, and the establishment of stable political authority all contributed to a decline in the attractiveness of battlefield martyrdom. Dissenters could still look to the early activist ideal, but mainstream communities (both Sunni and sectarian) would necessarily develop a quietist orientation. It is this emergence of a quietist outlook that would shape the understanding of martyrdom by most Muslims.

The earliest Muslims knew who was destined for Heaven. Members of the community were by definition ahl al-janna, people of Paradise; all others were ahl al-nār, people of the Fire. While individual piety was not irrelevant, for most Muslims it was membership rather than piety that marked one out for Paradise.[11] Those who fought "in the way of God" had a special status beyond the promise of Paradise: they are "mightier in rank with God" (Q.9:20); their sins will be forgiven (Q.61:12); whether slain or victorious they will receive a vast reward (Q.4:74). The Qur'an generally offers such rewards to all warriors, not simply to martyrs. The one reward unambiguously associated with martyrdom is immediate life in Paradise: "Do not say of those slain in God's way that they are dead; they are living, only you do not perceive" (Q.2:154; cf. 3:169). Beyond this, the Qur'an is not terribly concerned with battlefield martyrs as a group apart from other Muslims.

It is in the *ḥadīth* material that martyrs are clearly distinguished from ordinary Muslims. They not only enter Paradise immediately, skipping both the punishment of the tomb and the final judgement,[12] but they also ascend to the highest level, their souls alive and inhabiting the white (or green) birds in the lanterns hanging just beneath the Throne of God.[13] They occupy, according to one report, a special place in Paradise reserved otherwise for prophets, righteous men, just Imāms, and those who choose death over unbelief by refusing to renounce their faith under torture.[14] In another *ḥadīth*, the Prophet is made to reassure a grieving mother that her son is in the highest garden, the *jannat al-firdaws*.[15] Martyrs are also spared the pain of death, which to them is comparable to the pinch of a gnat.[16] God is even said to have spoken face-to-face with one of the martyrs of Uḥud, the Prophet's first major military defeat.[17] The Prophet in one report offers a useful list of the nine benefits enjoyed by the martyr. These include remission of sin at the moment his blood his shed; the privilege of immediately beholding his place in Paradise (i.e., there is no waiting until the Day of Judgement); avoidance of the punishment of the tomb; marriage to seventy houris; protection from the Great Terror; the wearing of the Crown of Dignity, each of whose jewels is better than the world and all it contains; and the right to intercede with God for seventy of his relatives.[18] All this is doubtless why martyrs are so pleased with their situation that they want nothing more than to return to earth to be martyred a second time.[19]

The afterlife benefits accorded martyrs are thus straightforward. Less so is the issue of just who qualifies for them. Not all casualties of war will receive a martyr's reward from God: most jurists require first of all that the war be fought against unbelievers (although for some, rebel Muslims suffice),[20] and second, that the warrior himself be properly motivated. Intention is central to the performance of all acts of piety in Islam; prayer or pilgrimage done without proper intention may be sufficient to qualify one as a Muslim in the social sense (they entitle one to marry and inherit from other Muslims and to be buried in a Muslim cemetery), but they do not fulfill the ritual requirement in God's eyes and will not earn one afterlife benefits. Martyrdom in *jihād* works precisely the same way. As several *ḥadīth* remind us, those who fight hypocritically, or chiefly in search of earthly reward, or out of zeal for fighting itself, or simply to display their bravery, are not in the final scheme of things martyrs. Only those who fight "desiring the face of God," or seeking to make the Word of God supreme, are martyrs in any ultimate sense.[21] And yet even the hypocritical warrior, should he die at the hands of the enemy, is to be buried as a martyr (i.e., his corpse remains unwashed, wrapped in its blood-stained clothing, and, according to some jurists, is not prayed over).[22] As we ourselves lack access to the intention and sincerity of others, we are to treat all battlefield deaths as martyrdom.

If death in battle is the only way to gain a martyr's funeral, the heavenly rewards themselves are more widely distributed. The *ḥadīth* and jurisprudential literatures stretch the category of *shahīd* to encompass far more than battlefield martyrdom. According to one frequently cited report, the Prophet granted the title of *shahīd* to victims of drowning, pleurisy, and plague, as well as to the innocent victims of accidental building collapse.[23] We also read of other ways to acquire direct access to Paradise: death in defense of one's property; death in childbirth; death by accident while engaged in *jihād*. Drowning is often mentioned, as is falling off the top of a mountain or being eaten by lions.[24]

In some of these cases, particularly those involving violent, sudden, or exceptionally painful death, the special rewards accorded the victims might reflect the continuing survival of ancient folk beliefs and their power to shape the lettered tradition. These forms of death had long been felt to deserve recompense; now, God shows Muslims His special favor by considering such deaths atonement for sin and thus as entitling these people to special treatment in the afterlife.[25] The inclusion of plague in the Prophet's list of martyrdoms is perhaps in part theologically inspired: God has sent plague as a mercy and martyrdom to the believers; those who die while remaining steadfast in their belief in God's decree are classed with the battlefield martyrs. In at least one report, the plague victim's boils are directly equated with the fallen warrior's wounds.[26]

We might understand all this as an attempt to make martyrdom available to more and more people in the post-conquest world. The Prophet himself would apparently agree: in reply to a companion's claim that only those killed in war are properly considered martyrs, the Prophet is reported to have said "in that case the martyrs of my community would be few," before going on to enumerate the other types of death that likewise earn one martyr status.[27] What this represents is an expansion of the category of "martyr" without any fundamental change in its nature. It is still through death that one earns a martyr's reward, even if battling unbelievers is no longer a central feature of the process.[28] But the religious scholars also go further and positively equate particular religious activities with martyrdom. Such a tendency is clear, for example, in the assurance that the soul of the pilgrim who dies on *hajj* goes immediately to Paradise. The great scholar Shāfiʿī (d. 820) tells the story of the bedouin pilgrim kicked to death by his camel: the Prophet orders that he be buried as a battlefield martyr, as he died "while occupied with worship, and the traces of that worship should be left on him just as with the [wounds of] the warrior who is martyred [in battle]."[29] Worship itself becomes a form of martyrdom, and the identity of ritual obligations and warfare "in the way of God" is elsewhere made absolutely explicit: "He who fasts and uses God's verses in performing the ritual prayer obediently, until the warriors have returned, is equal to the zealous in God's way," as one *hadīth* has it.[30]

It is thus not merely death while fulfilling religious duties that earns one martyrdom; the very fulfillment of such duties might in some circumstances bring one to that level. Interpreting one of his companion's dreams, the Prophet explains why the believer who died in bed after two colleagues had died on *jihād* was in fact given priority at the gates of Paradise: "No one is more virtuous in God's eyes than the believer who lives long in Islam, and is able to go on praising and glorifying God, and making the profession of faith."[31] A similar logic lies behind those Traditions in which, for example, the Qurʾan reciter is promised a martyr's reward, or the prayer caller is said to receive the reward of 40,000 martyrs.[32] More than simply an expansion of the category, this amounts to a change in the very conception of martyrdom.

In their revaluation of martyrdom, the legal scholars were driven chiefly by a quietist impulse. While there was often no love lost between the scholars and the rulers of the day, the former were no rebels. Despite the activist model of the Prophet, the scholars were as a whole distinctly uncomfortable with sedition and political upheaval, lest the moral life of the community be endangered. As the collective bearers of religious authority in the Muslim world, they were generally willing to tolerate far from ideal political arrangements, as long as these arrangements did not jeopardize the private, scholarly elaboration of religious law. Even dissenting movements, at least those which managed to survive beyond the first three centuries of Islam, came eventually to reconcile activist ideals with quietist necessity.[33] It was generally the idealistic dissenters, those who insisted on actively resisting the ruler's armies at the cost of their lives, that Sunnī and sectarian religious scholars had in mind when seeking to demilitarize martyrdom. Battlefield martyrdom was a powerful tool for cementing loyalty within dissenting groups. Perhaps the single most important martyrdom in this sense was that of Ḥusayn ibn 'Alī, whose death at Karbalā' in 680 helped create a deep emotional loyalty to the 'Alid house, and to this day has helped Shī'ites sustain what is the chief sectarian divide within Islam. Other dissenters also made much of their martyrs. Those rebels known as Khārijites ("seceders") also called themselves Shurāt ("vendors"); that is, those who sell their lives in exchange for Paradise, with apparent reference to Qur'an 4:74 and 9:112.[34] It is easy to see a notion of martyrdom behind this designation.

It is in Khārijite circles that we see most clearly the cluster of practices against which the religious scholars would aim their fire: activism, asceticism, and the deliberate seeking of martyrdom in battle. The first is represented by the Khārijite practice of *hijra*, exodus from the society of unbelievers to one of the group's own camps. It was, in the first Islamic century, through *hijra* to the garrison towns that one generally acquired a place in Muslim society; Khārijite encampments would similarly serve as *hijra* sites, from which active resistance to state power could be launched. For Khārijites, as for other Muslims, it was through *hijra* that one became a member of the community, that one joined the People of Paradise. *Hijra* and *jihād* are closely linked in the Qur'an, in Khārijite teaching, and in anti-Khārijite polemic. It is the Khārijites, in fact, who are most commonly associated in our sources with *ṭalab al-shahāda*, the deliberate seeking of martyrdom on the battlefield.[35]

The connection between *hijra* and *jihād* was only deepened by the prevailing ascetic culture of the camps. The early Khārijites are described as pious ascetics both by their opponents and by authors of a moderate Khārijite (Ibāḍī) persuasion; in an Ibāḍī work of the twelfth century, for example, a group of early Khārijite martyrs are said to have had "foreheads and knees as thick as camels from the intensity of their devotions."[36] Some Khārijites in the seventh and eighth centuries were called "Yellows" (Ṣufriyya), a comment not on the depth of their bravery but on their ascetic piety: the color yellow is sometimes associated with renunciatory practices in early Islam. The late seventh-century Ṣufrite rebel and martyr in Mesopotamia, Ṣāliḥ ibn Musarriḥ, is said to have gone yellow in the face as a consequence of his extreme devotion.[37]

The practice of asceticism is relevant here not only because it helped cement the collective identity of these groups but also because of its connection to *hijra*, *jihād*, and the deliberate seeking of martyrdom. Najda ibn 'Āmir, a Khārijite leader of the time, is reported to have promoted among his followers the desire for martyrdom and Paradise, as well as ascetic renunciation of the world.[38] Likewise, in a speech to his followers given just before launching an attack, the Ṣufrite Ṣāliḥ ibn Musarriḥ plays on the relationship between ascetic renunciation, death in battle, and the martyr's reward in Paradise:

> I commend to you fear of God, austerity in this world, desire for the afterlife, [and] frequent pondering of death. . . . Austerity in this world makes one desire what is with God and frees one's body for acts of obedience to God; frequent recollection of death makes one fear God and cry out for Him and humbly submit to Him. . . . Prepare, then, to strive against the . . . unjust leaders of error, and to go out (*khurūj*) from the Abode of Transience to the Abode of Eternity and join our believing, convinced brothers who have sold (*bā'ū*) this world for the next, and spent their wealth in quest of God's good pleasure in the final reckoning. Do not fear being killed for the sake of God, for being killed is easier than dying naturally. Natural death comes upon you when you least expect it, separating you from your fathers and your sons, from your wives and from this world. If your anxiety and aversion to this is too strong, then, indeed, sell your souls to God obediently, and your wealth, and you'll enter Paradise in security and embrace the black-eyed houris.[39]

The relationship between the ascetic piety of the Khārijites and their willingness to die as martyrs is clear here. Ṣāliḥ not only recommends asceticism in this world but also asserts that it is precisely such asceticism that cultivates in his followers a desire for martyrdom. His use of the term *khurūj*, going out (here, from the abode of transience to the abode of eternity, but often simply in rebellion or as an act of *hijra*), echoes the very name of his group and nicely underscores the centrality of *hijra*, asceticism, and martyrdom to Khārijite identity. Something similar can be made of the verb "to sell," used in two places here. That the Khārijites self-identified as "Vendors" on the basis of Qur'an 4:74 has already been mentioned, and Ṣāliḥ's use of the verb "to sell" (in the sense of selling this world for the next) has the effect of placing martyrdom front and center in his followers' minds.[40]

That asceticism, battle, and martyrdom are connected should be of no surprise; they went hand-in-hand in the Near East long before the Islamic period, and the connection is well attested outside of Khārijite circles in early Islamic times.[41] Moreover, in a Muslim context Ṣāliḥ had a real point. The model of Muhammad's career undeniably did call for action against injustice, and the tribal milieux in which both Ṣāliḥ and (earlier) the Prophet himself operated glorified death in battle.[42] Ṣāliḥ and those like him could not easily be dismissed by the religious scholars. This is why the *ḥadīth* collections contain a number of reports which both implicitly and explicitly praise the longing for death and martyrdom. The Prophet, for example, is made to say that he wishes he could have been present at every raid, and killed each time.[43] The Caliph 'Umar expresses at once a desire to be martyred in battle and also to die in Medina, the city of the Prophet, located in his day far from the scene of any fighting.[44] In one report, God is said to bestow martyrdom on all who seek it. The term used here for seeking martyrdom is *ṭalab al-shahāda*, precisely the phrase employed in polemic against the extreme Khārijites, who sold their lives in war against the political authorities. In this *ḥadīth*, it has an entirely positive sense.[45]

Such reports are, however, exceptional and do not reflect the general flavor of the classical material. Far more commonly, the tradition seeks to broaden the definition of martyrdom in order to make it politically safe and its rewards available to the growing number of settled Muslims with no interest in dying on the battlefield. We have seen some examples of this type of material above. One more should be adduced here, though, as it bears directly on the praise of *ṭalab al-shahāda* referred to at the end of the previous paragraph. The scholars know of a report which they normally treat as simply a variant on the one praising *ṭalab al-shahāda*: "One who *prays for* martyrdom sincerely: God will place him among the ranks of the martyrs even if he dies in his bed."[46] It is possible that this final clause emerged to reassure war veterans who missed their chance to earn Paradise on the battlefield. But the change in language from "seeking martyrdom" to "praying for martyrdom," when set against the more general tendency of the tradition to emphasize nonbattlefield *shahāda*, may well suggest something else. By displacing the phrase commonly associated with militant Khārijite dissent, the scholars may well have sought a means to praise martyrdom itself without jeopardizing social peace.[47]

The Muslim understanding of martyrdom was not static in the early period. It evolved along with Muslim society itself and was significantly shaped by the tension between the activist model of the Prophet and the later pragmatic quietism of the scholars. As a rule, the *ḥadīth* expresses the values of the religious scholars, even if in form it preserves the words of the Prophet. Here, the Prophet appears as the chief spokesman for a view of martyrdom consistent with the quietist outlook of classical Islam and of the scholars who made it. This is brought home strongly in those *ḥadīth* where the Prophet ranks the scholars higher than the martyrs and declares that on the Day of Judgment, the ink of the scholars will weigh more heavily with God than the blood of the martyrs.[48] We can only hope so.

Notes

1. For many of these parallels, see A. J. Wensinck, *The Oriental Doctrine of the Martyrs* (Amsterdam, 1921), 10–13. This work, along with a few rich pages from the second volume of I. Goldziher's *Muslim Studies* (London, 1971), are fundamental to any discussion of Muslim martyrdom. See now E. Kohlberg, "Medieval Muslim Views on Martyrdom," Koninklijke Nederlandse Akademie van Wetenschappen, Afd. Letterkunde, 60 (1997), 281–307; and *Encyclopaedia of Islam*, 2nd ed. (Leiden, continuing), s.v. Shahid (Kohlberg). Each appeared too late to be considered in this chapter.

2. Cf. A. Noth, *Heiliger Krieg und Heiliger Kampf in Islam und Christentum* (Bonn, 1966), 27f.

3. See, for example, Ṭabarī, *Jāmiʿ al-bayān* (Beirut, 1408/1988), iii, 106 *ad* Q. 3:140 ("So that God may know who are the believers, and may take witnesses [*shuhadā'*] from among you"), and v, 162f. *ad* Q. 4:69 ("Whoever obeys God and the Messenger—they are with those whom God has blessed, prophets, just men, *shuhadā'*, the righteous; Good companions they!"). And cf. the comments of the modernist translator and exegete Yusuf ʿAli, who writes *ad* Q. 4:69 that the *shuhadā'* are "the noble army of Witnesses who testify to the truth. The testimony may be by martyrdom" (*The Holy Qur'an* [Washington, D.C., 1946]).

4. Goldziher, *Muslim Studies*, ii, 350f.

5. Nawawī, *Ṣaḥīḥ Muslim bi-sharḥ al-Nawawī* (18 vols., Beirut, n.d.), iii, 24; Qasṭallānī, *Irshād al-sārī li-sharḥ ṣaḥīḥ al-Bukhārī* (15 vols., Beirut, 1990), ii, 334; ʿAbd al-Razzāq, *Muṣannaf* (11 vols., Beirut, 1972), nos. 6633f.

6. Sarakhsī, *Mabsūṭ* (30 vols., Beirut, 1409/1989), ii, 53f., concerning the martyr status of village women killed in raids. Cf. also Wensinck, *Oriental Doctrine*, 25, where the custom of burying martyrs unwashed and in their bloody clothes is traced to folk beliefs about the vulnerability of the dead to demonic attack. Note also that in Shīʿite tradition, the martyr Ḥusayn remains acephalous at the Day of Judgment, with the physical traces of his martyrdom serving as a terrifying reminder to those who murdered him and his family (M. Ayoub, "Martyrdom in Christianity and Islam," in R. Antoun and M. Hegland [eds.], *Religious Resurgence: Contemporary Cases in Islam, Christianity, and Judaism* [Syracuse, N.Y., 1987], 73).

7. But before being himself martyred at Karbalā', Ḥusayn (whose martyrdom, exceptionally, does reverberate throughout the tradition, particularly among Shīʿites) invokes Ḥamza, "Lord of the Martyrs" (Ṭabarī, *Ta'rīkh al-rusul wa-'l-mulūk*, ed. M. J. de Goeje, 15 vols. [Leiden, 1879–1901], ii, 329).

Generally, those killed at Badr and Uḥud survive mainly as legal proof-texts in arguments about burial practices; see, e.g., 'Abd al-Razzāq, *Muṣannaf*, nos. 6633, 6635, 6637, 6643–46, 6653. The martyr status even of the early Caliphs who died violently ('Umar, 'Uthmān, and 'Alī) is for Sunnīs more a matter of law than anything else; cf. Sarakhsī, *Mabsūṭ*, ii, 51. For Shī'ites under the spell of Ḥusayn's martyrdom, 'Alī's own violent death may have acquired more martyrological resonance, and this may have contributed to the popularity of his nickname Abū Turāb ("soil covered" or "dusty"); see E. Kohlberg, "Abū Turāb," *Bulletin of the School of Oriental and African Studies*, 41 (1978), 351f.

8. M. Hodgson, "A comparison of Islam and Christianity as a framework for religious life," *Diogenes*, 32 (1960), 53, 58. The article as a whole is to be recommended as an insightful comparative treatment of the two faiths.

9. For Syriac conceptions of the martyr-saint as an athlete anointing himself for battle in the arena, see Wensinck, *Oriental Doctrine*, 18ff.

10. For the Qur'anic emphasis on struggle rather than death, see Noth, *Heiliger Krieg*, 25.

11. J. van Ess, *Theologie und Gesellschaft im 2. und 3. Jahrhundert Hidschra* (Berlin, 1991), i, 20f.

12. They share this honor, according to one report, with those who die in early infancy (*mawlūd*) and the victims of female infanticide (*wa'īd*); Abū Dāwūd, *Sunan* (4 vols., Beirut, n.d.), 15:25. On the martyr's escape from the punishment of the tomb, see Nasā'i, *Ṣaḥīḥ sunan al-Nasā'ī* (3 vols., Riyad, 1408/1988), 21:112. The bodies of martyrs are also spared decomposition in the tomb; see J. Smith and Y. Haddad, *The Islamic Understanding of Death and Resurrection* (Albany, N.Y., 1981), 32.

13. 'Abd al-Razzāq, *Muṣannaf*, nos. 9553ff.

14. 'Abd al-Razzāq, *Muṣannaf*, no. 9560. Sumayya, sometimes called "the first martyr in Islam," may be the model for this last category. She is said to have died at the hands of the Meccan idolaters after refusing to renounce the faith.

15. Bukhārī, *Ṣaḥīḥ*, 64:9.

16. Aḥmad ibn Ḥanbal, *Musnad* (6 vols., Beirut, n.d.), iii, 297.

17. Tirmidhī, *al-Jāmi' al-Ṣaḥīḥ* (5 vols., Beirut, 1987), tafsīr, sūra 3, 18 (no. 3010).

18. 'Abd al-Razzāq, *Muṣannaf*, no. 9559; an abbreviated version of the list at Aḥmad ibn Ḥanbal, *Musnad*, iv, 200.

19. Muslim, *Ṣaḥīḥ*, 33:59.

20. J. Kraemer, "Apostates, rebels, and brigands," *Israel Oriental Studies*, 10 (1980), 58.

21. 'Abd al-Razzāq, *Muṣannaf*, nos. 9563, 9573 (a hypocrite at Khaybar is said by the Prophet to be in Hell); Aḥmad ibn Ḥanbal, *Musnad*, i, 416; Muslim, *Ṣaḥīḥ*, 33:86.

22. See the discussions in Sarakhsī, *Mabsūṭ*, ii, 49ff.; and Ibn Qudāma, *al-Mughnī* (10 vols., Beirut, 1405/1985), i, 398; and the *ḥadīth* at 'Abd al-Razzāq, *Muṣannaf*, nos. 6633, 6635, 6637, 6643–46, 5549, 6653, and 9580–9606.

23. Mālik, *Muwaṭṭa'* (Beirut, n.d.), no. 290; Bukhārī, *Ṣaḥīḥ*, 10:32, where a fifth category, that of battlefield martyr, is added to the list. Bukhārī's commentator notes that only the final type is the true martyrdom; the previous four are metaphorically called *shahīds*, as they receive the rewards of the true martyr (Qasṭallānī, *Irshād*, ii, 334).

24. 'Abd al-Razzāq, *Muṣannaf*, nos. 18562, 18565–71, 9572, 9574; Aḥmad ibn Ḥanbal, *Musnad*, i, 78f.; Ibn Qudāma, *Mughnī*, i, 399; Abū Dāwūd, *Sunan*, 15:14.

25. See Wensinck, *Oriental Doctrine*, 27.

26. For plague as martyrdom, see, e.g., Bukhārī, *Ṣaḥīḥ*, 60:54: Plague is a mercy to the believers, and one who remains patiently in an infested area, knowing that nothing happens except by God's decree, will have a martyr's reward, even if he ultimately dies by something other than the epidemic. This last clause is explained by Bukhārī's commentator: There are many sorts of martyrs; in this case, the victim is like one who leaves home intending to participate in the *jihād*, but dies for an unrelated reason. God judges him on the basis of his intention (Qasṭallānī, *Irshād*, vii, 488). On the theological and medical issues surrounding the plague victim as martyr, see M. Dols, *The Black Plague in the Middle East* (Princeton, 1977), 109–15.

27. Muslim, *Ṣaḥīḥ*, 33:97.

28. Nawawī (*Ṣaḥīḥ Muslim*, xiii, 63) distinguishes three types of martyr: the *shahīd* both with respect to this world and the afterlife (i.e., the sincere warrior killed in the *jihad*, who should be buried as a martyr and who will be recognized as such by God); the *shahīd* only with respect to the afterlife (i.e., victims of plague, drowning, and so forth, who will receive a martyr's reward but are not to be buried as such); and the *shahīd* only with respect to this world (i.e., the warrior who receives a martyr's burial, but not a martyr's reward in Paradise, as he has violated basic rules of *jihād*). Note also the wide-ranging discussion of different categories of martyrdom in Tihānawī, *Kashshāf iṣṭilāḥāt al-funūn* (2 vols., Hyderabad, 1862), i, 740.

29. Cited in Sarakhsī, *Mabsūṭ*, ii, 52.

30. Muslim, *Ṣaḥīḥ*, 33:110. Note also the report cited by Wensinck in which those who performed *ṣalāt*, gave alms, and suffered for a good cause are also free from the Final Reckoning (*Oriental Doctrine*, 8).

31. Aḥmad ibn Ḥanbal, *Musnad*, i, 163; cf. the similar point made at Abū Dāwūd, *Sunan*, 15:27 (no. 2524). But see the contrary Traditions, in which participation in *jihād* is ranked above other religious obligations, adduced by Noth, *Heiliger Krieg*, 51f., and at note 187. Note also that the formal practices of praising and glorifying God (*tasbīḥ* and *takbīr*), and professing the faith (*tahlīl*), are recommended to warriors themselves in the *ḥadīth* literature (ibid., 55, note 209).

32. Aḥmad ibn Ḥnbal, *Musnad*, iv, 437, cited in Goldziher, *Muslim Studies*, ii, 352f.; the prayer caller Tradition is cited by E. Kohlberg, "The development of the Imāmī Shī'ī doctrine of *jihād*," in id., *Belief and Law in Imāmī Shī'ism* (Brookfield, Vt.: 1991), xv, 67.

33. See, for example, B. Lewis, "On the quietist and activist traditions in Islamic political writing," *Bulletin of the School of Oriental and African Studies*, 10 (1986), 141–47. On the growth of Shī'ite quietism, in particular, see M. Hodgson, "How did the early Shī'a become sectarian?" *Journal of the American Oriental Society*, 75 (1955), 1–13.

34. The term "Khārijite" may well have originated as an echo of Qur'an 4:99, which speaks of those who leave their homes "emigrating to God." On emigration (*hijra*) see the following discussion. For martyrdom as central to Khārijite self-definition, and the use of the term "Shurāt" in Khārijite poetry, see K. Pampus, *Über die rolle der Hariǧīya im frühen Islam* (Bonn, 1980), 28f.

35. On Khārijite *hijra*, and its connection to *jihād*, see van Ess, *Theologie und Gesellschaft*, i, 8; and P. Crone, "The first-century concept of *hiǧra*," *Arabica*, 12 (1994), 380f.

36. Qalhātī, *al-Kashf wa-'l-Bayān* (Ar. ms., Br. Mus. Or., 2606), fol. 106a. For similar comments by Sunnī authors, see, e.g., Ibn al-Jawzī, *Talbīs Iblīs* (Cairo, 1368), 91; and Malaṭī, *al-Tanbīh wa-'l-Radd 'alā Ahl al-Ahwā' wa-'l-Bida'* (Istanbul, 1936), 41.

37. On Ṣāliḥ's ascetic piety, and for the interpretation of Ṣufriyya as "Yellows," see K. Lewinstein, "Making and unmaking a sect: the heresiographers and the Ṣufriyya," *Studia Islamica*, 76 (1992), especially 93–96. Note also the *ḥadīth* in which anyone wounded "in the way of God" will have the mark of the martyrs on him at the Day of Judgment and will appear the color of saffron; Aḥmad ibn Ḥanbal, *Musnad*, v, 244.

38. Balādhurī, *Ansāb al-Ashrāf*, xi (*Anonyme arabische Chronik*), ed. W. Ahlwardt (Greifswald, 1883), 133.

39. Ṭabarī, *Ta'rīkh*, ii, 883f. (The translation here is E. Rowson's, *The Marwanid Restoration* [Albany, N.Y., 1989], 33f.)

40. The Qur'an unfortunately uses a different verb, though one with the same meaning. The deliberate seeking of martyrdom, *ṭalab al-shahāda*, is met with in Khārijite circles outside of Ṣāliḥ's own group. The early Khārijite leader, Qaṭarī ibn al-Fujā'a, was himself called "The Prince of Death"; see E. Salem, *Political Theory and Institutions of the Khawārij* (Baltimore, 1956), 95f.

41. See Noth, *Heiliger Krieg*, 55–58. Note the conception of the ascetic as martyr in the seventh-century Syriac mystic Isaac of Niniveh (Wensinck, *Oriental Doctrine*, 16). Asceticism preparatory to battle is well attested in the Hebrew Bible; see, e.g., Judges 20:26.

42. M. Bravmann has argued that even the term *islām*, classically understood as "humble submission to God," had an originally secular sense in pre-Islamic Arabia of "giving up one's life in battle," and expresses the idea that one should fight to the death rather than give oneself up to the enemy (*The Spiritual Background of Early Islam* [Leiden, 1972], 8ff.).

43. E.g., Aḥmad ibn Ḥanbal, *Musnad*, ii, 231, and elsewhere.

44. Mālik, *Muwaṭṭa'*, 236 (no. 997).

45. Muslim, *Ṣaḥīḥ*, 33:90.

46. Emphasis added. The report appears just above the parallel cited in note 44; the commentator makes nothing of the different wording.

47. For the scholars' reaction against Khārijite *ṭalab al-shahāda*, see Goldziher, *Muslim Studies*, ii, 352. This is nicely parallel to the classical tradition's revaluation of both *hijra* and *jihād*. See Crone, "First-century concept of *hiǧra*"; and *Encyclopaedia of Islam*, 2nd ed. (Leiden, in progress), s.v. djihād.

48. Cited at Goldziher, *Muslim Studies*, ii, 353; and at Kohlberg, "*Jihād*," 66.

SIX

CONTEMPLATIVE DEATH IN JEWISH MYSTICAL TRADITION

Lawrence Fine

A feature normally assumed essential to martyrdom is that it results in physical death. This essay, however, focuses on a variety of traditions in which martyrdom has to do with something other than actual dying. In certain Jewish mystical traditions, particularly medieval Kabbalah and Eastern European Hasidism, we discover a range of rituals that encourage the practice of *contemplative* or *imagined* martyrdom. The study of such traditions expands our conception of the meaning of religious martyrdom. Fascination with the realities of evil, death, and the demonic is a quintessential and distinctive feature of medieval kabbalistic thought. Whereas medieval philosophic rationalists had little place in their systems for such questions, kabbalists unabashedly cultivated a powerful interest in them. One of the ways in which the concern with death expressed itself was in the development of various rituals intended to enable an adept to surrender himself to God in a devotional act of contemplative martyrdom.

"Falling upon the Face" in the *Zohar*

As is the case with so many other kabbalistic themes and rituals, we look to the *Zohar*, the seminal work of thirteenth-century Spanish Kabbalah, for our point of departure. The *Zohar* has some rather striking views concerning the practice of a certain section of traditional rabbinic liturgy known in Hebrew as *Taḥanun*, meaning supplication.

Coming immediately after a series of prayers known as the *Amidah* ("Standing Prayer"), or *Shemoneh Esreh* ("Eighteen Blessings"), the central portion of the morning service, *Taḥanun* is actually "a varied mosaic of biblical verses and prayers from different periods."[1] The technical term for this supplicatory prayer is "Falling upon the Face," or *Nefilat Appayim* in Hebrew. "Falling upon the Face" was a type of prostration customary in Babylonia at the beginning of the third century, performed during the recitation of *Taḥanun*. According to the Mishnah, the ritual of prostration before God goes back to a practice in the ancient Temple in Jerusalem: "The Levites recited the psalm. When they reached the end of the section they blew the shofar, and the people prostrated themselves. For every section the shofar was blown, and for every blowing of the shofar there was a prostration" (*Tamid* 7:3).

After its destruction by the Romans in 70 C.E., this custom was transferred from the Temple to the synagogues. Following the *Shemoneh Esreh*, the opportunity was given to every individual to express heartfelt devotion to God in an entirely private and personal way. Although they began as private, unfixed prayers, eventually a collection of liturgical passages evolved, whose main themes were confession of sin, the worshiper's unworthiness, and petitions for divine mercy. Now, according to the *Zohar*, while praying the *Shemoneh Esreh*, an individual gains in spiritual strength and brings about the unification of the male and female dimensions *(sefirot)* of divinity, *Tiferet* and *Malkhut/Shekhinah*, respectively.[2] From this state of spiritual exaltation the adept engages in an act of voluntary, contemplative death while reciting the *Taḥanun*. One "hands over one's soul" (*moser et nafsho*) in an act of mystical death, the purpose of which is to serve as atonement for one's sins:

> Come and see: When a person prays in this way, with [appropriate] actions and word, and establishes the union [of above and below], by virtue of his deeds upper and lower worlds are blessed. Then a person must regard himself, after he completes the *Shemoneh Esreh*, as if he has departed this world, and has separated himself from the Tree of Life, and died near the Tree of Death, which returns his pledge to him, as it is said: " . . . he (Jacob) gathered up his feet into the bed [and expired, and was gathered unto his people]" (Gen. 49:33) as he confessed his sins and prayed on account of them. Now he must be gathered near the Tree of Death, and fall [upon his face] saying: "'Unto Thee, O Lord, do I lift up my soul' (Ps. 25:1). At first glance I gave her (i.e., my soul) to Thee as a pledge; now that I have effected unification and performed act and word properly, and confessed on account of my sins, behold, I

surrender my soul to Thee completely." A person ought to regard himself as if he has departed this world, that his soul has surrendered to this sphere of death. Therefore, there is no [letter] *vav* in it (i.e., in the acrostic of Psalm 25), for *vav* represents the Tree of Life, and this [Psalm] signifies the Tree of Death. What does this mean to us? The mystery is that there are sins which are not expiated until a person leaves this world, as it is written: "Surely this iniquity shall not be expiated by you until you die" (Is. 22:14). And this person submits himself completely to death and surrenders his soul to this region, not in a pledge as at night, but as one who has truly left this world. One must perform this devotion with sincerity of heart; then the Holy One, blessed be He, will take pity on him and forgive his sins.[3]

While praying the *Shemoneh Esreh* the adept sustains the unity of above and below (that is, the divine realm of the *sefirot* and the natural world), and between male (*Tiferet*) and female (*Malkhut*) aspects of the divine persona, symbolized by the Tree of Life and the Tree of Death, respectively. However, when the devotee passes to the *Taḥanun* prayer in which he confesses his sins, he severs this holy relationship, separating himself from the Tree of Life (*Tiferet*) and binding himself to the Tree of Death (*Malkhut/Shekhinah*). Whereas at night while asleep, one merely entrusts one's soul "as a pledge" to the *Shekhinah*, in the course of *Nefilat Appayim* one gives himself completely to Her, falling upon the face, as if one were actually departing from this world.

In other words, the kabbalist, at his most vulnerable moment, the confession of sin, stands fully exposed and ready to accept the consequences of his deeds—death itself. No longer attached to life, he throws himself into the abyss of existence in the ultimate act of submission (*mesirat nefesh*) before God. Only divine mercy enables him to survive intact, his sins having been expiated through a momentary experience of voluntary "death." Unsatisfied with the partial atonement possible in this world, the kabbalist chooses mystical death as a means of achieving total purification of the soul, otherwise available only through physical death.

Commenting on the Zoharic passage cited above, Moses Cordovero (1522–1570) indicates that when a person performs this exercise he should prostrate himself and appear as if truly dead.[4] In so doing, the adept, whose body represents *Tiferet*, cleaves to the earth (symbolic of the feminine *Shekhinah*), thus unifying divine male and female. Furthermore, according to Cordovero, he must regard such death as being on account of having desecrated God's name, a transgression for which death alone can atone.

Contemplative Death in the Teachings
of Isaac Luria

Isaac Luria (1534–1572) was among the greatest kabbalists in the history
of Judaism and the preeminent figure in the great sixteenth-century
renaissance of mystical life which took place in the village of Safed nestled
high in the mountains of the upper Galilee. Luria's teachings are replete
with exceedingly detailed meditative instructions (*kavvanot*) for the performance of liturgical prayer. Luria's *kavvanot* for *Nefilat Appayim* are based
on the mythologems found in the *Zohar* that we have already described.
According to Luria, having raised his soul up to the highest spiritual
"World" known as *Atsilut* ("Emanation") as a result of praying the
Shemoneh Esreh, and having unified the "Four Worlds" which comprise
the cosmos, the male adept *himself* cleaves, as in an act of sexual intimacy,
to the divine feminine. The latter is known in Lurianic terminology, not
simply as *Malkhut* or *Shekhinah*, but as *Nuqba de-Zeir*. From this extraordinary state of strength and exaltation, the adept—while still praying *Nefilat
Appayim*—imaginatively "descends below to the farthest end of the [low-
est] world of *Assiyah* ("Making"), as a person who throws himself from
the top of a roof to the ground below."[5] That is, he hurls himself into
the lowest depths of the world, the scene of material existence and the
home of evil, the realm of the *qelippot* ("shells").

The erotic nature of this ritual is obvious. The devotee's ecstatic
descent constitutes an orgasmic release, resulting in exhaustion and a
depletion of energy akin to death. Once below he concentrates on
gathering "female waters" and divine sparks concealed in each of the
"Four Worlds," beginning with the world of *Assiyah* and moving
progressively upward through the worlds of *Beri'ah* ("Creation") and
Yetsirah ("Formation") until he returns to the place from which he
began, *Atsilut*. He facilitates the ascent of the "female waters" and liberates or redeems these sparks by attaching them to the various elements
of his own soul: in the lowest world of *Assiyah*, he joins sparks to his
lowest dimension of soul, *nefesh*. In the next highest world of *Yetsirah*,
he joins them to the aspect of his soul known as *ruah*, while in the world
of *Beri'ah*, he binds sparks to his highest grade of soul, *neshamah*. Having done this, the worshiper proceeds to bind these three aspects of his
soul—along with the collected sparks—to the *male* gradation within
Nuqba de-Zeir, some of whose light flows into the soul of the adept
himself, providing him with powerful spiritual inspiration. The kabbalistic devotee, then, becomes a conduit for the distribution of both

divine masculine and feminine seminal fluids in the course of performing this ritual.

Importantly, Luria compares this process to what the rabbis of the
Talmud taught regarding the fate of the righteous following death.[6] They
descend to the netherworld (Gehinnom), the site of the soul's punishment after death, grasp the afflicted who are found there, and retrieve
them. This is made possible by the fact that at the moment of their death,
righteous individuals unify the divine masculine and feminine, endowing
themselves with the spiritual power with which to extricate sinful persons from the consequences of their deeds.[7] Luria thus likens the imagined death and ecstatic moment of Nefilat Appayim to the actual death
of various individuals. Such a parallel makes it clear that Luria considered the descent into the realm of evil akin to a genuine act of offering
up one's life, at least momentarily. This action is said to be "in the nature
of true death," inasmuch as the realm of the qelippot is indeed a place of
death. The adept aspires to such a death since this is the only way in
which to rescue certain divine sparks from the grip of evil. In this paradoxical construction, then, death is a redemptive act, calling back to life
those souls trapped in a place of death.

On the other hand, one needs to take care so as to avoid ensnarement
by the qelippot, lest he become permanently mired himself in the depths
of the netherworld. Given the danger which this entails, not everyone
who aspires to practice this complex ritual should do so. Only an individual who is perfectly righteous—free of any moral or spiritual
blemish—has the capacity to struggle successfully against the forces of
death. If one is not wholly qualified, the only chance to succeed rests
on perfect and absolute concentration during the entire experience.
Otherwise, one runs the risk of not only not accomplishing one's goal,
but also far worse, of sinking inexorably into the complete grasp of evil.
While a person who is less than perfectly qualified may actually succeed in extricating himself from the depths, even if he does not reach
his goal, this is not the case with one who is substantially tainted. His
fate will be to remain trapped below along with the souls of other sinners. This explanation enables us to understand what the ancient sages
intended when they taught that "the wicked in their lifetime are called
dead."[8] These are the people who, in the practice of Nefilat Appayim,
succumb to the qelippot by virtue of their sins, thereby receiving a new
soul whose nature is entirely corrupt.

If the dangers are considerable, the successful adept achieves a great
deal at the experiential level. He elevates his soul to the highest sphere
within the divine realms, is filled with supernal light, and revitalizes his

soul with the abundance of divine life. According to Moses Yonah, one of Luria's most important disciples, such a person becomes "newly created" as one who has actually died and left this world. He receives the spiritual strength with which to struggle against the evil inclination, resist all further sin, and achieve new levels of inspiration by which he can comprehend the innermost mysteries of the Torah.[9] *Nefilat Appayim* thus accomplishes several related goals simultaneously. As an act of cosmic mending (*tiqqun*) it serves the purpose of raising up sparks of holiness from the *qelippot*, along with those that reside within the three lower spiritual worlds. At the same time, the adept undergoes an ecstatic experience in which he enjoys powerful spiritual rejuvenation.

The *Shema Yisrael*, another prayer central to daily Jewish liturgy, was conceived by Luria to be a medium for contemplative death as well. As is well known, the *Shema* is associated in Jewish tradition with physical martyrdom (*qiddush ha-shem*, literally, "sanctification of God's name"), Rabbi Akiba (2nd century) having recited this prayer in the act of sanctifying God's name while being tortured to death by the Romans.[10] According to Luria, imagined death performed while reciting the *Shema* is actually superior to *Nefilat Appayim*. In the former, the devotee finalizes the sacred union of the divine qualities of being (*sefirot*) known as *Hokhmah/Abba* ("Father") and *Binah/Imma* ("Mother"), a union that is higher than that realized through *Nefilat Appayim*, namely, the *hieros gamos* of *Tiferet* and *Malkhut*:

> In the recitation of the *Shema* . . . it is not enough that we surrender our souls through the mystery of death, but rather through that of martyrdom (*qiddush ha-shem*), this being surrender of the soul to [the extent of actual] death. Therefore, one must concentrate on the [divine] name YAHDVNH'Y when uttering the word "One" [in the *Shema*], and imagine the four types of [punishment by] death, meted out by a rabbinic court of law (*Bet Din*): stoning, burning, decapitation, and strangulation. And this is the mystery which our rabbis taught in connection with Rabbi Akiba who ascended to [the grade of] Divine Thought (*Mahshavah*), that is, *Hokhmah* ("Wisdom"), in the mystery of the surrender of his soul unto death.[11]

In this passage the emphasis is on the level within the divine hierarchy to which the adept's soul ascends, and the nature of the union that takes place in the upper world rather than the gathering of trapped souls, as seen above. The divine union brought about by an act of martyrdom (*qiddush ha-shem*), whether actual or merely intended martyrdom, is perfect and exalted. Up until the period of Rabbi Akiba and the so-called Ten Martyrs, the *sefirot Tiferet* and *Malkhut* enjoyed sufficient illumination with which to raise up the "female waters" to the divine grade of *Binah*, requiring only a limited degree of help from the righteous, who surrendered their souls through imagined death in the course of reciting the *Shema*. In the period during which Rabbi Akiba and his comrades lived, however, the sun and the moon became dark on account of the sins of that generation, leaving them deprived of the strength to raise up the "female waters." Upon the death of Akiba and the other martyrs, their very souls served to illuminate *Tiferet* and *Malkhut* and thus to elevate the "female waters" so as to draw down the influx of the "male waters" from the realm of Divine Thought once again. Thus, martyrdom—be it actual physical death or imagined death—along with the recitation of the *Shema* prayer, has the enormous power to generate the dynamic processes of divine unification and cosmic mending.

The messianic implications of such martyrdom are suggested by the fact that death by martyrdom is, according to Luria, comparable to the role played by the precursor to the Messiah, namely, the Messiah, the son of Joseph. The martyrological death of the latter was believed to set the stage for the arrival of the Messiah, the son of David. Presumably, these Lurianic notions were influenced not only by earlier kabbalistic literary traditions but also by the examples of recent contemporary martyrs, most notably a certain Solomon Molcho. We know, for example, that Molcho's death as a martyr in the early sixteenth century inspired a famous contemporary of Luria's in Safed, Joseph Karo, to aspire to be burnt at the stake! Karo frequently spoke of the burning of worldly thoughts in the "strawfire" of meditation on the unity of God during the *Shema* prayer, and his desire to be burnt at the stake.[12]

These themes reverberate in the writing of still other Safed kabbalists, including Eleazar Azikri, according to whom "it is a positive obligation to sanctify God's name if one is being forced to renounce his religion . . . and he should meditate on this in his heart when he recites the *Shema* . . . and fully resolve that should he be so tested he will strengthen himself and hand over his soul and worldly goods with joy . . . and he should consider such resolve to be tantamount to having actually performed such an act."[13] It turns out, then, that Isaac Luria conceived of a number of different ways to accomplish quite similar goals. Two involved imagined death, either in the course of *Nefilat Appayim* or the martyrological recitation of the *Shema*, and two involved physical death, the natural death of righteous individuals, or recital of the *Shema* in the midst of actual martyrdom.

Rituals of voluntary, symbolic death are a well-attested phenomenon in the history of religions. Death, real or imagined, especially in archaic and traditional cultures, is typically considered a creative event, a spiritual rebirth. The ritual of imagined, ecstatic death, as we have seen in our case, is an *initiation* of sorts, a mythic passage from one mode of existence to another in the course of which one becomes revitalized. The Lurianic ritual of *Nefilat Appayim*, in particular, is akin to other perilous descents to a dangerous world, strikingly reminiscent of shamanic voyages to the underworld for the purpose of gathering sick souls and bringing them back to the land of the living. One of the most fundamental features of shamanic activity is to descend to the subterranean world so as to journey among the sick and the dead. Thus, for example, among the shamans of Siberia and Inner Asia the purpose of such a journey is to search out and retrieve the soul of a sick individual which is believed to have wandered away from his body or to have been carried off by demonic forces.[14] Moreover, just as Luria cautions that one who engages in such a journey runs the risk of being ensnared by evil forces in the netherworld, so too the shaman's ecstatic experiences "at the same time make him vulnerable, and frequently, through his constant struggling with evil spirits, he falls into their power . . . by being really 'possessed.'"[15]

Sabbatai Sevi's Apostasy as Martyrdom

The notion that one endangers oneself, flirts with death itself in the process of extricating the holy from the grasp of evil, became a fundamental tenet of the Sabbatian movement. In the seventeenth century, the most significant, not to mention turbulent, expression of kabbalistic life was the messianic movement known as Sabbatianism, which galvanized around the charismatic but highly troubled personality of the Turkish Jew Sabbatai Sevi (1626–1676). Sevi became infamous for his dramatic mood swings, his practice of violating Jewish law, and his ultimate apostasy when he converted to Islam under duress. We are hardly surprised that Sabbatianism specifically appropriated the Lurianic ritual of *Nefilat Appayim* as one way of explaining Sabbatai Sevi's apostasy; it served as a perfect example of how he deliberately descended into the abyss of the netherworld (the realm of the *qelippot*) in order to complete the yet unfinished task of cosmic redemption. This view is set forth in a letter written about 1673–4 by Sabbatianism's most important ideologist and theologian, Nathan of Gaza:

> It is well-known that the reason behind every [legal] prohibition is that it causes one's soul to become impure. If this is so, why are the righ-

teous permitted to enter into the realm of impurity? Even more, [why is] one not called righteous unless he performs such an act? We have seen a wonderful meditative intention of Isaac Luria, may he be blessed, concerning *Nefilat Appayim* [to the effect] that a righteous individual must hurl himself into the depths of the *qelippot*. Now, this is similar to one who transgresses all of the prohibitions of the Torah. Because he is capable of extricating himself from there he is permitted to commit such an enormous transgression.[16]

In another letter, Nathan explicitly defines this activity as a form of martyrdom, writing that *Nefilat Appayim* may be likened to a man who casts himself into the dangerous realm of the *qelippot* and thereby martyrs himself in order to extract divine sparks from the clutches of evil. Such was the nature of Sabbatai Sevi's apostasy, according to Nathan!

While others who labored for redemption had remained aloof from danger, the Messiah, that is, Sevi himself, alone dared to assume the frightful task of struggling with evil on its own terms, and on its own territory. While in Sabbatianism such struggle was believed to necessitate antinomian behavior, the violation of Jewish law, and ultimately apostasy, in Lurianism we find nothing of the sort. On the contrary, exposing oneself to the dangers involved required that the worshiper be in as complete a state of holiness as possible.

Contemplative Death in Eastern European Jewish Ritual and Thought

In the eighteenth century there were Eastern European teachers who were no less enthusiastic about the practice of contemplative martyrdom. If anything, our sources suggest an even more intense feeling for this type of activity. This was presumably inspired, in part, by the traumatizing experience of actual martyrdom that occurred in Poland in the middle of the seventeenth century. Bogdan Chmielnicki (1595–1657) was the leader of the Cossack and peasant uprising against Polish rule in the Ukraine in 1648 which resulted in the destruction of hundreds of Jewish communities and the deaths of tens of thousands of Jews. These events—the "Chmielnicki massacres"—left a lasting scar on the psyche of Polish Jewry.

Jacob Emden (1697–1776), a famous Polish rabbi and kabbalist whose life was perpetually at the center of some controversy, and who devoted much of his energy to combating the continuing effects of Sabbatianism,

considered *Nefilat Appayim* to be a rite of great significance. In his popular prayer book, *House of Jacob*, Emden distinguishes between surren-
dering one's soul to God while reciting the *Shema* and doing so during
Nefilat Appayim. In the former case a person resolves to surrender his
life through *qiddush ha-shem* and to be killed in any of the terrible ways
that might befall him. However, in performing *Nefilat Appayim*, one
goes further and considers himself as actually having died as he pros-
trates himself. Only this more radical expression of submission can ensure
that one's sins will be forgiven, especially those for which only death
atones, such as having desecrated God's name.

Without any doubt, the most fervent proponent of the practice
of spiritual martyrdom during this period was an ascetic Lithuanian
kabbalist, Alexander Susskind of Grodno (d. 1793). In addition to cit-
ing the Zoharic and Lurianic traditions that we have discussed, Susskind
also stresses the importance of glorifying God's great name and expressing one's love for Him, rather than atoning for one's sins. In contrast
to Luria, Susskind advances a far simpler contemplative strategy,
devoid of complex Lurianic symbolism:

> By means of this form of worship a person performs tremendous mend-
> ing (*tiqqunim*) in the worlds on high. . . . I refer to the devotion of
> martyrdom, even though he only suffers it potentially, not in actual-
> ity. . . . This type of worship comes to the man who has a great long-
> ing and love for his Maker and Creator, may He be exalted, which
> burns in his heart so that he expresses, *in potentia*, that is, in his thoughts,
> his willingness to suffer martyrdom, whether in those passages of the
> liturgy in which God, may He be exalted, is praised and thanked, or
> in those passages which speak of the absence of God's glory in this bit-
> ter exile. As a result of this martyrdom, albeit only *in potentia*, in his
> thoughts, with great rapture and with the intention of sanctifying God's
> name through all the worlds, the great Name of our Maker and
> Creator, may He be exalted, is elevated and sanctified in all worlds,
> both those on high and those here below.[17]

Although Susskind calls this action only *in potentia*, it is clear that he
has in mind not mere resolve, but rather the attempt to come as close
to experiencing actual martyrdom as possible:

> Now it is obvious that this martyrdom, even though it is only *in poten-
> tia*, must be whole-hearted and not with a remote heart. For the
> Creator, blessed be He and exalted, searches all hearts. For it is clear
> that a mere thought on a man's part that he is ready to suffer martyr-
> dom for the sanctification of God's name does not mean anything un-

less he really makes the firmest resolve that he will certainly survive the test, allowing himself to be threatened with every kind of death by torture rather than be false to his holy religion. And he should depict to himself that at this moment they are actually carrying out these forms of death, and he should depict the pain and the sufferings that will be his, and yet he survives the test. The Creator, blessed be He and exalted, who searches all hearts, sees his thoughts and the manner in which he depicts to himself the deaths and the tortures inflicted upon him, and yet he survives the test. This is real martyrdom even though it is only *in potentia.*[18]

A variety of Hasidic masters also took up the theme of contemplative death, building on many of the motifs that we have already seen. For example, Elimelech of Lizensk (1717–1787) formulates this idea by advocating that a person not confine such experiences to climactic liturgical moments:

> Whenever an individual is free of the study of Torah, and particularly when he is sitting idly by himself in a room, or lying in bed unable to sleep, he ought to meditate upon the positive commandment: "And I shall be sanctified in the midst of the children of Israel" (Lev. 22:32). He should imagine to himself and visualize in his mind as if a great and awesome fire burned before him, reaching to the heart of heaven. Breaking his natural instinct for the sake of sanctifying His blessed name (*bishvil qedushat ha-Shem*), he casts himself into that very fire. . . . Even while eating and having marital relations, he ought to meditate as described above. As soon as he begins to experience sensual pleasure he should visualize to himself the image described. He should immediately say to himself that he would take far more delight in fulfillment of the positive commandment, "And I will be sanctified in the midst of the children of Israel," than from the pleasure which he derives from this sensual enjoyment.[19]

In a poignant prayer, the famous Hasidic master Nahman of Bratslav (1772–1811) expresses a similar sentiment. He prays that God grant him the strength with which to surrender his soul in the manner of *qiddush ha-shem*, particularly during the recitation of the *Shema*. Nahman yearns to imagine all the terrible deaths which a martyr experiences, to the point where he feels as if the experience is real. So genuine should this experience seem that he will have to restrain himself lest he actually die! "For it is not Your desire," he says to God, "to take my soul before the proper time, God forbid." Nahman further prays that his own sacrifice will bind him to the actual sacrifices of those who went to their deaths in the course of Jewish history. This, he hopes, will extricate him from exile and draw him near to God in love. "Let our death atone for our transgressions and raise up our souls to You in purity and clean-ness. Let our souls be bound up in the bond of eternal life with the Lord our God."[20]

Conclusions

The practice of spiritual death was inspired by a wide range of motiva-tions, of which one or more appears to have been paramount at a particular time or for a particular individual. Atoning for one's sins, glorifying the name of God and drawing near to Him in love, waging war against the forces of evil, raising up the *Shekhinah* from exile, mend-ing the "body" of God: all these were kabbalistic and Hasidic goals which could be accomplished through an imagined act of death, more often than not conceived within the framework of martyrdom. While Jewish mystics had a wide range of strategies and techniques for achieving these goals, this particular strategy seems to have been especially com-pelling. It is not difficult to understand why this should have been so. Death was regarded as the ultimate, most perfect rite of initiation, a change in ontological status in which a person dies to this world and is born to a new one. From a spiritual point of view, death was seen as much as a beginning as an end. Like other forms of initiation, death is preceded by a process of ordeal through which one must pass in order to achieve new life.

Anticipatory death, for the writers and individuals we have described here, is concomitantly characterized by divestment of one's attachment to and reliance on the things for which a person longs in this world. It consists in stripping away the material and overcoming the limitations of physical existence. It means ridding oneself of worldly attachment and offering oneself to God in utter devotion and purity. To surrender oneself in death, even if only imaginatively, is to lay oneself open to the presence of God.

Finally, we are faced here with the fact that Jewish martyrdom was radically transformed by certain Kabbalists and Hasidim, from a fate to be avoided where possible, to one to be *sought* after. In the course of time, as medieval Jewish communities experienced the grim reality of actual martyrdom, it came to be idealized as a uniquely noble way to die. What better way to make religious and spiritual sense of the hor-ror of such violence and victimization? It is not a very long step from privileging death by martyrdom when there is no other choice, to ac-tively seeking to *enact* it in contemplative ways. There is not such a vast psychological difference between glorifying a death that is unavoidable by construing it as a unique spiritual opportunity, on the one hand, and volunteering to pursue the experience of martyrdom, on the other. Still, these traditions and mystical rites leave us somewhat startled. Christians who aspired to experience the ultimate form of suffering had, of course, the paradigm of Jesus' martyrdom after which to pattern their lives. And Muslims cultivated the practice of martyrdom in the course of *jihād*, holy striving, as a fundamental virtue. In Judaism, however, life was normally considered to be an absolutely precious gift, not to be surrendered except when faced with a worse alternative, namely, the coerced violation of certain unbreachable standards of human conduct.[21] This is, after all, a tradition that teaches that a pillow should not be removed from beneath a dying person's head lest it hasten death, and that regards as sinful the taking of one's own life. In this light, the practice of contemplative death—in which one *yearns* for death—suggests to me a simple truth about the history of Jewish spirituality: Jewish ascetics, pietists, and mystics, no less than their counterparts in other religious traditions, pursued every path available to them in their quest for self-perfection and in their impassioned search for God.

Notes

1. Concerning the development of *Taḥanun*, see A. Z. Idelsohn, *Jewish Liturgy and Its Development* (New York: Schocken, 1972), 110–112; S. Freehof, "The Origin of the Taḥanun," *Hebrew Union College,* 1 (1925), 339–350; and I. Elbogen, *Jewish Liturgy: A Comprehensive Survey,* translated by R. Scheindlin (Philadelphia and New York: Jewish Publication Society, 1993), 66–72.

2. The conception of the ten *sefirot* is fundamental to theurgical or theosophical Kabbalah. The *sefirot* are ten "faces" or dimensions of the divine persona, ten qualities of divine being, all of which emanate from within the concealed mystery of *Ein-Sof,* the infinite, nameless source of all reality. Whereas *Ein-Sof* is beyond human imagination and comprehension, the *sefirot* are accessible to the imagination in manifold ways. For introductions to Kabbalah, see A. Green, "The Zohar: Jewish Mysticism in Medieval Spain," in Lawrence Fine, ed., *Essential Papers on Kabbalah* (New York: New York University Press, 1995), 27–66; L. Fine, "Kabbalistic Texts," in Barry Holtz, ed., *Back to the Sources—Reading the Classic Jewish Texts* (New York: Summit Books, 1984), 305–359; and D. Matt, *The Essential Kabbalah* (New York: Harper Row, 1995).

3. *Zohar* 3: 120b-121a. Psalm 25 is written acrostically, but the letter *vav* is lacking. For variations on this motif, see *Zohar* 2: 202b; 3: 176b, 241b. For discussions of the *Zohar's* treatment of *Nefilat Appayim,* see I. Tishby, *The Wisdom of the Zohar* (Oxford: Littman Library of Jewish Civilization, 1989), vol. 2, 970–

971; E. Wolfson, *Through a Speculum that Shines* (Princeton: Princeton University Press, 1994), 339–340; and especially the analysis of this ritual and motif in M. Fishbane, *The Kiss of God—Spiritual and Mystical Death in Judaism* (Seattle and London: University of Washington Press, 1994), 107–110.

4. Moses Cordovero, *Siddur Tefillah le-Moshe* (Przemysl: 1892), 112a. Cf. Fishbane, *The Kiss of God*, 110–112.

5. Hayyim Vital, *Sha'ar ha-Kavvanot* of the *Shemonah She'arim*, 301–314. All references to the collection of Lurianic teachings known as the *Shemonah She'arim* ("Eight Gates"), edited by Hayyim Vital, Luria's chief disciple, are from the Yehudah Ashlag edition (Jerusalem: 1962). See Y. Liebes, *Studies in the Zohar* (Albany: State University of New York Press, 1993), 52–55; and Fishbane, *The Kiss of God*, 112–116.

6. Babylonian Talmud, *Hagigah* 15b.

7. *Sha'ar ha-Mitsvot* of the *Shemonah She'arim*, 112a–b.

8. Hayyim Vital, *Sha'ar ha-Kavvanot*, 305a.

9. Moses Yonah, *Kanfei Yonah* (Lemberg: 1884), 50c.

10. In rabbinic tradition, sanctifying God's name by way of martyrdom was considered to be a religious obligation, based on Leviticus 22:31–33: "You shall faithfully observe my commandments: I am the Lord. You shall not profane my holy name, that I might be sanctified in the midst of the Israelite people—I the Lord who sanctify you, I who brought you out of the land of Egypt to be your God, I the Lord." These verses were eventually construed to signify the requirement to surrender one's life to God under particular circumstances. According to the Babylonian Talmud, *Sanhedrin* 74a, "if a man is commanded (i.e., coerced): 'Transgress [some religious precept] and do not suffer death,' he may transgress and not suffer death, except [in the case where he is coerced to commit] idolatry, incest (i.e., illicit sex), and murder." In other words, with the exception of these latter three "cardinal" transgressions, a person may transgress *all other* religious precepts in order to save his life in a situation of coercion. In the case of these three transgressions, however, he is obligated to "sanctify God's name" by giving up his life. Based on this religious obligation, significant numbers of Jews martyred themselves under duress, the most famous example of which occurred during the First Crusade of 1096 in the Rhineland. For a brief overview of this subject, see the entry "Persecution" in *The Encyclopedia of Religion*, ed. Mircea Eliade (New York: MacMillan, 1987), vol. 1, 249–251.

11. Hayyim Vital, *Sha'ar ha-Kavvanot, Inyan Qeri'at Shema*, 137.

12. Concerning Karo's yearning for martyrdom, see R. J. Zwi Werblowsky, *Joseph Karo* (Oxford: Oxford University Press, 1962), 152.

13. Eleazar Azikri, *Sefer Haredim* (Venice: 1601), pt. 1, ch. 1, par. 16. See Werblowsky, *Karo*, 152, n.4.

14. See the classic study by Mircea Eliade, *Shamanism—Archaic Techniques of Ecstasy* (New York: Bollingen Foundation, 1964), especially chapters 6–7. For a brief, general overview of the phenomenon of shamanism, see the entry "Shamanism" in *The Encyclopedia of Religion*, vol. 13, 201–208.

15. Eliade, *Shamanism*, 236.

16. Letter by Nathan of Gaza to Sabbatai Sevi's brother, in J. Sasportas, *Sefer Sisat Nobel Sevi*, published from manuscript by Z. Scwarz, ed. I. Tishby (Jerusalem: 1954), 201–202. Concerning the question of Sabbatai Sevi's apostasy more generally, see G. Scholem, *Sabbatai Sevi* (Princeton: Princeton University Press, 1973), 687–820.

17. Alexander Susskind, *Yesod ve-Shoresh ha-Avodah* (Jerusalem: 1965), ch. 11, 33–35. The present translation is from L. Jacobs, *Jewish Mystical Testimonies* (New York: Schocken, 1997), 217–218. Concerning still another Polish kabbalist for whom the visualization of martyrdom was exceedingly important, Tsvi Hirsh Kaidanover, see M. Verman, *The History and Varieties of Jewish Meditation* (Northvale, N.J.: Jason Aronson, 1996), 106–107.

18. Jacobs, *Jewish Mystical Testimonies*, 218–219.

19. Elimelech of Lizensk, *Tzetyl Qatan*, found at the beginning of the various editions of his work *No'am Elimelech* (Cracow: 1896). Concerning Elimelech of Lizensk and still other Hasidic teachers who advocated spiritual death, see Fishbane, *The Kiss of God*, 117–124.

20. Nahman of Bratslav, *Liqqutei Tefilot* (Jerusalem: 1957), paragraph 87. For a study of the life and teachings of this Hasidic master, see A. Green, *Tormented Master—A Life of Rabbi Nahman of Bratslav* (University, Ala.: University of Alabama Press, 1979).

21. See note 10.

SEVEN

MARTYRDOM IN SUNNI
REVIVALIST THOUGHT

Daniel Brown

Sunni Islam is not where the primary action is when it comes to Muslim ideas about martyrdom. Our attention, with regard to martyrdom, should more naturally be drawn toward Shī'ite Islam. It is Shī'ite Muslims whose willingness to die has left an enduring mark on the world during the last two decades—in the Iranian Revolution; in the Iran-Iraq war; in the bitterness of the Lebanese civil war. Moreover, modern Shī'ite ideologues—Ṭāliqānī, Sharī'atī, Muṭahharī—have created out of the Shī'ite doctrine of martyrdom a sophisticated ideology of social and political activism and revolution. And at the level of popular religion, it is among Shī'ite Muslims that martyrdom has formed the basis of an elaborate cultus and the foundation of a theology of redemptive suffering. Shī'ite Islam presents us with an enduring and dramatic modern case of a system of belief for which martyrdom is a central value, and Shī'ite ideas must be reckoned with in any serious attempt to make sense of the phenomenon of martyrdom.

Shī'ites have not been alone in their preoccupation with martyrdom, however; among Sunni revivalists there have also been some who have made an ideology of martyrdom central to their program. Sunni revivalists are those individuals and groups who seek a resurgent, revitalized, reinvigorated, and self-assertive Islam modeled after the early Muslim community of Medina. Westerners often perceive Muslim revivalist movements as prone to violence, hostile to Western geopolitical interests, and committed to a reactionary social agenda; and so they sometimes are. But even if these images are not entirely false, they miss the point. What gives revivalist movements their strength is simply the fact that they are *revivalist*; they promise to bring Islam back to life. They claim to represent a vision of renewed Islam which is not only authentic to the ideal Islamic past but also adapted to the modern situation of Muslims. Reality belies the common stereotype of Islamic revivalism as a defensive and reactionary movement, born of frustration, anger, and fear at the encroachment of Western cultural values. Revivalist ideas are appealing to many Muslims precisely because they are forward-looking and confident.[1]

The ongoing struggle to reinvigorate and restore Islam to ascendancy in a world that has turned away from God is the single most important characteristic of revivalism. Nowhere is this self-confident, assertive, sometimes militant attitude better reflected than in the revivalist emphasis on *jihād fi sabīl Allāh*—struggle in the way of God. It is, in turn, the revivalist doctrine of *jihād* that provides the foundation for a revivalist ideology of martyrdom. What I will set out to do here is as follows: first, I will describe in rough outline the main features of the classical Muslim doctrines of *jihād* and martyrdom; second, I will describe in more detail the revivalist reaction against these classical doctrines; finally, I will explore what the revivalist case might tell us about Muslim constructions of martyrdom more generally.

First, the classical background.[2] Many medieval Muslim scholars would likely have been uncomfortable with the most basic assumption underlying the modern understanding of martyrdom: namely, that violent death is its most significant precondition. Just as the doctrine of *jihād* was spiritualized and assimilated to the internal spiritual struggle of the believer, so also the doctrine of martyrdom had its most characteristic classical expression in the spiritualization of martyrdom and its assimilation to the inward sacrifice of the believer. This tendency found its clearest expression in the distinction between a lesser and a greater *jihād*. The lesser *jihād* is a struggle against unbelievers, the greater *jihād* a struggle against the tendencies toward evil within the human spirit. A believer did not have to go to a battlefield to wage the greater *jihād*, and by extension did not necessarily need to die violently to be a martyr. A tendency which marked classical Muslim legal thinking—the tendency to focus on the spiritual value of an act rather than its externals—contributed directly to the spiritualization of martyrdom. For Muslim legists and theologians, what mattered was not primarily the external performance of an act but the intention with which it was performed. There was no reason, then, why the value of martyrdom couldn't be transferred to other pious acts so long as the intention was to testify to the truth. Martyrs include not only those who die in battle but also those who testify to the truth through argument; those engaged in the *jihād* of the pen are thus equally eligible for the privileges of martyrdom. Such an idea was bound to appeal to a scholarly audience.

Naturally, death remained the preferred means of achieving martyrdom, but the manner of death ceased to be of primary concern in defining martyrdom or in allocating its rewards. In theory, there was no need to find a battlefield or unbelievers to fight. Almost any kind of death would do. The believer might as well stay at home waiting for an epidemic of plague or an earthquake. Indeed, a Muslim who died peacefully in bed might still achieve martyrdom, so long as his heart was really in it.[3] Conversely, dying in the battlefield was no guarantee of martyrdom. One had to fight with the right motives. Death, while certainly the preferred means of martyrdom, was not its decisive defining element. What really mattered was purity of intention and willingness to testify to the truth.

We observe in the medieval Muslim treatment of the subject a serious dilution of the value of martyrdom. Rather than a valuable commodity, available only at a very high price, martyrdom became common currency, readily accessible to any pious believer. There are several possible explanations. The doctrine of martyrdom was shaped by scholars and scholars tend to be quietists. Scholars could tolerate the rule of a tyrant; they could not handle anarchy. Thus, the doctrine of martyrdom probably represents, at least in part, a scholarly reaction against the militancy of early Islamic rebels in favor of peace and quiet. The pervasive influence of sufism and the emphasis placed by sufis on internal spiritual experience above outward ritual and duty further encouraged a deemphasis on physical martyrdom. Probably, the inflated rewards of martyrdom also contributed. Martyrs avoid all those stages of the afterlife that Muslims most dread; they go directly to Paradise without passing go, so to speak. And once there they enjoy attractive benefits. Surely, it would seem rather cheap to confine rewards like this to the few who had the opportunity to die in battle. Finally, it is certainly the case that the classical doctrine of martyrdom reflects a time when there were fewer and fewer real opportunities for martyrdom on the battlefield.

If medieval Muslim scholars lacked the opportunity, the necessity, or the desire for physical martyrdom, modern Muslim experience has provided all three in abundance. Western ascendancy, the colonial experience, and the political and economic dislocation that followed in their wake have led modern Muslims to reopen the questions of *jihād* and martyrdom. For some Muslims, the modern experience has clearly presented both an enemy worth fighting and a cause worth dying for. The story of modern Muslim soul-searching on the question of *jihād* is long and complex, and I can only summarize here.[4] One of the first and quite natural reactions to colonialism was the emergence of militant *jihād* movements that sought to throw the infidels out: the *jihād* of Sayyid Ahmad in India, the Mahdist movement in the Sudan, and the Sanusiyya movement in North Africa. This first wave of *jihād* movements was followed in the nineteenth century by a return to quietism among leading Muslim intellectuals. The generation of Sir Sayyid Ahmad Khan, Chirāgh 'Ali, Sayyid Amīr 'Ali, and Muhammad 'Abduh was less concerned with reviving militant *jihād* than with showing the West that *jihād* was not militant. These so-called modernists sought to counter Western polemics which portrayed Islam as a religion of violence, "spread by the sword." They emphasized the greater *jihād* of internal spiritual struggle and argued that physical *jihād* was intended to be purely defensive. The modernists had neither inclination for nor interest in martyrdom.[5]

It is against this background that we we must place Sunni revivalist ideas about *jihād* and martyrdom. In the twentieth century, Sunni revivalists have reacted against the quietism of both the modernists and the classical Islamic tradition. One of the most important products of this reaction has been a revival of the doctrine of *jihād*, and along with it the emergence of a reinvigorated ideology of martyrdom.

The ways in which revivalist ideas about *jihād* differ from classical doctrine can be adequately summarized under three headings: first, revivalists have emphasized the superiority of the physical *jihād* (i.e., armed struggle) over other spiritual or metaphorical understandings of the idea; second, they have insisted that under modern conditions participating in *jihād* has become an individual duty, incumbent on all Muslims; third, revivalists began to transfer the focus of *jihād* away from foreign, external enemies and toward their own governments. Each of these elements of the revivalist program has contributed to the development of a characteristic revivalist ideology of martyrdom.

Revivalist emphasis on the physical *jihād* is not difficult to account for once we recognize the context in which revivalism grew. Sunni revivalism first took institutional form in the 1930s and 1940s in two separate but similar organizations, the Jamā'at-i-Islāmī in the Indian subcontinent and the Muslim Brotherhood in Egypt and Syria. Both of these movements grew up in the context of prolonged movements for national liberation directed at colonial regimes. It should be no surprise that an activist interpretation of *jihād* was perceived to be of more utility in the fight against colonialism than a passive one.

The emphasis on reviving the physical *jihād* is especially evident in the writings of Ḥasan al-Bannā', the founder of the Muslim Brotherhood. Bannā' is scornful of those who try to divert people from the importance of fighting and preparing for combat by proposing other interpretations of *jihād*. The distinction between a lesser *jihād* and a greater *jihād* is merely a fiction, he claims, and the traditions on which this distinction is based are unreliable at best. Those who minimize the importance of fighting are not true to the faith. The success of the Muslim community, the *umma*, depends on its ability and willingness to carry out *jihād*.[6] These arguments have been taken up by numerous later revivalists as well. In the words of an ideologue from the radical group that succeeded in assassinating Anwar Sadat: "The idols of this world can only be made to disappear through the power of the sword."[7]

If *jihād* must take on concrete form, then so too must martyrdom. Just as the only true *jihād* is the physical *jihād*, so the only true martyrs are those who die in the struggle. The Muslim Brotherhood and its successors did not reject the application of *jihād* to intellectual effort or to other forms of nonviolent struggle, and they did not abandon the classical doctrines of *jihād* and martyrdom altogether. Revivalists often do not even reject the traditions that extend the rewards of martyrdom to those who die of the plague or die in earthquakes. What they insist is that these are a different and lesser category of martyrs. The supreme reward of martyrdom, according to Bannā', is reserved for those who are killed in the way of God. What revivalists find offensive in classical ideas about martyrdom is the suggestion that someone who dies of seasickness is equal in merit before God to one who dies struggling against unbelief. In contrast to classical doctrine and the apologetic of the modernists, revivalists insist that *jihād* should be understood in its primary sense as fighting, and true martyrdom can only be achieved by death in the way of God.

The second defining characteristic of the revivalist ideology of *jihād* is the argument that *jihād* is a duty incumbent on all Muslims *as individuals*. It is, in modern times, an individual duty (*farḍ 'ayn*) rather than a collective obligation (*farḍ kifāyah*). *Jihād*, according to Bannā', has become, like prayer and fasting, a religious duty imposed by God on every Muslim. Conversely, abstention from *jihād* is a major sin, which will guarantee damnation. A favorite tradition among revivalists who write on this topic states that "whoever dies and has not fought, or had not resolved to fight, has died as if he had never been a Muslim."[8]

Classical juristic arguments are mustered in support of this position. According to classical manuals, *jihād* is a collective duty so long as the enemy is an external one. But when an enemy invades and occupies Muslim territory, it becomes the duty of every individual to participate in the *jihād* in order to liberate the land of the Muslims. Clearly, the colonial situation matched these conditions. The reason, in fact, for the subservience of the Muslim community can be attributed largely to the neglect of the doctrine of *jihād*.

But God does not simply command the performance of *jihād*, he also offers a program of voluntary incentives. Revivalist literature on *jihād* is liberally sprinkled with traditions on the merits of *jihād* and the rewards of the martyrs, both in this world and the next. These we do not need to rehearse, for they follow closely the classical doctrine of martyrdom.

A more important theme, for our purposes, is an emphasis, especially in Ḥasan al-Bannā''s writings, on the potential martyr's preparation for death. If *jihād* is an individual duty, then it is incumbent on Muslims to prepare themselves. Here it is worth quoting at length:

> Brothers! God gives the umma that is skilled in the practice of death and that knows how to die a noble death, an exalted life in this world and eternal felicity in the next. What is the fantasy that has reduced us to loving this world and hating death? If you gird yourselves for a lofty deed and yearn for death, life shall be given to you. . . . Know, then, that death is inevitable, and that it can only happen once. If you suffer it in the way of God, it will profit you in this world and bring you reward in the next.[9]

Several phrases here are striking. Bannā' calls on Muslims to be "skilled in the practice of death" and to "know how" to die a noble death. Elsewhere in his writings he talks of the "art of death"—*fann al-mawt*.[10] What does it mean to be skilled at dying or to have mastered the art of death? Bannā' almost certainly has in mind the sort of transaction talked about in the Qur'an, where those who die in battle are described as "those who sell the life of this world for the next" (Q. 4:74). Martyrdom is the calculated exchange of one commodity—life—for other much more valuable commodities. Bannā' emphasizes that the rewards of martyrdom are not just heavenly—they are also quite worldly. To be skilled in the practice of death is to know how to get the most out of this exchange. Since we all must die, Bannā' is saying, let us die in a way that will make a difference for the cause of Islam. The art of death is mastered when Muslims put aside the love of life and choose to love death. Only in this way will they be free to expend their lives on that which matters most. The success of the Muslim community rests on *jihād*, and the success of *jihād* depends on a collective willingness to die.

Death and martyrdom are not just an unfortunate by-product of *jihād*, for which God will provide a healthy recompense. Rather, death is the very goal of *jihād*, and willingness to die is the key to its success. Here Bannā' comes dangerously close to encouraging the seeking out of martyrdom, *ṭalab al-shahāda*, a practice unequivocally condemned in classical scholarship because of its association with the Khārijite rebels.

Bannā''s construction of martyrdom as an exchange of the imperfect for a higher perfection invites comparison with the work of two modern Shī'ite thinkers, Ayatullāh Ṭāliqānī and 'Ali Sharī'atī. Ṭāliqānī borrows a metaphor from the sufi poet Rumi. Vegetation, he writes, is eaten by a lamb and in dying it becomes flesh and blood. The flesh of the lamb, when eaten by a human, is transformed into thought and energy. In the same way, when a person becomes a martyr, he enters into a higher state of being because he partakes in a higher cause. In the words of Rumi: "From the inanimate I died and became vegetation; from vegetation I died and became animal; from an animal I died and I became human; I am not afraid of death; death has never made me lesser." Thus, martyrdom, according to Ṭāliqānī, is part of a chain of sacrifice leading to perfection.[11]

Sharī'atī presents similar ideas in a less mystical metaphor. If I donate a thousand dollars toward a just cause, then my thousand dollars is, in a sense, transformed into justice. Before the transaction money is worthless paper. But after it is expended—after losing its existence—it becomes valuable in proportion to the value of the cause for which it was spent. Thus, the general principle is established that "everything obtains a similar value to that for which it has been spent." If the cause is permanent and valuable, a permanent and valuable legacy is left.[12] A martyr, then, is a person who expends his whole existence—his very life—for an ideal. The person exists no more as an individual, but the ideal for which he dies is given life through his martyrdom. Martyrs thus exchange their lives for something greater and more lasting.

We see a tendency in these Shī'ite thinkers, and also in Ḥasan al-Bannā', to emphasize the ideological value and rewards of martyrdom rather than the pleasures of the hereafter. Here is an ideology of martyrdom that could quite easily thrive in a secular context, where the individual has little hope for the afterlife, but wants to leave behind a lasting legacy.

The relevance of revivalist ideas about *jihād* and martyrdom to the actual situation in which revivalist movements emerged is clear. The Muslim Brothers did not just talk about martyrdom, they willingly, perhaps zealously, became martyrs—particularly in the struggle against Zionists in Palestine and also in the struggle against the continuing British presence in Egypt. Ḥasan al-Bannā' himself became the movement's most prominent martyr when he was assassinated in 1949. In 1952, the Brothers were at the forefront of "liberation battalions" fighting the British in the Suez Canal Zone. These were only the beginning of what has become a long stream of martyrs from among revivalists in Egypt. This stream of martyrs has, in turn, fed the development of a revivalist ideology of martyrdom. Through martyrdom, whether in the *jihād* against the British, in Palestine, or at the hands of their own govern-ments, revivalists have joined the ranks of the heroes of Islam. Litera-ture in praise of the new martyrs has proliferated.

After the 1950s we can see an important evolution in revivalist ideas about *jihād* and martyrdom. For Ḥasan al-Bannā', *jihād* was still directed outward toward the British, toward Palestine. Revivalist martyrs were those who fought in these conflicts. We can see an important change in the pattern of martyrdom after the revolution, however. From this point on, the revivalists have no need to look abroad to find opportu-nities for martyrdom—they can achieve martyrdom quite easily at home at the hands of their own government. Revivalist leaders in Egypt have been sent to the gallows by their own government at regular intervals over the last forty years—in 1954, in 1966, in 1975, 1978, 1982—a pattern that Hosni Mubarak's regime has continued with some zeal.

This pattern of martyrdom at the hands of other Muslims serves to introduce the third and final element of the revivalist doctrine of *jihād*: The revivalist *jihād* is not just directed at external and overt enemies of Islam, but first and foremost at anti-Islamic elements within Muslim society itself. This tendency can be traced in the first instance to Mawdūdī, the founder of the Jamā'at-i-Islāmī. Mawdūdī sets out to portray *jihād* not as ordinary warfare, but as a sort of social revolution— a struggle to transform society and to throw off all forms of oppression and tyranny that prevent real obedience to God. Any force which op-poses the sovereignty of God, Muslim or not, external or internal, thus becomes the legitimate focus of *jihād*. Mawdūdī consciously adopts rhetoric borrowed from Western political thought—his Urdu text is peppered with English phrases like "revolutionary struggle," "social revolution," and "class war." The importance of this construction of *jihād* is that it makes a tyrannical or impious Muslim regime just as much the object of *jihād* as any external enemy. Because *jihād* is a struggle for the remaking of society on a truly Islamic basis, the enemy is both without *and within*. In fact, according to Mawdūdī, modern Muslim societies have reverted to a religious social climate that is similar to the situation in pre-Islamic Arabia—a period known to Muslims as *jāhiliyya*, the time of ignorance.[13]

Interestingly enough, however, Mawdūdī does not advance these ideas in order to advocate armed struggle against existing power structures—nor does he have much to say about martyrdom. This important reminder shows that revivalist thought on this issue is not monolithic. The Jamā'at-i-Islāmī recognized martyrs in Pakistan's conflicts with India, especially in Kashmir, but it has neither taken up arms against the Pakistani government, nor have its members become martyrs. Instead the organization consciously adopted a gradualist approach, choosing to work within existing political structures rather than promoting violent revolution.

In Egypt, however, similar ideas have been used quite differently. Among radicals within the Egyptian revivalist movement, beginning with Sayyid Qutb, the Egyptian government has become the chief focus of armed struggle. *Jihād* must be directed, in the first instance, against the enemy who is nearest. Clearly, the nearest enemy is an ungodly and corrupt regime. For early Muslim Brotherhood activists, the primary *jihād* was in Palestine; but later radical groups argued that the *jihād* in Palestine must take second place until the enemies of Islam in Egypt had been brought down. The last words of a leader of the Brotherhood at his execution in 1954 ring out in defiance of the godlessness of the regime: "Praise be to God that he has made me a martyr and may he make my blood a curse upon the men of the revolution."[14]

These attitudes toward *jihād* and martyrdom espoused by radicals within the revivalist movement harken back to the ideas of the Khārijite rebels of early Islam, who were all too ready to declare anyone who opposed them an apostate. What we have here, in fact, is a sort of neo-Khārijite ideology. The connection has certainly not been lost on the enemies of revivalism, especially in the government, who have applied the Khārijite label in an attempt to discredit revivalist ideology. By virtue of declaring other believers infidels, by withdrawing from the greater Muslim community, and by waging war against other Muslims, both the Khārijites and modern radical groups are guilty of inciting division and civil war. This is not *jihād* but *fitna*. In this way, the construction of *jihād*, and of martyrdom, has become an important focus of debate in modern Muslim discourse. To government authorities, those who die at the gallows are neo-Khārijite rebels; to radical groups they are martyrs.

One of the most striking characteristics of the Muslim experience with martyrdom—throughout Islamic history—is that all the martyrs who matter die at the hands of other Muslims. This is the opposite of what the core of Muslim teaching on martyrdom, beginning with the Qur'an, would have led us to expect. In theory, martyrdom is related to *jihād*, and *jihād* is directed against the unbelievers. But the martyrs that have lived on, so to speak, are those who died symbolic deaths in the context of struggles internal to the Islamic world—the Khārijites, the Shī'ite martyrs, and the great sufi martyr, al-Hallāj, all fit this pattern. So too the martyrs of the Iranian revolution and the Sunni revivalist martyrs I have described. These martyrs died not to spread Islam, but in an effort to shape or alter its course, and we know their names. Most of the martyrs who died on the battlefield, as soldiers in the *jihād* against unbelievers, remain nameless. This pattern may provide an important insight for a broader understanding of martyrdom in comparative context. It reminds us, in particular, of something we all know but are perhaps prone to overlook—that is, that martyrs can only be identified by a community that recognizes them as such and finds meaning in their death.

Notes

1. For a defense of this interpretation of revivalism, see my *Rethinking Tradition in Modern Islamic Thought* (Cambridge: Cambridge University Press, 1996).

2. For general treatment of the classical background, see A. J. Wensinck, "The Oriental Doctrine of the Martyrs," *Semietische Studien uit Nalatenschap* (Leiden: A. W. Sijthoff, 1941), 90–113.

3. Ibid., 95.

4. For background see Rudolph Peters, *Islam and Colonialism: The doctrine of Jihad in Modern History* (The Hague: Mouton, 1979).

5. See, for example, Chirāgh 'Alī, *A Critical Exposition of the Popular Jihad* (Calcutta: Thacker, Spink & Co., 1885), and Syed Ameer Ali, *The Spirit of Islam* (London: Christophers, 1922), 204–221.

6. Ḥasan al-Bannā', *al-jihād fī sabīl Allāh* (Cairo: Dar al-Jihad, 1977).

7. "Al-Farīḍah al-Ghaibah," *The Neglected Duty: The Creed of Sadat's Assassins and Islamic Resurgence in the Middle East*, trans. Johannes J. G. Jansen (New York: Macmillan, 1986), 161.

8. Richard P. Mitchell, *Society of the Muslim Brothers* (Oxford: Oxford University Press, 1993), 207.

9. Ḥasan al-Bannā', *Five tracts of Hasan al-Banna (1906–1949): A Selection from the Majmuat rasail al-Imam al-shahid Hasan al-Banna*, trans. Charles Wendell (Berkeley: University of California Press, 1978), 156.

10. Ḥasan al-Bannā', "Fann al-mawt," in *al-Ikhwān al-Muslimīn*, 16 August 1946. Cited by Mitchell, *Society of the Muslim Brothers*, 207.

11. Mahmud Ṭāliqānī, "Jihad and Shahadat," in *Jihad and Shahadat: Struggle and Martyrdom in Islam*, ed. Mehdi Abedi and Gary Legenhausen (Houston: Institute for Research and Islamic Studies, 1986), 69.

12. Alī Sharī'atī, "A Discussion of Shahid," in Abedi and Legenhausen, eds., *Jihad and Shahadat*, 232.

13. Syed Abul Ala Maudoodi, *Jihad in Islam* (Lahore: Islamic Publications, 1976).

14. Mitchell, *Society of the Muslim Brothers*, 161.

EIGHT

TRUTH AND SACRIFICE:
SATĪ IMMOLATIONS IN INDIA

Lindsey Harlan

To associate the *satī*, a term referring to a woman who immolates herself on her husband's funeral pyre, with the martyr, a word with indisputably positive valuation in Christianity and other traditions originating in European and Middle Eastern antiquity, is to invite charges of insensitivity from many people engaged in moral discourse outside India and from those opposed to *satī* immolation and worship within India.[1] As Ashis Nandy has shown, educated urban elites as well as feminists in India have been adamant in their condemnation of *satī* immolation, which they view as a horrifying practice and an embarrassing legacy of the Hindu past.[2] It was therefore with trepidation that I accepted an invitation to contemplate the issue of *satī* immolation within the context of a colloquium on martyrdom.

However inconceivable the immolation of living women might be to those of us who do not see *satī*s as venerable or exemplary, it cannot be denied that those who worship *satī*s regard them in a very positive light. For them a *satī* is sacred and divine. This essay proposes to shed further light on ways in which *satī*s are represented and valued by those who hold them to be divinities worthy of veneration, and to reflect on what the concept of *satī* might share with the concept of martyr. Necessarily brief, it cannot consider in a comprehensive way how the *satī* might be equated with or analogized to the martyr. Such a determination would mandate defining "martyr" in terms sufficiently abstract to embrace the term *satī* and a variety of terms from Hinduism as well as other religious traditions.[3] I will devote this essay to considering one aspect of *satī* immolation that I think will be of interest to those concerning themselves in various ways with the notion of martyrdom: the idea that the *satī* who dies on the pyre embodies and affirms truth.

As noted elsewhere in this volume, as well as in the literature on martyrdom, the term "martyr" derives from the Greek and refers to the act of witnessing. So construed, the term implies a witnessing of truth that is in turn witnessed by others. The martyr both sees and illustrates truth. The term can be compared in a limited but fruitful way to the Sanskrit and Hindi term *darśan*, which refers to the acts of seeing, and also being seen, by the divine.[4] Whereas the Christian martyr sees the truth of the divine and his act of martyrdom provides access to that divine truth for others, the *satī*, whose very name is cognate with *sat*, referring to the "real" or the "true," not only sees transcendent truth but also literally embodies it. As we shall see, *sat* is a substance as well as a quality; while burning on the pyre, the *satī* metamorphoses into a divinity whose verity is witnessed by those attending her ritual procession to the pyre and subsequent immolation.[5]

Before detailing the notion that the *satī* embodies and reveals truth, however, it will be useful to gain familiarity with the ethnographic context in which *satī* immolation has recently occurred. The following provides some background on the practice in the state of Rajasthan, where I have conducted fieldwork over the course of the past decade.[6]

Satī Immolation and Rajasthan: A Sketch

Rajasthan is a vast and arid area in northwest India, a land of sand and rocks. It becomes increasingly hot and dusty as one travels westward. Bifurcated by the Aravalli range, its territory has as its westernmost feature the formidable Thar desert, which forms a natural border between India and Pakistan. Much of my work in Rajasthan has focused on the Rajputs, members of a military caste that once ruled most of the kingdoms that were combined to form the state of Rajasthan (literally: "Land of the Kings") after Indian Independence in 1947. The practice of *satī* immolation in Rajasthan is generally, though not exclusively, associated with this group.[7]

The history of Rajasthan is a history of war: Rajput rulers often found themselves defending or expanding their territories. They fought with each other, with tribal groups who resisted domination, and with Muslims who ruled much of the subcontinent during medieval times, but could never bring many Rajput kingdoms under control. Some of the Rajputs living in the twelfth through the sixteenth centuries are frequently represented today as "freedom fighters," who repelled the attacks of Muslim monarchs based in Delhi and its environs.[8]

Some of the most famous *satīs* in India are women who perished on the pyre after their husbands died fighting Muslims. Many Rajasthanis believe that these medieval *satīs*, who followed their husbands in death, glorified their husbands and honored their families, both their *sasurāls* (husband's families) and *pīhars* (natal families). Perishing in flames rather than risk violation by conquerors, such a *satī* preserved her shame (*lāj*) and remained pure. In doing so, she also preserved the honor and integrity of her conjugal family's blood line. The Muslims in the stories about famous *satīs* are often portrayed as exceptionally villainous and lecherous, though women as booty is hardly a concept foreign to Hindu tradition.[9]

Many Rajasthanis believe that women whose husbands did not die on the battlefield were also justified and laudable for dying on their husbands' pyres. Dying as a *satī* proved a wife's commitment to *strīdharma*, a "woman's duty," as well as her love for her departed and his family. Dying as a *satī* assured that she would not be an alluring or lustful widow, one who might tarnish the family's reputation.[10]

During the 1980s, *satī* immolation emerged as a highly charged and politically volatile issue. In 1987, a young Rajput woman named Roop Kanwar burned on her husband's pyre in a village quite near Jaipur, Rajasthan's capital, which is located just a few hours' drive from Delhi. In the weeks following the immolation, as many as 200,000 pilgrims visited the village to pay their respects and seek blessings from Roop Kanwar, whose death was understood to transform her into a *satīmātā*, a benevolent supernatural protectress.[11]

The immolation and subsequent influx of pilgrims offended and angered feminists in Jaipur and Delhi, who organized anti-*satī* demonstrations. These were followed by pro-*satī* demonstrations, attended by well-known politicians and some influential religious leaders. For many of those defending the immolation, the *satī* became emblematic of *Hindutva*, "Hinduness." Clearly, feminist outrage was not solely responsible for catalyzing these pro-*satī*, pro-*Hindutva*, demonstrations. Rather, these demonstrations reflected the anger of many Hindus with the Indian government, which had made *satī* illegal and which had, in their eyes, failed to protect other important Hindu values formerly nurtured by Rajput rulers.[12] Moreover, supporting Hinduness, as it were, the protests implicitly—and sometimes explicitly—contrasted Hinduness with Muslimness. Many Hindus felt that whereas the Constitution protects religious freedom of the Muslim minority, it fails to safeguard the religious freedom of the Hindu majority.[13]

The reaction to Roop Kanwar's death occurred during a time of Hindu-Muslim tensions that slowly built into several years of sporadic and bloody rioting. The culmination was widespread mayhem and bloodletting after Hindus stormed and destroyed a Muslim mosque, which they believed to be situated on the birth site of Rāma, hero of the much beloved Rāmāyaṇa epic and incarnation of the Hindu god Viṣṇu. Suffice it to say, the *satī* became an emblem in the midst of communitarian turmoil.

This is a nutshell version of a very complex controversy, but provides at least rudimentary understanding of the context in which *satī* has been interpreted and analyzed over the past few years and some sense of what is at stake when considering the juxtaposition of the terms *satī* and martyr. To contemplate the relation between the terms, let us reflect directly on the idea that martyrdom involves choice: martyrs choose death rather than embrace what is false. Having done so, we may then turn to examine the *satī* ideal as represented in some Rajasthani folksongs and in one very rich *satī* narrative. These sources shed light on the nature of the *satī*'s presumed choice: the choice of self-sacrifice as an expression of truth.

Witnessing Truth, Choosing Death

Frequently a martyr is someone who dies and who is willing to die, but is also understood as being forced to choose to die, contradictory as that may seem.[14] A martyr defends a principle, a notion of truth, which he or she cannot surrender. The idea that a martyr chooses to defend truth unto death but does not choose death itself makes the martyr heroic and denies the accusation that the martyr embraces suicide, for the martyr's death serves and is effected by a compelling cause.[15] Such a martyr sees no other way to affirm, defend, and propagate truth. Whereas suicide is selfish—it represents a failure of nerve, endurance, or patience and often an inability to go on despite grief, pain, dissatisfaction, or deprivation—martyrdom is selfless.

An example that readily comes to mind is the whisky priest in Graham Greene's *Power and the Glory*. In this novel, the whisky priest is the last priest left in Mexico during an anticlerical purge. He is a terrible priest, an alcoholic with an illegitimate child. He runs from the police because of his fear of execution and therefore regards himself as a coward. He could renounce Catholicism and be spared, but he cannot consider this option, so sure is he of God's damnation and the tortures that await him beyond the grave. His faith in God, his conviction of unworthiness, and his belief that performing mass is God's will keep him a priest and enable him to persevere in his running and preaching. Ultimately, he is shot and pronounced a martyr.

The whisky priest may not be the most pristine martyr—he is certainly no paradigm of virtue—but his story shows how amazing it seems that any human, full of imperfections as humans tend to be, can be a martyr.[16] The human who lives and the martyr who dies are polar opposites. The frailty, the inconstancy, and the selfishness of the human being make the courage of the martyr who dies the perfect, sacrificial death all the more wondrous.

This paradox applies in the case of the *satī*. Many Hindus in Rajasthan praise and venerate women who immolated themselves on their husbands' pyres. Yet *satī* traditions illustrated by legends and songs do not eagerly embrace the idea that a woman can achieve the moral perfection, the utter selflessness, it takes to be a *satī*. There are many narratives in which women who have taken a vow to become a *satī* are doubted, ridiculed, and even reviled. The hostility is surely due in part to the fact that *satī*s are women and women are thought to be even less perfect and less perfectible than men.[17]

To illustrate the ambivalence found in traditions of *satī* veneration, let me contrast two *satī* songs that are quite similar in subject matter but very different in emphasis.[18] These are *rātijagā* (literally, "night-wake" songs) that are sung by women to celebrate auspicious occasions such as birth and marriage. The first song provides a picture of the ideal *satī*, literally, "good woman," who is eager to join her husband on the pyre:

> Buy me a forehead ornament—do it quickly little brother-in-law
> I will follow my husband [as a *satī*]
> Dear younger brother-in-law—yes, O dear little brother-in-law
> Cool the *satī* under a shady banyan tree
>
> Bring me a nose ring—do it quickly . . .
> Buy a necklace—do it quickly . . .
> Buy me bangles—do it quickly . . .
> Buy a saffron-colored sari . . . [and] a blouse piece—do it quickly . . .
> Buy toe-rings—do it quickly . . .[19]

As I have said, this song conveys an ideal picture of an impatient wife hurrying to accompany her husband to the cremation ground. She repeatedly orders her helper to do everything quickly; she cannot wait.

Ideally, there should be no wait whatsoever. In fact, the term often used for such a *satī*, *sahagāminī*, literally, "one who goes [dies] with" [the husband], creates a temporal fiction whereby the woman's death is simultaneous with the husband's.[20] There should be no interval between his death and hers, no break in the togetherness that was symbolically established when the garments of groom and bride were tied together during the marriage ceremony.[21]

In this song, the *satī* is helped by her *devar*, younger brother-in-law. According to popular convention, the *devar* is a wife's closest ally in the family. She spoils him and dotes on him; he adores her and confides in her. Of all the people in the family, except for children, he is the one who will surely miss her the most. Here he is portrayed as dallying—he has lost a brother, now also his friend. The song conveys a difficult moment for the *devar*, who is contrasted with the eager wife awaiting reunion with her husband.

Also worth noting is the fact that the *satī*, preparing to die, demands lots of ornamentation. A *satī* is expected to adorn herself in her very best things before processing to the pyre. She puts on the jewels given her as a bride when she entered her *sasurāl*. Her procession to the pyre confirms her status as wife now and in the future. Ideas about her future vary: she will be reincarnated with him; she will accompany him to heaven; both will be liberated from rebirth by her meritorious sacrifice. In any case, as she leaves this life, she is once again a bride on the margin of marriage. She is entering a new relationship with her husband in some other place, birth, and state.

It is interesting that the *satī* wants the *devar* to buy her jewelry. Either for some reason, perhaps poverty, she lacks these items (she never had them, she no longer has them) or the ones she has are inadequate for such a momentous occasion. The demand for jewelry is a favorite one in women's songs. The jewelry given by parents at the time of wedding indicates the value of the gift (*dān*, i.e., the bride) they are giving the groom and his family. More jewelry, especially that given by the husband, indicates the success the wife has had in earning her husband's affection through loving service and by sacrificing her desires to fulfill his. In short, it is symbolic of her very status as a beloved and dutiful wife—a *pativratā*—one who has sworn (literally, taken a vow, *vrat*) to protect and serve her husband (*pati*).

Whereas the jewelry listed in the song evokes an image of marital union, the clothing evokes an image of renunciation. Brides wear red; this *satī* demands saffron, the color worn by many ascetics and by warriors who know they are entering a battle in which they are sure to perish. The saffron color conveys the idea that the *satī* detaches herself from all social responsibilities in order to die with her husband.[22]

The saffron-donning hero who dies in battle is often described as a sacrificial goat in the sacrifice of battle; the *satī*'s immolation is often called a *balidān*, a "gift (*dān*) of a sacrificial victim (*bali*)."[23] Thus, like an ascetic, she renounces social ties to pursue a higher cause; like a warrior facing unbeatable odds, she renounces as an immediate prelude to death.

Here I might note that the cremation ceremony is itself an act of sacrifice. The ritual, which is Vedic in origin, reenacts the sacrifice of the primal man Puruṣa, which creates the cosmos.[24] The joint cremation of the *satī* and her husband is thus a double sacrifice. The *satī* is not only a sacrifice, she is also her husband's sacrificer. Ideally, she lights the flame. In one legendary instance, the *satī* makes herself an oblation on her husband's funeral fire. Having placed her husband's body on a pyre, she cuts her body into twenty-four bloody bits, which she offers as oblations on the sacrifice, combining the role of sacrificer and victim.[25]

The actions of this legendary *satī*, who carves herself up, and of the song's *satī*, who chooses saffron clothing, illustrate the understanding of the *satī* as agent and victim, one who sacrifices and one sacrificed (*bali*). As a wife, the *satī* wanted her husband to live and aspired to fulfill her duty to nurture her husband; she did not wish to end up dying after him or "with" him, for that matter. Yet forced by circumstance, she chooses the flames or even cuts herself up as she burns her flesh on the flame.

Now let us focus for a moment on the refrain. The *satī*'s instructions to her brother-in-law are repeatedly punctuated by the singers' instruction to "cool the *satī* under a shady banyan tree." A *satī* is thought to become increasingly hot as she prepares to die. Through the many self-sacrificial actions she performed as a devoted wife, she has built up *sat* (meaning, as we have seen, both "truth" and "goodness"), which inheres in the blood. This *sat*, as it accumulates, acts like a fuel that generates heat and fervor—the fervor to engage in more sacrificial acts and so to accumulate more *sat*. When the *sat*-saturated woman learns of her husband's death, the theory goes, the *sat* ignites a fire inside, which eventually causes her body to ignite on the funeral pyre. Thus, although the pyre is often lit by a relative, usually the son, the *satī*'s fire is thought to consume the bodies of husband and wife and to unite husband and wife through the commingling of ashes.

The command to "cool the *satī* under a shady banyan tree" could mean that the *satī* is to be cooled and comforted en route to the pyre.

Or it could mean that she is to be bathed under the tree. This second possibility is given support by the fact that the term used, *sīlāo*, means both cool and dampen. Moreover, banyan trees are often found near tanks where bathing occurs. Yet another possibility is that the cooling refers not to the *satī* before she dies, but to the *satī* as she is represented in an icon after she dies. *Satī* memorial stelai, like those of heroes and other venerated ancestors, are often placed under shady trees—a gesture of consideration and perhaps purification. The stone, infused with sanctity, is already hot with *sat*; it should be cooled and protected from the brutal Rajasthani sun.

The manifestation of *sat* as flames is seen as a natural consequence of previous virtuous actions, but this does not mean that the *satī* is understood as having no choice as to whether she will die a *satī*. Rather, the *satī* takes a vow that indicates her intention to die as a *satī*. At this point, the *sat* inside her generates the power to perform miracles: she can confer blessings to petitioners or curse and destroy those who doubt her ability to die a *satī* or would try to interfere with her actions.

Satī lore abounds in stories about people who dispute the ability of women to decide to become *satīs* or who question the propriety of allowing women to decide to become *satīs*. These stories depict society as being willing to accept the idea of *satī*, in general, but being unwilling to believe that individual women could possibly perfect themselves and literally burn with truth. Before examining one such story in detail, let me pause for a moment to recite the opening verses of another song, one that sounds very similar to the eager *satī* song we just heard but whose message is very different.

Satīmātā, take a forehead ornament and wear it.
O take a forehead ornament and wear it.
Why the delay for the forehead ornament, Satīmātā? [i.e., hurry up!]
Your husband's litter is waiting under the balcony.
Your young man's litter is waiting under the balcony.
Waiting under the balcony, waiting under the balcony windows.

O Satīmātā, take your earrings and wear them.
O Satīmātā, take your earrings and wear them.
Why the delay for the earrings, Satīmātā?
Your husband's litter is waiting under the balcony . . .

O Satīmātā, take your nose ring and wear it.
O Satīmātā, take your nose ring and wear it.
Why the delay for the nose ring . . .[26]

In this song a *satī* is being aided by anonymous people, presumably members of her *sasurāl*. Here eagerness characterizes not the *satī* but these other people who feel the *satī* simply is not going fast enough for their taste. Is she just slow and deliberate or is she dallying? They repeatedly ask, "Why the delay?"

The song seems to express anxiety that this "satīmātā" won't carry out her vow and so will not turn out to be a satīmātā after all. If she fails to die on the pyre, her *vrat* could not have been an expression of *sat* but of other things: pride, stupidity, or insincerity. This kind of failure would reflect badly on her and on her family.

The hurrying along of this *satī* gives one the impression that the *satī* is being pressured. This is interesting because ideally the *satī* should not be pressured. A woman who dies for any reason besides loyalty to the husband (and by extension his family and his village) is not considered a *satī*: her death is suicide. While a genuine *satī* could not be pressured into dying because death is her decision, the logic goes, this *satī*, who is in fact being worshiped as a *satī* as her song is being sung, is being doubted. The song affirms that she is a *satī* who is worshiped yet expresses the worry that attends the *satī*'s transformation. Can this woman really be a *satī*?

The question arises in story and song again and again, and while it is inevitably answered in the affirmative, it shows how dubious the *satī*'s *vrat* strikes people, including and perhaps especially, those who know her. Death by fire is just too difficult to imagine; how can any woman who is known manage to go through that? The narratives do not doubt the existence of *satī*s, in general, but do question the existence of *satī*s in particular.

It should be mentioned that the same suspicion does not occur in narratives about great heroes who die in battle and are worshiped as supernatural protectors. In such narratives, saffron-donning heroes who know they are going to die in battle—they are facing unbeatable odds— are not interrogated. In some songs, various relatives try to stop a hero from riding off to war, but they do not doubt his ability to succeed at dying. They are all too confident that the hero can go forth and die a hero's death. Although heroes and *satī*s are worshiped as natural counterparts—many hero stelai are also *satī* stelai, the reunited husband and wife (or wives) appearing together—the heroes, sons of the lineage, are portrayed as accepted from the moment they decide to go to war, whereas wives who take vows to become *satī*s may well have to earn acceptance by demonstrating supernatural power.[27]

Recently, I translated a rather long *satī* story that is a virtual chronicle of anxiety and doubt. In the story of Godāvarī, a musical miniepic of sorts, people worry that Godāvarī, a village woman who has taken a vow to die as a *satī*, will fail to die on the pyre.[28] Her mother-in-law, one of the many who does not believe she can succeed, refuses to unlock the doors to their house so that Godāvarī can put on her fine clothes and jewelry. Godāvarī has to call on her ally Sūraj, the Sun, to help her. He breaks the lock with a mighty sunbeam.

Godāvarī's neighbors, too, disbelieve her. One remarks that just the other day he saw her burn her finger when she was making bread and "she jumped like a baby camel." The villagers contrive plot after plot to try to stop her from going to her husband's pyre because they are worried that she might get as far as jumping into the flames before losing her nerve. Then "burned and half burned," she would run through the village setting everything on fire.[29]

The plots all end in failure. When the villagers bring Godāvarī's friend to dissuade her from trying to become a *satī*, Godāvarī curses the friend to be a leper: immediately the girl's toes and fingers fall off and the remaining stumps shrivel up like little peanuts. When the village lord (*ṭhākur*) tries to stop her, she turns him into a babbling idiot: his tongue grows "thick as a tree trunk" and he cannot pronounce anything. There are more such episodes. Each curse that comes true demonstrates Godāvarī's possession of *sat* to a skeptical crowd. Finally, the villagers simply give up and let her go to the pyre, where she does manage to die without losing her nerve.

The plots serve not only to demonstrate the reservations the villagers have about according Godāvarī *satī* status, but also to exonerate the villagers from allowing Godāvarī to become a *satī*, which would make their village illustrious. Burning with *sat*, Godāvarī is simply too hot to handle. When she does succeed, they are blameless.

The question of blame arises specifically in the story. The villagers are not worried about their consciences, particularly; they are worried that the police will beat them when Godāvarī's death becomes known.[30] Thus, the many plots they hatch serve as protests, but it seems to me that the villagers protest too much. They do not believe Godāvarī can become a *satī*—"burned and half burned she'll set the town on fire"— but if she does become a *satī*, let it be known that death was the *satī's* choice: no one helped her in the least. It was all her idea.

This is not to say that women who die on their husbands' pyres have, in fact, had freedom of choice. Women who are worshiped as *satī*s,

however, are deemed by devotees to have chosen to immolate themselves because they could not live without their husbands. Most *satīs*
are ancestral *satīs*—they are venerated by descendants. Devotees wor-
shiping their own *satīs* may be especially skeptical of nonancestral *satīs*.
Thus, for example, there were many Rajputs I knew who venerated
their ancestral *satīs* but who rejected the notion that Roop Kanwar was
in fact a *satī*. Some said she was drugged; some said she was pushed;
some said she was unfaithful to her husband before he died, so she could
not have become a *satī*, whether or not she went to the pyre of her
own free will. Such accounts portray Roop Kanwar's death as murder
or suicide, not as a consequence of the manifestation of *sat*.

Being a *satī*, then, is to have accumulated *sat*—truth/goodness/virtue—
and to have expressed this *sat* by enacting the self-sacrificing *satī* scenario.
The *satī*'s vow is thought to transform her into a supernatural being with
great power. Godāvarī, like the heroines in many *satī* stories, exercises
this power by cursing people who doubt her. According to a rumor that
circulated widely around Rajasthan in the months after Roop Kanwar's
death, Roop Kanwar demonstrated her power when her *sat* burned the
hand of someone who tried to prevent her from dying. The stories about
Godāvarī and Roop Kanwar illustrate how *satīs* are understood not only
as choosing to die as *satīs* but also as persisting in their quests to die as
satīs, when living no longer seems an option.

In sum, devotees who worship a given *satī* understand that *satī* as an
incarnation or embodiment of truth and a self-sacrificial victim and agent
of that truth. Like the martyr, the *satī* has no choice, it seems, but to
choose death. That a woman could make such a choice is hard to
believe—and the continuing tradition of *satī* veneration makes that perfectly clear.

Notes

1. Even the term "martyr" is positive only for those who have faith in the
possibility of martyrdom and in the person being accorded that status. As Arthur
Droge and James Tabor have so succinctly stated the matter: "Whether one is
a 'martyr' or a 'fanatic,' a 'hero' or a 'fool' is a matter of commitment." See
A Noble Death: Suicide and Martyrdom among Christians and Jews in Antiquity
(San Francisco: HarperSanFrancisco, 1992), 4.

2. Ashis Nandy, "Sati as Profit versus Sati as a Spectacle: The Public Debate
on Roop Kanwar's Death," in *Sati, the Blessing and the Curse*, ed. John Stratton
Hawley (New York: Oxford University Press, 1995), 131–49.

3. For informative discussion of the pitfalls inherent in employing the term
comparatively, see Droge and Tabor, *A Noble Death*, 3–4. On related notions

in Hinduism, see Lindsey Harlan, *The Goddesses' Henchmen* (New York: Oxford University Press, in press).

4. See Diana Eck, *Darśan: Seeing the Divine Image in India*, 2nd rev. ed. (Chambersburg, Pa.: Anima Press, 1985).

5. For a more elaborate discussion of *sat* and *satī* ritual, see Lindsey Harlan, "Perfection and Devotion: Sati Tradition in Rajasthan," in *Sati, the Blessing and the Curse*, 79–99.

6. On Rajasthan generally, see also Lindsey Harlan, *Religion and Rajput Women: The Ethic of Protection in Contemporary Narratives* (Berkeley: University of California Press, 1992). For a thorough introduction to Rajasthan, see *The Idea of Rajasthan: Explorations in Regional Identity*, 2 vols., ed. Karine Schomer et al. (Manohar: New Delhi, 1994).

7. See Lindsey Harlan, *Religion and Rajput Women*, and "The Story of Godāvarī: Satī Veneration in Rajasthan," in *Devī: Goddesses of India*, ed. John Stratton Hawley (Berkeley: University of California Press, 1996), 227–49. On *satī* and martial groups throughout India, see Romila Thapar, "In History," *Seminar* 342, "Satī: A Symposium on Widow Immolation and It's Social Context" (February 1988): 14–19.

8. On heroes as freedom-fighters, see Lindsey Harlan, "Tale of a Headless Warrior: Kalaji Rathor," paper delivered at the 26th Annual Conference on South Asia, Oct. 17, 1997 and also *The Goddesses' Henchmen*.

9. According to the *Mānavadharmaśāstra*, written at the beginning of the Common Era, the abduction of women is a legitimate form of marriage. For a recent translation of the relevant passage (5.3.1), see *Textual Sources for the Study of Hinduism*, ed. Wendy Doniger O'Flaherty (Chicago: University of Chicago Press, 1990), 103.

10. The word *raṇḍ*, from which the English "randy" is derived, means both widow and prostitute.

11. For more comprehensive discussion of this event, see the introduction and various essays in *Sati, the Blessing and the Curse*. See also Hawley's essay, "Hinduism: Satī and Its Defenders," in *Fundamentalism and Gender*, ed. John Stratton Hawley (New York: Oxford University Press, 1994), 79–110.

12. For discussion of the emblematic character of the *satī*, see Lindsey Harlan, "The Story of Godāvarī," in *Devī: Goddesses of India*; Veena Talwar Oldenberg, "The Continuing Invention of Sati Tradition," in *Sati, the Blessing and the Curse*, 170, as well as her essay "The Roop Kanwar Case: Feminist Responses," ibid., 110. Vivid usage of the *satī* as a summarizing symbol is found in Kalyan Singh Kalvi's comment that the issue of *satī* functions to bind together "Motherland, religion, and woman," *India Today*, October 31, 1987, 20, quoted in *Sati, the Blessing and the Curse*, 177.

13. The Roop Kanwar case was often compared to the case of the Muslim woman Shah Bano, who was divorced and abandoned by her husband. Some Hindu supporters of *satī* immolation said that the Hindu practice should be protected from government interference as should the Muslim practice of allowing a man to divorce his wife without providing support. For recent

discussions of the comparison, see three articles from *Sati, the Blessing and the Curse*: Veena Talwar Oldenberg, "The Roop Kanwar Case," 122–23; Ashis Nandy, "Sati as Profit versus Sati as a Spectacle," 142–43; and John Stratton Hawley's "Afterword," 177. See also Peter Awn, "Indian Islam: The Shah Bano Affair," in *Fundamentalism and Gender*, 63–78.

14. The characterization conflates the first two sorts of martyrdom in Arthur Droge and James Tabor's typology. Focusing primarily on the Judeo-Christian tradition, they say, "The martyrs are portrayed as going to their death in one of three ways: either as a result of being sought out, by deliberately volunteering, or by actually taking their own lives," *A Noble Death*, 156. A similar conflation is noted elsewhere in their text: see the discussion of the ambiguous nature of Perpetua's martyrdom, 2.

15. Extensive discussion of the oppositional nature of the categories "martyr" and "suicide" is found in Arthur Droge and James Tabor, *A Noble Death*.

16. For a fine example of sinfulness and noble/heroic death, see Droge and Tabor, *A Noble Death*, 87.

17. In much of Indian religious tradition, women are seen as less spiritually inclined and able than men. Many traditions require women to be reborn as a man before achieving great spiritual progress. For more extensive discussion of the imperfectibility of women and the idea of the *sati*, see Lindsey Harlan, "The Story of Godāvarī."

18. General treatment of these songs also appears in Lindsey Harlan, "Women's Songs for Auspicious Occasions," Donald Lopez, ed., *The Religions of India in Practice* (Princeton: Princeton University Press, 1995), 269–80.

19. Ibid., 271–72.

20. According to the Vedic concept of death, death is not complete until the skull is broken during the funeral and the immaterial self is allowed to depart. This concept, which does not necessarily comport with popular notions of death, brings the deaths of husband and wife much closer together. On death ritual and the Vedas, see Jonathan Parry, "Sacrificial Death and the Necrophagous Ascetic," in *Death and the Regeneration of Life*, ed. Maurice Bloch and Jonathan Parry (Cambridge: Cambridge University Press, 1982), 74–110, and David Knipe, "Sapiṇḍīkaraṇa: The Hindu Rite of Entry into Heaven," in *Religious Encounters with Death: Insights from the History and Anthropology of Religion*, ed. E. Reynolds and E. H. Waugh (University Park, Pa.: Pennsylvania State University Press, 1977), 111–24.

21. Because the *sati* escapes widowhood and joins her husband in the afterlife, she is expected to die with a happy countenance. The absence of tears is considered one of the telling indications of true *sati* status. For a compelling analysis of the tendency to omit reference to pain in discussions of *sati* immolation, see Rajeshwari Sundar Rajan, "The Subject of Satī: Pain and Death in Contemporary Discourse on Satī," *Yale Journal of Criticism* 3:2 (1990): 1–23.

22. The symbolic nexus between social renunciation and death is vivid in India. Male renouncers or *sannyāsīs* cremate an effigy of themselves to indicate their death to society. Some *sannyāsīs* frequent cremation grounds and

rub themselves with the ash of cremation fires. As *satīs* bent on self-immolation, women renounce their responsibilities as family members, including motherhood. The question of whether a pregnant woman should immolate herself has always been controversial. There are many stories of women cutting babies out of their wombs before throwing themselves on the pyre. There are also stories of pregnant women immolating themselves and even of women sacrificing their children.

23. To be worshiped, heroes must die in battle. Heroes who die in bed are admired and honored, but they do not tend to generate cultic followings. See Harlan, *The Goddesses' Henchmen.*

24. For detailed analysis of death and sacrifice, see Jonathan P. Parry, *Death in Banaras* (Cambridge: Cambridge University Press, 1994) and Knipe, "Sapiṇḍīkaraṇa."

25. See Harlan, *The Goddesses' Henchmen* and "Tale of a Headless Warrior."

26. See Harlan, "Women's Songs for Auspicious Occasions," 272–73.

27. Harlan, *The Goddesses' Henchmen.*

28. Harlan, "The Story of Godāvarī."

29. The image is reminiscent of the scene in the *Rāmāyaṇa*: Hanumān sets Lanka on fire with his tail.

30. Under Indian law, it is a crime to aid a woman intent on becoming a *satī*. The story does not give many clues as to the time period in which the events it narrates are supposed to have occurred. There are various references to contemporary phenomena, including disco music, but these may well be anachronisms. See Harlan, "The Story of Godāvarī."

NINE

SELF-SACRIFICE AS TRUTH IN INDIA

D. Dennis Hudson

On January 30, 1948, in Delhi, a young Hindu deeply offended by the work of Mohandas Karamachand Gandhi for peace and unity between Muslims and Hindus shot him. M. K. Gandhi died with the name of Ram on his lips. If we take seriously the statements he had made a few days earlier, he died believing that Ram willed his death, because he believed that Ram was his only protector in the midst of India's violence.[1] For over forty years he had lived as a witness to *ahimsa*, to the desire not to cause injury, a desire he believed to be both grounded on truth and the means to it. Yet it appears that Ram had let him die while he clung to him as the truth, whose power acts through an absence—the absence of the ego's desire to injure anyone, including itself.

Gandhi was a martyr to *satya*, which is "truth," or "true being," or "being true," whose power he believed to be active and transformative. Truth's power radiates through the person who participates in it by eliminating the personal ego-centered passion that distorts it. Truth is God whom Gandhi called Ram. To serve Ram as a pure conduit for his gracious power in the middle of India's violent political life, Gandhi had tried for years to reduce himself to "zero." As he stated at the end of his serialized autobiography in 1925, when he was fifty-six years old, "I must reduce myself to zero. So long as a man does not of his own free will put himself last among his fellow creatures, there is no salvation for him. *Ahimsa* is the farthest limit of humility."[2]

M. K. Gandhi represented an ancient mode of Indian thought about martyrdom that he applied to modern society, and this chapter will ex-

plore some of its sources. We shall begin with a story that Gandhi himself said had been highly influential in his life.

At the age of twelve, sometime around 1881, he saw a play in his
hometown about the ancient legendary king Harischandra. At the age
of fifty-six, he wrote about it:

> This play—*Harishchandra*—captured my heart. I could never be tired
> of seeing it. But how often should I be permitted to go? It haunted me
> and I must have acted *Harishchandra* to myself times without number.
> "Why should not all be truthful like Harishchandra?" was the question
> I asked myself day and night. To follow truth and to go through all the
> ordeals Harishchandra went through was the one ideal it inspired in
> me. I literally believed in the story of Harishchandra. The thought of it
> all often made me weep.[3]

Although by fifty-six he thought that Harischandra must have been
legendary, still he was sure that if he read that play again it would move
him in the same way. In my judgment, that story provides the pattern
that guided Gandhi's understanding of himself as it developed in South
Africa through the philosophy and strategy of *satyagraha*. To understand
him, therefore, let us consider the story of Harischandra.

The Story of Harischandra

Harischandra was a righteous king in an earlier more perfect age who
fulfilled his duties perfectly so that his kingdom prospered.[4] Those duties
were to give gifts to Brahmins who fulfill vows, to protect his subjects
who live in fear, and to make war on his enemies. The story begins
with the first duty (gifts to Brahmins performing vows), it ends with
the second duty (protection of his subjects), and illustrates throughout
the third duty (to make war on his enemies). In this case, the enemy is
the king's own sense of "my" and "mine."

One day while hunting deer, Harischandra heard a woman's voice
yelling for help. Since his duty was to protect, he rushed to her aid.
Instead of a woman he found the great Brahmin sage Vishvamitra; he
was just about to seize Knowledge by fulfilling a vow of asceticism,
and it was Knowledge who had cried out. At that moment a demon,
who felt threatened by Vishvamitra's near grasp of Knowledge, seized
this opportunity to thwart the sage by entering into the king and cre-
ating furious anger within him toward the ascetic. The possessed
Harischandra threatened to kill Vishvamitra. The sage himself then
became enraged, and because he had thereby lost control of himself,

Knowledge slipped out of his grip. She and the demon who had possessed the king then vanished.

Now free of the demon and its anger, Harischandra was left prostrate before Vishvamitra, pleading for him not to be angry, for he had not really left the path of righteousness. "If you are truly righteous," Vishvamitra said, "then give me a gift, for I am a Brahmin." Harischandra joyously responded, "Whatever you ask, whatever is in my power to give, is as if already given." Vishvamitra said, "I accept your offer. You must also give me the fee for the sacrifice which I shall make for you." Harischandra promised. Only then did the ascetic name the gift the king had already agreed to give: "Whatever you have, excepting your wife, your son, and your own body, give to me. Keep nothing else." The king said of course, "As you have ordered, so shall it be."

Harischandra had now given away his kingdom and his wealth to Vishvamitra, so Vishvamitra ordered him to dress in bark cloth and leave the kingdom with his wife and son. Yet as they were leaving, Vishvamitra blocked their way and said, "Where are you going? You have still not given me the fee for the sacrifice." Now that he had no resources at all, the king promised to give him the fee in one month. Lamented by the kingdom, he then left with his queen and the prince.

On the last day of the month, the king, queen, and prince entered Benares, where they found Vishvamitra waiting for his fee. Harischandra begged for half a day more and out of despair thought of suicide. His wife, however, urged him to remain faithful to his word, because his only protection now was righteousness. Since she had borne a son, she was already fulfilled, so now it was his turn. To enable him to be fulfilled by being true to his promise as king, she said, "Sell me and give the money as the fee." With excruciating agony, Harischandra agreed. He then sold her to a Brahmin. But when her new owner dragged her away by the hair, their son, the prince, clung to her, so the Brahmin had to buy the boy as well.

Left grieving for wife and son, Harischandra still did not have enough money for the fee, so he decided to sell himself into slavery and use the money to keep his word. Thereupon the god named Dharma, or Righteousness, took the form of a polluted executioner and corpse-burner, appeared before Harischandra, and offered to buy him. But Harischandra refused to sell himself to a corpse-burner, because it was unrighteous for a royal person to be a slave to an untouchable. Vishvamitra then appeared and demanded the fee, so Harischandra fell at his feet, begged for mercy, and offered himself as slave to Vishvamitra. "Whatever you command," he said, "I shall do. I shall keep only your welfare and comfort in my mind." Vishvamitra took him as his slave and then turned around and sold him to the corpse-burner. Nevertheless, the enslaved king remained true to his word and merely replied, "As you command."

Now destitute and suffering, Harischandra spent an anguished year working at cremation pyres, thinking only of his son and wife, until dementia erased even that memory. Then one day, his wife appeared at the cremation ground with the body of their son for burning. When they recognized each other they realized with horror that not only was the prince dead, but also the queen was the wife of an enslaved and untouchable corpse-burner. Harischandra was so grieved that he decided to mount the pyre himself and burn with his son's body; his anguish had erased any concern in him for the sin such an act would generate. The queen decided to join him. But before they mounted the pyre, they stood before it to pray to the gods who dwell deep within the human heart—and suddenly the gods Indra and Dharma and others appeared with Vishvamitra before them.

First, the god Dharma spoke. He said that Harischandra's self-control, patience, and truth were so pure that he and his wife and son could now ascend directly to heaven. Yet Harischandra was a slave and, just as a slave should, he replied that he could not ascend to heaven without the permission of his corpse-burning master. The god Dharma then revealed himself to be that corpse-burner, which meant that Harischandra was the slave of Dharma as he had been all along.

Next, Indra, the king of the gods, spoke. He urged Harischandra to ascend to the highest heaven suitable to such a righteous king. Still, the slave of Dharma remained true to his royal duties and replied that people in his kingdom were grieving because of his absence; they depended on him and were devoted to him, and therefore he could not abandon them. "O king of the gods," he said, "if they go to heaven with me, then I shall go; otherwise I shall go to hell with them. Whatever good deeds I have performed, I have performed because of them. I cannot abandon them now because of mere desire for heaven. Whatever merit I have gained by deeds or prayer or alms, belongs to them as well as to me." That final self-sacrificing faithfulness to the truth of his royal being ends the story, for it caused Harischandra, his queen, the crown prince, and all their subjects to ascend to heaven, where they now dwell in a city surrounded by high walls and ramparts.

As M. K. Gandhi told us, that story had been deeply important to him from the age of twelve. How does it illuminate his life? I think it contains four patterns of thought salient to premodern Indian civilization that helped shape his career as a martyr.

We first learn from the story that a royal person consists of three bodies: the king, the queen, and the prince, with the kingdom of subjects as a fourth. Those four "bodies" constitute a single whole. The prince is the king reborn through the queen, for as ancient poets said, the husband's wife becomes his "mother" through the birth of himself as son; thus, when the husband-father looks at his son, it is as if he looks in a mirror and sees himself. When, in *Mahabharata* 1.68, Sakuntala argued with the emperor Duhsanta about the fact that her son was his, which he pretended not to believe, she said: "A son, the wise say, is the man himself born from himself; therefore a man will look upon the mother of his son as his own mother. The son born from his wife is as a man's face in a mirror; and looking at him brings as much joy to a father as finding heaven brings to a saint."[5]

That complex notion of a person explains why Vishvamitra banished all three from the kingdom and not only Harischandra. It also explains why in the course of the story, Harischandra had to be stripped of all the "bodies" that fed his ordinary ego-centered sense of "I," "My," and "Mine." In order for the power of true being to redeem the whole person in all four "bodies," Harischandra had to be reduced to "zero."

Following from that lesson is the second, that the excruciating pain felt by the king when he sold his wife and then his son is the pain that is felt when one part of that whole person dismembers itself for the sake of itself, and, in the long run, for the sake of the others. As the queen argued to Harischandra, she could be sold because she had already fulfilled herself by giving birth to the prince; she had already become her husband's "mother" by giving birth to the continuation of his patrilineage. The little prince clung to her because he, as Harischandra's son, belonged to her as the mirror image of her husband. Nevertheless, one-third of that whole remained unfulfilled, namely, the king, who could not be fulfilled, except by being true to his royal role and nature. Sakuntala made that argument about truth to the emperor Duhsanta as her final and most persuasive point: "There is no Law higher than truth, nothing excels truth; and no evil is bitterer on earth than a lie. Truth, O king, is the supreme Brahman, truth is the sovereign covenant. Do not forsake your covenant, king, the truth shall be your alliance."[6]

The third lesson is that conscious intent is the factor crucial to being true. To keep his promise, Harischandra had to be true to his nature as king, which meant that as long as he was a free actor he could not raise the money for his fee by intentionally enslaving himself to an untouchable corpse-burner, although he could enslave himself to a Brahmin. Yet once he had become the Brahmin's slave, he had to remain true to the intent he voiced when he offered himself—"Whatever you command me I shall do"—and obediently became the untouchable's slave, despite the fact that as a free actor he was forbidden to choose that solution. His intent was righteous even when the change in contexts resulted in a conflict with the letter of the law. That pure intent was sustained even when he and his wife stood before their son's cremation pyre in the midst of the most degraded and polluting setting with a sinful action in mind, for in that defiled external context they turned inward to the gods inside their own hearts. Turning to the true being at the center of their own consciousness while standing in that highly polluting context was apparently such a powerful act that it caused the gods to appear before them.

The fourth lesson, then, is that power emanates from a person who persists in being true to a standard of self-giving that transcends even the gods. Even after the royal whole of king, queen, and prince had been restored, Harischandra would not go to heaven without the permission of his untouchable master. And when that master turned out to be the god Dharma himself, Harischandra would not go to heaven without his subjects, for his salvation was their salvation; they shared a single "body" because kings are kings only because they have subjects. As the story reveals, ritual and political leaders like kings, who pursue truth through faithful self-sacrifice, will produce concrete social and political benefits for the realm.

To my mind, these patterns of thought account for much of Gandhi's "experiments with truth," as he called his career. The legendary Harischandra lived in a more perfect age in the past, but, as an excerpt from a writing of his from 1925 reveals, Gandhi found his example relevant to this much less perfect age of "history." The following statement can be read as Gandhi's appropriation of Harischandra's self-sacrificing persistence in truth as a means to bring his subjects to a "heavenly realm":

> The spiritual weapon of self-purification, intangible as it seems, is the most potent means of revolutionizing one's environment and loosening external shackles. It works subtly and invisibly; it is an intense process though it might often seem a weary and long-drawn process, it is the straightest way to liberation, the surest and quickest and no effort can be too great for it. What it requires is faith—an unshakable mountain-like faith that flinches from nothing.[7]

Gandhi's remarkable career—in which he included his wife and sons in his "experiments with truth," as if they were extensions of himself or parts of a single whole—resembles a modern Harischandra. Unlike the king who did not calculate the power his truthful self-sacrifice would generate, however, Gandhi consciously believed that persistence in truth by means of self-sacrificing noninjury would purify the realm through the power of truth itself. The basis for his belief, it appears, is the ancient South Asian idea of the person as a collective whole.

The Sacrifice of the Primordial Person

An early paradigm for that idea appears in the poems of the vedic fire sacrifice collected in the Rig Veda about 1000 B.C.E. or earlier. The highly influential poem called "Praise of the Person" (*Purusa-sukta*) portrays God or the Person as a collective whole. God as primordial Person is the Father who is also the Mother through whom he becomes the Son.[8] The poem encapsulates fundamental ideas of the fire sacrifice and has remained to this day basic to much Hindu worship. Following the lead of later interpretations, for example the *Bhagavad-gita* (13–16) (a text that Gandhi considered his "mother") and the accounts of cosmogony in the *Bhagavata Purana* (2–3), we may understand its cryptic outline of the way our universe of space and time begins and operates this way.[9]

The Person of true being who is omniscient, omnipotent, and omnipresent stretches out to make heaven and earth, and then populates heaven with *devas* or gods. At this "moment," earth is neither populated nor manifest and there is no chronological time. To populate earth and make time, the primordial Person produces a female womb which is matter. He inseminates that uterine matter and gestates the "seed" into himself as Son. Since he is compounded of the nonmaterial Father and the material Mother, the Son is the primordial Person in a slightly less "true" mode.

The primordial Person then sponsors a fire-sacrifice on earth. He has the *devas* serve as priests and gives himself as Son to be the victim. Accordingly, the priestly *devas* suffocate the Son, dismember him, and cook his body parts in the fire, which transforms them into the manifest earthly realm of directional space and chronological time: into the sun and moon to measure time, into heaven, atmosphere, earth, and the four directions to measure space, into wilderness and civilization, into wild and domestic animals, into the four classes of humans, and into the words, poems, and actions of sacrificial ceremonies that sustain that realm. Since he is now the complex and ever-moving unity of space and time, the Son is the primordial Person in an even less "true" mode.

According to that view, the universe exists because the Father gives birth to himself through the Mother as Son, and then sacrifices the Son to himself through himself as the rites of the fire. Consequently, all creatures are transformations of the Son, tiny replicas of him existing inside his own reorganized and ever-moving body. Among such beings, however, we humans are more like the Son than any others and are envied even by the gods. Yet we, too, live inside space and time as subjects of the continuous sacrificial process that the sun and the moon measure, for it is chronological time that gives us birth, sustains us, and eats us up, only to give us birth again somewhere in the cosmos. Wandering by means of death from birth to birth normally lasts as long as the Son lasts in the transformed mode of manifest space and time.

There is, however, a way to transcend that wandering. Through the knowledge (*veda*) that emerges with the primordial sacrifice of the Son, humans may participate in the true being of the Father and Mother even while recycling inside the Son. Those who know the nature of reality know that if they identify themselves with the Son in his cosmic wholeness, they will become more "true," because the Son is a "truer" version of the Father than they. And the degree to which they participate in the Father's mode of being, which is unchanging and unlimited, is the degree to which they will be beyond the limits of chronological time and directional space.

How does one identify with the Son? There are various methods, but an important one is to imitate the Son's act of giving himself away as victim in order that everything, including himself, may exist. In Gandhi's terms, it is to reduce oneself to "zero," to become "empty" (*sunya*). An "emptied" person allows the primordial Father's true being to emerge through him into those around him, a process that Gandhi encoded in the name, "the grasping of truth" (*satyagraha*), which he coined for the discipline of nonviolence (*ahimsa*) he had developed in South Africa. The truly "emptied" person eventually will attain the true being of the Father. As Gandhi put it in 1925, "What I want to achieve—what I have been striving and pining to achieve these thirty years—is self-realization, to see God face to face, to attain *Moksha*."[10] Emancipation, or Moksha, is freedom from entanglement in the Son's manifest and changing body, and eternal participation with the Mother in the unchanging and unmanifest body of the Father.

Stories of King Sibi

The theme of a royal person who, like Harischandra, voluntarily gives himself away to others appears repeatedly in Indian stories. There is, for example, the story of Harischandra's father-in-law, king Sibi, in

Mahabharata 3.131.[11] While sitting on his throne one day, a dove flew onto king Sibi's lap. He was seeking refuge from a hawk in hot pursuit. The hawk demanded the dove as his food, but the king refused to give it because the dove had taken refuge in him, and a king's duty is to protect his fearful subjects. The hawk responded that he had been fashioned to eat doves, and that if he did not eat, he would starve, and his wife and son would perish. By protecting the dove, the king would kill many.

King Sibi was caught between his royal duty to protect his subjects and his royal duty to feed them. He resolved the dilemma by taking the place of the dove and feeding his own flesh to the hawk. Scales were brought and the dove was placed on one side. The king lopped off a piece of his own flesh and placed it on the other side to balance the dove. Yet the scale would not balance, and repeatedly he cut off pieces of himself. Only when he climbed into the scale entirely did it balance. As in the case of Harischandra, king Sibi's faithfulness to his duty—his truthfulness—turned out to be his power. The hawk then revealed himself to be Indra, king of the gods, and the dove revealed himself to be Agni, the vedic fire. They had been testing Sibi to see if his glory was greater than Indra's, and it was.

The story repeats the sacrifice of the primordial Person as it was reenacted by the patron of the vedic rites based on the "Hymn of the Person." Just as the patron employed priests to pour various substances representing himself into the fire to feed the gods represented by their king Indra, so too king Sibi offered pieces of his own body to feed the hawk, who was Indra, by means of the dove, who was the fire.

The Buddhists also told the Sibi story, but removed it some distance from the vedic fire sacrifice while keeping the theme of sacrificial feeding. In place of the vedic fire, the Buddhists put purity of intent; in place of the duty to protect, they put the delight in giving oneself to others; and in place of the renewal of the giver's personhood, they put new insight. True being, the story says, is true seeing, which is gained through true giving. When a Buddhist gives food to worthy others before eating, he or she imitates in a small way the future Buddha (*bodhisattva*), whose great acts of giving over many births generated the merit needed to produce the true insight that made him the Sakyamuni Buddha. One's food, it appears, represents one's body.

According to the "Sivi-Jataka" of the *Jataka*, or birth-story, collection, the *bodhisattva* was once born as king Sibi, renowned for his giving.[12] On a full moon day, when worthy persons are to be ritually fed, king Sibi sat thinking that he would like to give something of himself. He resolved to give whatever was asked of him that day, even if it were his eyes. Indra decided to test him and took the form of a blind old Brahmin and entered the giving-hall. The old Brahmin stretched out his hand to king Sibi and asked for one of his eyes to replace one of his. Delighted, the king ordered the surgeon to take out one of his eyes. Accordingly, the surgeon put powders on the royal right eye and brought it out dangling on its socket and dripping with blood. Urged on by the *bodhisattva*, who by now was in great pain, the surgeon cut the tendon and laid the eye in the king's hand. King Sibi then called the Brahmin to him, stated that he did this because the eye of omniscience is of much greater value than this fleshly eye and gave the eye to the Brahmin. The blind Brahmin put it into his eye socket. Overjoyed, king Sibi immediately gave his other eye. Indra in the guise of the old Brahmin then left the hall and returned to heaven.

Now that he was blind, king Sibi could no longer rule. Keeping in mind the gift he had made, he left the palace for a grove of trees where he would become an ascetic and die. Indra then went to the grove and offered the blind king a gift, but because he was now blind and could not rule, Sibi wanted nothing except death. Indra told him that if, when he gave his eyes, his intention had been pure, that act had been "true" and the power of its truth could restore his eyesight. Following Indra's advice, the *bodhisattva* formally stated that his gift had indeed been pure, and immediately one eye grew in its socket. He repeated another similar statement, and immediately the other eye grew in its socket. Yet the new eyes were different. They were the eyes of "Truth Absolute and Perfect" that can see through everything. As Sibi observed, "Through rock and wall, o'er hill and dale, whatever bar may be / A hundred leagues on every side these eyes of mine can see."

In order to celebrate the pure gift that had produced such pure perception, king Sibi built a hall, assembled his people, and taught them the moral of the story:

> Self-sacrifice in all men mortal living,
> > Of all things is most fine:
> I sacrificed a mortal eye; and giving,
> > Received an eye divine.
> See, people! see, give ere ye eat, let others have a share.
> > This done with your best will and care,
> > Blameless to heaven you shall repair.

Giving one's food to others before eating, we thus learn, is the first step toward the goal of giving oneself away. Giving food leads only to heaven, but giving oneself leads to omniscience.

Other Buddhist stories explain further steps one may take. In the *Lotus Sutra*, for example, we learn of the *bodhisattva* named "Seen with Joy by All Living Beings," who lived in another world during the time of the Buddha named "Pure and Bright Excellence of Sun and Moon."[13] That *bodhisattva*, who was a monk, heard the teaching of the *Lotus Sutra* and decided to cultivate painful practices, and by means of them he attained a mode of enstatic consciousness or *samadhi*. While in that *samadhi* he made mental offerings to the Buddha, which are the purest of offerings. When he came out of *samadhi*, however, he was dissatisfied. He decided to offer more of himself. Anointing his body, he drank fragrant oils, wrapped himself in a jewelled garment, took a vow, and burned his body as an offering to the Buddha. Buddhas in all world spheres praised that vigorous perseverance in giving as the prime gift.

For 1,200 years, the *bodhisattva* "Seen with Joy by All Living Beings" burned. After he was finally consumed, he took rebirth in the same Buddha land, this time as a prince sitting cross-legged. Immediately he went to the Buddha "Pure and Bright Excellence of Sun and Moon," whose final extinguishing or *parinirvana* was due. The Buddha asked the *bodhisattva* prince to prepare his couch and seat, and he entrusted to him those parts of his body that would remain after his cremation. He was to distribute them in several thousand burial mounds. Accordingly, the *bodhisattva* prince cremated the Buddha's body and distributed his relics in 84,000 stupas. Each stupa embodied a piece of the Buddha's body and was itself a Buddha-body; and the 84,000 stupas altogether embodied the 84,000 pieces that had constituted the Buddha's original body.[14]

Still, the *bodhisattva* prince was not satisfied with the level of his giving. He therefore stood before the 84,000 stupas—that is, he stood before the complete body of the Buddha—and burned his forearm as an offering. That burning lasted 72,000 years and it enabled multitudes of observers to attain *samadhi*, yet it upset the gods, men, asuras, and others who watched because now the *bodhisattva* had only one arm. In response to their distress, he called on the purity of his intent when he destroyed his arm as a means to generate it again. After an incalculable number of such gifts of his body parts and their regeneration, that *bodhisattva* came to be born into our world as the "Medicine King."

He became king of medicine, we may suppose, because he had specialized successfully in healing his own self-injured body. In other words, his power to heal in this world derived from the purity with which, in other worlds, he had dismembered himself in offerings to the Buddha, echoing in Buddhist terms the story of the primordial Person of the *Purusa-sukta*. Like the story of the *bodhisattva* who was king Sibi, this story of the *bodhisattva* who was the "Medicine King" teaches us that each of us can imitate complete self-sacrifice, even if only minimally, and that doing so will enable us to be "true" to some degree. Even though this world and age limits human consciousness and action severely, in it, mercifully, a small gift produces a disproportionately huge benefit. According to the *Lotus Sutra* account, for example, anyone who can burn a finger or even a toe as an offering to a Buddha stupa will be giving a gift to the Buddha greater than the gift of a realm or a walled city, of a wife or of children, or even of all lands, mountains, forests, rivers, ponds, and so forth. Of even greater merit than such a giver, it says, is the person who keeps just one of its verses in mind.

That means that in our world and age, the purity of consciousness equivalent to a true act of self-sacrifice can be obtained merely by memorizing a stanza of the *Lotus Sutra* and keeping it in mind. Yet perhaps that is not so easy either: To keep a stanza in mind for very long is difficult and requires self-sacrifice, because to be mindful of one thing only leaves no room for the multiple thoughts and desires that constitute a normal person in society. And the sacrifice of one's own normality is no small gift, as Harischandra learned.

Burning oneself, or a part of oneself, as an offering to the Buddha is not merely found in scripture. Living in Sumatra at the end of the seventh century, after years spent in India, the Chinese Buddhist monk I-Tsing wrote to China: "I hear of late that the youths bravely devoting themselves to the practice of the Law, consider the burning of the body a means of attaining Buddhahood, and abandon their lives one after another."[15] I-Tsing probably had in mind young Chinese monks who were following the Indian models depicted in texts like the *Lotus Sutra*, but perhaps he meant Indians. In any case, he did not approve of young monks anywhere burning themselves, because in his judgment it went against the monastic discipline to which they were committed. Referring apparently to the story of king Sibi who gave himself for a dove, he also wrote, "It is not seemly for a Sramana to cut the flesh from his body in order to give it away instead of a living pigeon. It is not in our power to imitate a *Bodhisattva.*"

Behind that statement probably lay a rite in which people seeking to imitate Sibi's self-sacrifice released pigeons or doves they had purchased to substitute for pieces of their own flesh. Such a substitutionary rite, however, suggests that there were some people who literally gave pieces of themselves away, just as some young monks were burning themselves instead of something else. Yet I-Tsing's statements made clear that he was criticizing only *monks* who performed such acts, not householders. Perhaps Buddhist laypeople were in his opinion free to follow the *bodhisattva* path by burning themselves for the good of others or by giving away pieces of themselves, even if he personally did not like the practice, for they had not committed themselves to a monastic discipline that disallowed such rites.

Likewise, kings and emperors giving themselves away was not merely literary convention. Another Chinese Buddhist monk, Hsuan-Tsang, traveled throughout India in the middle of the seventh century and was himself the honored guest at an extravagant giving ceremony conducted in 643 by the emperor Harsa. Harsa had conducted the ceremony every five years during his more than thirty years of rule; it was his way to purify himself of sin. He performed it again with Hsuan-Tsang as the honored guest.[16]

The "giving" rite took place at the confluence of the Ganga and Yamuna rivers because the purity or "merit" (*punya*) generated there was believed to be a thousand times greater than elsewhere. The ceremonies lasted about 75 days, involved representatives from all over Harsa's empire, and appear to have been done in imitation of the *Bodhisattva* Vessantara (or Visvamtara), a prince in the Sibi dynasty whose own extraordinary acts of giving himself away had purified him so well that in his next birth he became the Buddha Sakyamuni. The Vessantara story pushes the stories of his Sibi ancestors to the extreme, so that the *bodhisattva*'s total self-giving as Vessantara led to his total awakening as Sakyamuni.[17] It also evokes the rite of the fire sacrifice in which the sponsor, imitating the primordial Son, gives himself in pieces to Brahmin priests to pour into the fire in order that he may become true like the Father.

As heir to the Sibi throne, Vessantara specialized in the perfection of giving. One day, he gave the elephant that represented the kingdom he was to rule to Brahmins who asked for it. That provoked a rebellion by his subjects who forced his father to exile him. As the prince left the capital with his wife and two children in a chariot, he gave away the remaining constituents of his royal self. He first gave away all his wealth to beggars. He next gave away his horses to Brahmins who asked for them, leaving himself and his wife to pull the chariot. Then in response to another Brahmin he gave away the chariot, and he and his wife carried the children. A year after he had established the family in a hut on a mountainside, yet another Brahmin came while his wife was away and asked for his children, and he gave them. The grief that consumed him when he heard their pitiful cries and pleas as they were led away reminds us of the pain he had felt as king Sibi, whose right eye dangled on its tendon. Finally, of course, he gave his wife to a Brahmin. With her he had given away the last part of himself as householder, except for his own body. Before he could give that away, too, Indra revealed himself to be the Brahmin who had taken his wife and the whole drama came to a halt. The gods then gave back his wife and his children; and with himself whole again, they restored him to the kingdom. Vessantara's purity was now so great that when he died, he ascended to the heaven from which *bodhisattvas* who become Buddhas are born on earth. Perfection in giving thus leads to perfection in seeing.

Let us return to the emperor Harsa. Presumably, he believed that his own ceremonial self-giving would similarly free him from impurity so that in another birth he too would "awaken." By his order, 500,000 people had assembled at the confluence of the Ganga and Yamuna rivers. On the first day he had a golden image of the Buddha installed within a thatched building where treasures were stored, a building that stood inside a compound designed as a mandala. Harsa then distributed his first gifts. On the second day an image of the god Vishnu (*Adityadeva*) was installed and he distributed his second gifts.[18] On the third day an image of the god Siva (*Isvaradeva*) was installed and he distributed his third gifts. Beginning with the fourth day, he gave away what remained of the imperial wealth collected over the five years since the previous ceremony. In the words of Hsuan-Tsang's biographer, he gave away everything, except "the horses, elephants, and military accoutrements which were necessary for maintaining order and protecting the royal estate."[19] In other words, he did not give away the "stick" (*danda*) by which he could keep the subordinate kings subordinate. Like Harischandra, who would not voluntarily violate his duty as king, Harsa would not violate his royal duty by giving up the force that enabled him to be an emperor who gave himself away.

The distribution of imperial wealth occurred according to the precedence of the recipients; apparently, the degree of purity generated for him by his gifts decreased as the worthiness of the recipients decreased. On the ceremony's fourth day, 10,000 Buddhist monks, in ranks of 100, received 100 pieces of gold, one pearl, one cotton garment, various drinks and meats, and flowers and perfumes. For the following twenty days, Brahmins received gifts. For the following ten days, "heretical" Vaishnavas and Saivas received gifts. Over the next ten days, those who had come long distances received gifts. During the following month, the poor, the orphans, and the destitute received gifts.[20]

By that time, Harsa had given away everything except his personal items. Now he gave them away too: "his gems and goods, his clothing and necklaces, ear-rings, bracelets, chaplets, neck-jewel and bright head-jewel, all these he freely gave without stint."[21] The king then borrowed a second-hand garment from his sister and worshiped the Buddhas of the ten regions. In his prayer we are told that he said: "In amassing all this wealth and treasure I ever feared that it was not safely stored in a strong place; but now having bestowed this treasure in the field of religious merit, I can safely say it is well bestowed. Oh that I (*Siladitya*) may in all my future births ever thus religiously give in charity to mankind my stores of wealth, and thus complete in myself the ten independent powers (*dasabalas*) [of a Buddha]."[22] The ceremonies were now complete. Nevertheless, the kings who attended understood what was expected of them as rulers loyal to their imperial sovereign. They used their own wealth to buy back "the royal necklaces, hair-jewels, court vestments, etc." and returned them to the king. After a few days, however, the sovereign ruler once again gave them away, and we may presume that again the kings bought them back and gave them to him,[23] for in ten days the treasury was full from the wealth of subordinate rulers anxious to attest their loyalty.[24]

Stories of Saiva Saints

To conclude, let us return to Hindu tradition and to the stories of saintly devotees of Siva as found in a twelfth-century hagiography in Tamil. It is entitled the "Purana of the Great" or the "Great Purana" (*Periya Puranam*). The saints of these stories number over sixty-three men and women who devotedly served the primordial Person whom they knew as "the auspicious one," Siva. They loved Siva inordinately and at least twenty-four of them did so in a manner that can only be described as violent and fanatical.[25] Tamil Saivas describe their love as "fierce" rather than "mild" and believe that it flows from a flood of love for Siva that arises without limits and ripens very quickly. Their flooding love resulted from previous lives, in which they had expressed "mild" love through temple and domestic liturgies. In other words, for Tamil Saivas, injurious "fierce" love is valued more than noninjurious "mild" love.

The lives of the fiercely loving saints include various acts of martyrdom. A memorable one is that of "Saint Ferocious Tiger." He served Siva by setting aside rice to be cooked in Siva temples. One day he went away to war and told each member of his household not to use the paddy while he was gone, for it was consecrated to Siva and would be defiled if they used any of it, because it would then be "leftover" and leftovers cannot be offered to Siva. But a famine came while he was gone and they ate from the store of consecrated rice, planning to replace it later. On his return, Saint Ferocious Tiger learned of that fact and acted quickly. He set a guard at the door of the house and slaughtered everyone in the household—his father, mother, wife, brothers, sisters, and all other relatives and also the servants. Only a baby boy remained. The guard asked that the baby be saved since he had not eaten from the paddy. "Yes, but he nursed from a woman who had," said the saint, and chopped off the baby's head. Siva then appeared and took the saint and all of those he had slain to dwell in heaven.

Judging from Siva's response to such "fierce" love, we may conclude that Saint Ferocious Tiger had rid himself of the sin his body parts had generated by lopping off the guilty members of his collective social body, including the infant who had imbibed the guilt. The whole of himself was then qualified for heaven. Perhaps that "fierce" love is what Jesus had in mind when, according to Matthew 5:29–30, he said: "If your right eye causes you to sin, pluck it out and throw it away; it is better that you lose one of your members than that your whole body be thrown into hell. And if your right hand causes you to sin, cut it off and throw it away; it is better that you lose one of your members than that your whole body go into hell."[26]

The difference, of course, is that Matthew's Jesus confined the offending body parts to the flesh-and-blood body of the actor, while the Saiva story extended them into an entire household. Yet the "fierce" devotion in both cases demands purifying and painful self-sacrifice.

Two other saints illustrate the complexities of martyrdom when "fierce" devotion is expressed in the service of "Siva's slaves." "Siva's slaves" are devotees who dress as Siva does, usually by wearing Siva's ashes and beads on their bodies, and sometimes by keeping their hair matted. Saivas believe that to serve such "slaves" is to serve Siva, because they wear Siva's emblems. The saints in question are "Saint Cutting Devotion" and a king known as the "Celebrated Chola Saint."

Saint Cutting Devotion used his battle-ax to chop up anyone who disrupted Siva's slaves in their service of the master they resembled. One day, which was the first day of a great festival for God and the king, a devotee was taking his usual basket of flowers to a Siva temple in the regional capital. The Chola king's royal elephant with five grooms rushed by on its way to its bath, seized the basket, and scattered the flowers. When Saint Cutting Devotion appeared on the scene and learned what had happened, he took off after the elephant, chopped off its trunk, and hacked the five grooms to death. Bloodily, the saint had purified the Chola king from the sin he had unknowingly committed through his elephant and grooms.

The king, however, was also a saint. He knew that the elephant and the grooms were royal extensions of himself, so as soon as he heard that they had been slaughtered, he rushed to the spot with his army. But all he found was a single man standing there dressed in Siva's ashes and beads. Immediately he realized that the elephant must have done something wrong to bring that slave of Siva to such anger. When the saint told him that the elephant had scattered the flowers of Siva, that the grooms had not stopped him, and that he therefore had killed them, the king grew anxious. Venerating the warrior-saint he said, "It isn't enough to kill the elephant and the grooms for the grievous crime of harming Siva's slaves. You must kill me too. But your own auspicious sword is more than I, a great criminal, deserve. It's not right to use it. Use instead my own sword," and he held it out to him.

Saint Cutting Devotion was astonished at the king's great love of Siva and hesitated to take the sword; but then realized that if he did not take it, the king might use it to kill himself. So he took it. The king then venerated the warrior-saint who held his own sword and said, "When this Siva devotee kills me with the sword, my sin will be cut away." But when Saint Cutting Devotion heard him say that, he anxiously thought to himself, "This celebrated Chola king wasn't at all sorrowful when he learned why his royal elephant and its grooms had died; not only that, he handed me his own sword and asked me to kill him—and I meant to give *him* trouble! The only thing to do is to kill myself first." So, holding the king's sword, Saint Cutting Devotion started to cut his own throat with it. Startled, the king quickly grabbed his arm and the sword and brought him to a halt.

As we ponder those two "fierce" saints standing face-to-face, the question arises: Why is a devoted slave of Siva, who wears Siva's beads and ashes, willing to slit his own throat out of love for Siva when, at the same time, he will not agree to kill another devotee who, out of the same love for Siva, asks him to? If Siva is represented by both oneself and the other, what criterion allows one to act from one perspective rather than the other? The answer, I think, is that each devotee sees Siva in the other's love, but not in his own. Even though Saint Cutting Devotion is dressed as Siva, and even though the Chola king sees him as Siva and treats him accordingly, he sees himself only as Siva's *slave* and therefore worthy of death.

The king had stated that if Saint Cutting Devotion slew him, he would be purified, presumably, because Siva's purifying grace would be expressed as death through his slave. At the same time, Saint Cutting Devotion did not want the king to kill himself, because he saw Siva in the king. According to this Saiva thought, loving Siva joins the lover and the beloved so that they are "not-two," though they are not entirely one either. That is the mystery of sharing love with Siva. Yet to the lover, Siva always appears as someone else, not as oneself. Only a third party can recognize the lover as an extension of the beloved. Even if Saint Cutting Devotion looked in a mirror, he would presumably see Siva in the clothes, ashes, and beads he was wearing and himself as the slave wearing them. Thus, those two saints, each thinking himself the sinner and the other Siva, prevented each other from committing bloody suicide, yet wanted to be killed themselves. By being killed, they would be purified of crimes against Siva; and by preventing the suicide of the other, they prevented injury to Siva.

Not surprisingly, Siva was moved by their love. He resurrected the elephant and the five grooms, and they went on to the palace with the king. The scattered flowers returned to the basket, and the devotee continued on to the temple. Saint Cutting Devotion continued in his warrior-like service to Siva, and eventually became the chief of Siva's assembly in Kailasa. And the Celebrated Chola Saint finally did manage to kill himself.

One day, when the Chola king's soldiers brought back the heads of those they had killed while attacking a ruler who refused to send the king tribute, the king spotted one head with matted locks on its top. He recognized it as the head of a slave of Siva and—on the basis that the soldiers were extensions of himself—he realized immediately that unwittingly he had sinned greatly. He had only one option. First, he turned his kingdom over to his son, and then he put the soldier's head in a golden pot, put the pot on his head, circumambulated a blazing fire, and while uttering Siva's Five-Syllable Mantra, stepped into the fire. From that fire he emerged in Siva's realm.

When we consider his act, it is significant, I think, that the Chola king performed a mode of self-immolation, prescribed for a warrior's faithful wife (*sati*) when her husband has died away from home. Holding a piece of her husband's clothing or his body, the wife was to burn herself on a pyre; and, as Lindsey Harlan has reported, "the *sati* is always described as dying with her husband's head in her lap."[27] In this story, the devotee's head in the golden pot represented the husband, and the Chola king holding the pot represented the wife.

This means, I think, that we are to regard the saints' love for Siva as a male version of the wife's absolute faithfulness to her husband (*pativrata*). The saints, almost all of whom were male and householders, were masculine versions of a South Asian belief about women: absolute and loving faithfulness to the husband as master purifies the wife and gives her a sacred power that can be destructive or salvific. It is not unlike the power that the sage Vishvamitra possessed in the Harischandra story when he pursued Knowledge. The saints were faithful to Siva in the same way that their own wives were faithful to them. In turn, Siva treated each saint in the same way that the saint treated his own wife: as an extension of himself, as an instrument of his will, as a slave to do his bidding, as a means for achieving paroxysms of pleasure, and as a companion in sharing love.

Conclusion

Now, perhaps, we understand better the martyrdom of Mohandas Karamachand Gandhi in its South Asian context. He died absolutely faithful to Truth, which he believed to be Ram, the primordial Person as Father and Mother, who gave birth to himself as Son. Imitating king Harischandra, Gandhi lived like a faithful wife married to Truth. He viewed himself as the slave of God, yet others insisted on seeing him as manifesting God and gave him the title "Mahatma" or "The Transcendent Self." But he rejected the title, because he never saw himself that way. He thought of himself only as Ram's slave and believed he was to give himself away for the sake of others and thereby become pure and free. He attempted to reduce himself to zero, to empty himself of ego-claiming "I," "My," and "Mine," so that Ram's true being as Father and Mother would act through him with cleansing and healing power for the world around him. By acting through him, that power of Truth, he believed, simultaneously would save his people from social and political degradation and would free him personally from further birth in the ever-changing body of the Son.

Notes

1. Judith M. Brown, *Gandhi: A Prisoner of Hope* (New Haven: Yale University Press, 1989), 382.

2. Mohandas K. Gandhi, *An Autobiography: The Story of My Experiments With Truth,* tr. from the Gujarti by Mahadev Desai (Boston: Beacon Press, 1957), 505. For his thoughts in his own words, see Mahatma Gandhi, *All Men*

Are Brothers: Autobiographical Reflections, comp. and ed. Krishna Kripalani (New York: Continuum, 1984).

3. Gandhi, *An Autobiography*, 7–8.

4. I have retold it from the translation of the Bengali version by Edward C. Dimock in *The Thief of Love* (Chicago: The University of Chicago Press, 1975), 135–68.

5. *The Mahabharata*, vol. 1, tr. and ed. J. A. B. van Buitenen (Chicago: The University of Chicago Press, 1973), 167.

6. *The Mahabharata*, vol. 1, 169–70.

7. From *Young India*, April 30, 1925, quoted in Gandhi, *All Men Are Brothers*, 76.

8. *Rig Veda* 10.90, translated by many, for example, R. C. Zaehner, *Hindu Scriptures* (New York: Dutton, 1966), 8–10.

9. For the Sanskrit text with translation, see J. A. B. van Buitenen, *The Bhagavadgita in the Mahabharata: Text and Translation* (Chicago: The University of Chicago Press, 1981); or R. C. Zaehner, *The Bhagavad-Gita: With a Commentary Based on the Original Sources* (London: Oxford University Press, 1969); and Swami Tapasyananda, *Srimad Bhagavata: The Holy Book of God*, vol. 1 (Madras: Sri Ramakrishna Math, 1980).

10. Gandhi, *An Autobiography*, xii.

11. *The Mahabharata*, vol. 2, tr. J. A. B. van Buitenen (Chicago: The University of Chicago Press, 1975), 470–72.

12. "Sivi-Jataka," *The Jataka or Stories of the Buddha's Former Births*, vol. 3, tr. H. T. Francis and R. A. Neil (London: Pali Text Society, 1981).

13. Chapter 23 of *Scripture of the Lotus Blossom of the Fine Dharma* (*The Lotus Sutra*), tr. Leon Hurvitz (New York: Columbia University Press, 1976), 293–302.

14. See John S. Strong, *The Legend of King Asoka: A Study and Translation of the Asokavadana* (Princeton: Princeton University Press, 1983).

15. I-Tsing, *A Record of the Buddhist Religion as Practised in India and the Malay Archipelago* (*A.D. 671–697*), tr. J. Takakusu (Delhi: Munshiram Manoharlal, 1966), 196–98.

16. The two ceremonies are summarized briefly in Hsuan-tsang's *Si-Yu-Ki: Buddhist Records of the Western World* (*Translated from the Chinese of Hiuen Tsiang* [*A.D. 629*]), by Samuel Beal, Trübner's Oriental Series, two volumes in one (London: Kegan Paul, Trench, Trübner and Co., n.d.), vol. 1, 214–15. Hsuan-tsang's biographer, Shaman Hwui Li, noted that the king arrived at Kanyakubja in the last month of the year. See *The Life of Hiuen-Tsiang by the Shaman Hwui Li. With an introduction containing an account of the works of I-Tsing*, by Samuel Beal, with a preface by L. Cranmer-Byng (London: Kegan Paul, Trench, Trübner and Co., 1914), 176. Vincent A. Smith gave the date in Thomas Watters, *On Yuan Chwang's Travels in India* (*A.D. 629–645*), two volumes in one, ed. T. W. Rhys Davids and S. W. Bushell, with two maps and an itinerary by Vincent A. Smith (Delhi: Munshi Ram Manohar Lal, 1961), vol. 2, 336. Five years forms one complete cycle of the Indian calendar of 360 days in which the discrepancy

between lunar and solar days is adjusted through intercalary months. The cycle
of five years and the cycle of twelve months produced a still larger cycle of
60 years.

17. The Sanskrit version by Arya Sura in the *Jatakamala* has been translated
by Peter Khoroche in *Once the Buddha Was a Monkey* (Chicago: The University
of Chicago Press, 1989), 58–73. The older Pali version in the *Jataka* has been
translated by Margaret Cone and Richard F. Gombrich in *The Perfect Generosity
of Prince Vessantara: A Buddhist epic translated from the Pali and illustrated by unpub-
lished paintings from Sinhalese temples* (Oxford: Clarendon Press, 1977).

18. Adityadeva means "the god who is the son of Aditi" and can denote
either the Sun or Vishnu, who took birth as the dwarf (*vamana*) through the
womb of Aditi in order to enslave the asura king, Bali. I think the latter is
most likely.

19. Shaman Hwui Li, *The Life*, 186.

20. The list is slightly different in Beal's translation of *Si-Yu-Ki: Buddhist
Records*, vol. 1, 233: After the offerings to the Buddha, "he offers his charity
to the residentiary priests; afterwards to the priests (from a distance) who are
present; afterwards to the men of distinguished talent; afterwards to the her-
etics who live in the place, following the ways of the world; and lastly, to the
widows and bereaved, orphans and desolate, poor." In Watter's summary in
On Yuan Chwang's Travels in India, vol. 1, 364, it reads: "the king went on to
bestow gifts on the resident Buddhist Brethren, next on the assembled con-
gregation, next on those who were conspicuous for great abilities and extensive learning, next on retired scholars and recluses of other religions, and lastly
on the kinless poor."

21. Shaman Hwui Li, *The Life*, 187.

22. Ibid.

23. Ibid.

24. See Hsuan-Tsang, *Si-Yu-Ki: Buddhist Records*, vol. 1, 233, and Watters,
On Yuan Chwang's Travels in India, vol. 1, 364.

25. See D. Dennis Hudson, "Violent and Fanatical Devotion Among the
Nayanars: A Study in the *Periya Puranam* of Cekkilar," in *Criminal Gods and
Demon Devotees: Essays on the Guardians of Popular Hinduism*, ed. Alf Hiltebeitel
(Albany, N.Y.: SUNY Press, 1989), 373–404.

26. *The Holy Bible: Revised Standard Version*. Reference Edition with Concise Concordance (New York: Thomas Nelson and Sons, 1959), 1023.

27. Lindsey Harlan, *Religion and Rajput Women: The Ethic of Protection in
Contemporary Narratives* (Berkeley: University of California Press, 1992), 131.

INDEX